blue
rider
press

OFF THE RADAR

ALSO BY CYRUS M. COPELAND

Farewell, Godspeed: The Greatest Eulogies of Our Time

A Wonderful Life: Fifty Eulogies to Lift the Spirit

Passwords: The Essential Guide to a Heartfelt Eulogy

OFF THE RADAR

A FATHER'S SECRET, A MOTHER'S HEROISM,

AND A SON'S QUEST

CYRUS M. COPELAND

BLUE RIDER PRESS
a member of Penguin Group (USA)
New York

blue
rider
press

Published by the Penguin Group
Penguin Group (USA) LLC
375 Hudson Street
New York, New York 10014

USA · Canada · UK · Ireland · Australia
New Zealand · India · South Africa · China

penguin.com
A Penguin Random House Company

Copyright © 2015 by Cyrus Copeland
Penguin supports copyright. Copyright fuels creativity, encourages diverse voices,
promotes free speech, and creates a vibrant culture. Thank you for buying an authorized
edition of this book and for complying with copyright laws by not reproducing, scanning,
or distributing any part of it in any form without permission. You are supporting
writers and allowing Penguin to continue to publish books for every reader.

Blue Rider Press is a registered trademark and its colophon
is a trademark of Penguin Group (USA) LLC

ISBN 978-0-399-15850-6

Printed in the United States of America
1   3   5   7   9   10   8   6   4   2

BOOK DESIGN BY MEIGHAN CAVANAUGH

For my parents, Shahin and Max,

who left home for the horizon

We are always saying farewell in this world, always standing at the edge of loss attempting to retrieve some memory, some human meaning from the silence—something which is precious and gone.

—ADLAI STEVENSON

CONTENTS

PROLOGUE

Max's Radar Affair, the handwriting across the file said. I recognized my mother's cursive—as well as her flair for drama. The story contained in this file had all the markings of a classical affair. Secret meetings. Unaccounted-for hours. Divided loyalties. For thirty years, the file had lain dormant at the bottom of this box—which had followed us Copelands from Iran to Pennsylvania, through four suburban homes, to the dusty corner of the library where it now resided. In a strange way, I believe it was my father's will that I found the file. Last week, a land prospector called with news of mineral rights that once belonged to my dad. "They're yours if you can prove ownership," she told my mother, who promptly dispatched me to the study to locate my father's will. I was buried deep in the wilderness of boxed diplomas, old address books, photos, tax files, and receipts, when from the bottom of a box of relics, the past coughed up a different nugget.

"Open it," my mother said. Into our laps spilled several documents. The first was a newspaper clipping dated November 27, 1979.

CIA Agent Smuggling Radar
Equipment Caught

November 27, 1979

TEHRAN—The Revolutionary Guards here arrested a CIA agent who was trying to smuggle eight console radar machines to the United States. Max Copeland, whose nationality was not identified yet, had booked eight boxes of radar equipment belonging to the Iranian Air Force at Mehrabad customs destined for the United States...

A succession of other documents fell from the file, their pages delicate and crisped by time. There was a formal rebuttal written by my father disputing the charges. An affidavit from Secretary of State Cyrus Vance. A packing list. A long letter from my mother to Iranian president Banisadr—a review of which brought tears to her eyes.

"You know, of course, your father was a CIA agent," she said.

It was not the first time I'd heard her say this. I suppose a review of salient facts did suggest a career in intelligence: low-profile jobs in defense and high-tech industries. Broad knowledge of Iran. And he was caught up in an international incident that somehow never got any play beyond those couple paragraphs in the *Tehran Times*. But a CIA agent? I remembered him as an academic whose greatest hours were spent in the company of books. A hunter. A mindful adventurer who could never quite get enough of mountain ranges, seascapes, and the oddities of different cultures. It irked me, hearing her call Dad a spy.

"Tell me about Dad's arrest," I said.

"Why must we talk about the past when you know it gives me a head-ache?" she replied—never mind that the past was all around us, splayed out in an accordion of yellowed documents. "Anyway, haven't you heard this story enough times?"

I knew the tale well enough, but somehow it had never sat right. My father was too sincere to traffic in government secrets. His love for Iran was genuine. But ever since the CIA had organized a revolution in 1953, Irani-ans have come to distrust the motivations of Americans. Just a couple of years ago, three American hikers had been accused of espionage after "in-advertently" crossing into Iran. It was of course a perfectly ridiculous claim—every bit as absurd as their choice of destination—but it prompted my mother into her latest act of volunteer diplomacy. She drew up a letter to Hillary Clinton offering personally to negotiate their freedom.

"I sacrificed much more for your father, a real-life spy, so why shouldn't I defend these innocents?" she said.

It didn't cross her mind that at eighty, she might no longer have the con-nections needed to pull it off. But even today, you cannot underestimate her.

Sadly, she did not hear back from Secretary of State Clinton. Or maybe she never got around to mailing the letter. But that afternoon for the gazil-lionth time, she recounted the events leading to my father's capture and resulting trial.

Through the years, with each retelling, I felt a deeper regret that I didn't know my father better. All children have unresolved questions about their parents, of course, but this was no trifling matter. Was he a spy? Then it struck me: I had a file on my father. If he had been a CIA agent, they'd have a file on him, too.

That week, in a bid to put the past to rest once and for all—for myself and my mother and sister—I filed a Freedom of Information Act request with the CIA. Passed into law by President Clinton, the act allows previ-ously classified documents that were more than twenty-five years old to be released. If my father were a CIA agent, his file would certainly meet these guidelines. A dead agent doesn't worry about his cover being blown, right? I also filed inquiries with the FBI, the Department of Defense, the State Department, and President Carter. A flurry of letters flew out into the world, each a bid to open my father's long-dormant past. I held out hope that someone, somewhere knew something—and, like the file I'd unearthed, that thing would fall gracefully into place.

Which just shows you how much I know about the world of intelligence.

While waiting for responses to come in, I began writing this book. My mother's story is easy to tell for she is an ardent, often glittering story-teller. My father's was trickier—the dead tell no tales. He was a notoriously private man. The story of his capture, imprisonment, and trial I pieced together from journals, notes, memories, and shards of conversation I recall from quieter moments. But much of his interior life and motivations had been shrouded from me.

While writing, a curious thing happened. At times I heard his voice in my head, which was lovely and disconcerting. I began to feel closer to him.

I have an American father and an Iranian mother. I have the blood of the Great Satan and the Axis of Evil in my veins. The year 1979 launched the Iranian revolution and Islamic fundamentalism on an unready world, and in revisiting that year and its dramatic events, I saw how the fracture between the two countries was written into my parents' marriage—and played itself out in microcosm while Iran and America did battle. Our story was a prism. While all eyes were on the hostages, our crisis played out in jail, in court, across international borders—and in private.

Was my dad a spy? Were the charges leveled against him true? Were my father alive today, he'd have pushed up his glasses and said in a voice that left little room for discussion, "Cyrus, I don't want to talk about it." But we Copelands had an adventure, a tale that goes back three decades to the fault lines between Iran and America. And it needs to be told.

PART 1

A Hunting
Expedition

SHAHIN

I n America, a peanut farmer rules the free world. Here a king is deposed from his peacock throne, ending twenty-five hundred years of monarchy. God have mercy, the revolution has arrived.

It's been months since the Shah left—leaving the country in the hands of bearded hooligans and a rotating roster of ministers, most of whom last barely longer than a carton of milk. The prisons have been emptied and refilled. Each day brings more prohibitions: ties, perfume, nail polish, makeup. And more executions: generals, SAVAK agents, Communists, drug offenders, Kurds, Bahais, intellectuals, political dissidents and holdovers from the prior regime, their names written on their foreheads for identification—their blood running from Evin's prison grounds.

Welcome to the Islamic Republic of Iran.

For the record, her name is Shahin Maleki Copeland. She is an inveterate royalist and always will be. Did the Shah not launch a White Revolution that gave women the vote, peasants the land they'd farmed, illiterates an education, industrial workers the right to profits, Iran's forests protection, and the farthest villages access to public healthcare? But you don't hear about any of that, for bloodless revolutions rarely make headlines. Better a red revolution to take Iran back a century.

Not only does she disavow herself of all this, Shahin notes with pleasure how the Islamic Republic was certified on April 1, when the gullible are taken for a good laugh. Her countrymen marched, fought, died, ransacked, burned, stared down the barrels of guns—and now celebrated. *The revolution has succeeded! Become martyrs in the path of righteousness!* It's as if they'd read the Che Guevara handbook on revolution, mixed it with fundamentalist Islam, and were now drunk on their unmixable principles. "Brother" and "sister," they called each other.

It was the best of times followed by the worst of times.

Mornings as she passes the newsstand, Shahin glances at the headlines and photographs of executed men. She wonders if it bothers her compatriots that blood flows freely and vengefully, or that Tehran's walls are defaced with ugly slogans calling for death. Death is all around them. By daylight and moonlight, men patrol the streets like hounds in search of Communist, royalist, traitor, and dissident—carting them off to destinations unknown. As SAVAK had done. Stories of abduction are whispered over tea: *Gereftanesh.* A single word, shorthand for capture and probable death: *"They got him."*

November 25, 1979: Today, as she sets the table, Shahin realizes Max still has not arrived. Usually he is home by seven, whistling in the stairwell. It's nine P.M. Kebabs and rice are on the table, losing steam. "Where is Dad?" the kids want to know.

"He went hunting," Shahin says, the facility of her lie surprising her.

"Hunting?" Katayoun asks.

"Hunting. Yes. Your father decided—spontaneously—to take a trip up north," Shahin says, expanding the lie and giving it room to breathe. "Now eat."

In truth she has no idea where Max might be.

Her thoughts turn to the American embassy. A couple of weeks ago, some ruffians seized the embassy for the second time. Shahin remembers that day; the gods had set the mood perfectly. A misty gloom hung over Tehran. A light rain fell. In the late afternoon, her sister Mahin had called with news of the takeover. Shahin turned on the TV to see a gleeful mob parading its blindfolded Americans, chanting death to Carter, death to imperialism. By now death was so invoked, so ingrained in the language that she thought she was immune to it. But this? She felt embarrassed that Iran's new face to the world was a horde of bloodthirsty hoodlums with no international etiquette.

Doubtless they'd been elated to discover the pile of documents, three CIA agents, and a cache of weapons—all of which confirmed their worst suspicions about America. Finally the revolution had found a unifying event. And hundreds of thousands took to the streets in jubilant agreement.

"This is not an occupation. We have thrown out the occupiers!" Ayatollah Khomeini proclaimed.

It does not take a Nobel laureate to appreciate that of all the times in Iran's history, this was the most inauspicious, the absolute worst, for Max to go missing. But over dinner Shahin feels a strange calm descend. After the kids retire to their rooms to finish homework, she remains anchored at the table watching the hours tick by.

Come midnight, Max is still missing.

Where, she wonders, does one search for a missing American husband? She'd been married to Max for twenty-plus years, mostly good, but ever since the revolution had ignited she'd sensed a growing rift. The night of the embassy takeover they'd argued fiercely. Where was the sense of international decency, Max wanted to know. The goddamn moral outrage? Where was the recognition that America had been riding roughshod over Iran for years, Shahin demanded. She'd not take any criticism of Iran, not now, not from an American, not when Carter had sold out her beloved Shah for a barrel of oil. The argument had ended the way most did, with Max seething and silent. That was a week ago. Now he was gone.

The following morning, she stops at Laleh hospital, a couple of blocks from home. The overwhelming nausea she's already feeling has nothing to do with the antiseptic smells wafting in the corridors.

"Have you admitted a Dr. Copeland? A tall American man."

"Does he work here?" the admitting clerk asks.

"Oh—no, he's not that kind of doctor. He's a Ph.D. And my husband."

"I see," the clerk says with a hint of derision. Unshaved, he barely looks at her. Yesterday people like him had washed her windows, clipped her hedges, and shined her shoes. "We have no record of him here."

"Thank you," she replies, the words like vinegar on her tongue.

For the next fifteen hours, this scene plays like a recurring nightmare: Surly, uninterested clerks who've forgotten their humble beginnings brushing her off. (Bad enough her husband is missing, Shahin's life has become a scene from a Marxist play.) The response is always the same. At the hospital, the police station, the prison, the morgue: *We have no record of him.* Shahin crisscrosses Tehran knowing that with every passing hour her chances of finding Max diminish.

One hour bleeds into the next.

One prayer gives way to a hundred.

At eleven P.M. she returns home husbandless. She has not eaten—a missing husband is a wonderful appetite suppressant—and collapses onto the sofa. "Will you rub my legs?" she asks Katayoun.

That night, Shahin prays formally for the first time in years. On a rug. Facing Mecca. This was the Islamic Republic, but the mullahs weren't the only ones with a line to God. Midprayer, she stops short, and in the way a piece of the puzzle eventually comes forward, she remembers Max's driver. *Surely he would know Max's last whereabouts.* She doesn't bother excusing herself from God, but gathers her skirt and leaves. An hour later, she stands in the alley outside Javad's house, and when he doesn't answer his buzzer, Shahin yells: "JAVAD!" He comes downstairs, looking like he's seen a ghost—which Shahin attributes to the surprise of seeing her at midnight minus makeup. In this dark alley on the other side of Tehran's tracks, the two of them are briefly stunned by the improbability of this rendezvous. Shahin pulls him into the shadows. "Dr. Copeland is missing—do you know where my husband is?"

"Sincere apologies, *khanoum,* nah."

"Where did you take him yesterday?"

"To the warehouse. I returned after lunch, but he wasn't there. I assumed he'd gotten a cab."

That sounded right. Max was in charge of closing out the affairs of Westinghouse's employees—selling their belongings to the public, returning to the warehouse after each sale to record the proceeds. But something is wrong. Javad won't look at her. So Shahin takes a step toward him and in a move that surprises her, a desperate and conceivably widowed woman, she puts her hand to his throat and pushes Javad against the wall.

"Tell me where my husband is. I have a gun in my purse and will shoot you."

A year ago, Shahin had been a woman of decorum—gliding through Iran's upper echelons and hobnobbing with university presidents and four-star generals. She had an American husband. Two children. They took yearly vacations to the European capitals. Educated at Georgetown, she prided herself on speaking five languages and having been the youngest woman to leave Iran, unchaperoned, at age seventeen to study abroad. In a year, all vestiges of her privileged life have disintegrated—leaving Shahin with the one unassailable trait she's always possessed. Practicality. To date, Shahin has never choked anyone, certainly never the help. But if violence is what it takes to shake down a lowly driver at this midnight hour, by Allah she will do it.

"Please, *khanoum,* let me go! I know nothing!"

She tightens her grip and Javad's veins start pulsing—then popping. She can smell the onions from dinner on his breath, which arrives in pungent, staccato bursts.

"Do you want your children to grow up fatherless? *Harf bezan, beechareh!*"[†]

---

[*]Honorific title for a woman.
[†]"Talk, you scalawag!"

Javad gasps and a tiny web of spittle lands on her hands. A thin crescent of blood appears where her thumbnail has pierced his neck. It pearls, then meanders down Shahin's thumb.

"*Grrftssshh.*"

"What?"

She releases her hold on him, and like the miserable stoolie he is, Javad pants forth a torrent of apologies. "*Gereftanesh,** *khanoum* . . . We were outside the warehouse and two Revolutionary Guards took him away . . . They had guns . . . Tell anyone and we'll come for you too, they said. *Khanoum,* I have a family! Debts! Imagine the trouble they would unleash on my poor head . . ." By now, Javad has recovered from his near strangulation and is beating himself on the head like a professional mourner. "My wife is upstairs right now, hiding with shattered nerves. *Vaaaay.* I'm sorry I didn't tell you, but I have a family! Debts! What is going to happen, *khanoum*? God help us, we are without hope!"

There it was; the well-worn phrase that ricocheted throughout Iran had landed with a thud. *Gereftanesh.* Frankly, she is relieved to hear someone has Max, but relief gives way to new questions: Why is he being held? What has Max done?

Naturally, she dismisses Javad. Once you choke someone, you can never be sure of their loyalties.

---

*"They got him."

CYRUS

I've been wanting a stronger father recently.

A father who'll tell me exactly how to behave. A do-this, do-that father. Instead, I have a father who makes pancakes and waffles, and dispenses bromides like "Be kind to your sister" or "Remember the little people." Which is well and good, but it does not tell a boy how to grow up. Little people? At six-foot-three, with a colossal intellect from reading Winston Churchill, my father is a Big Person. But I gather he's talking about something else. He says "Remember the little people" conspiratorially—like it's the secret to life—and it annoys me, because I really don't want to hear any sentimentality from him. He's already too gentle.

My father is a gentle man. He does not care for cocktails or cocktail conversation, or wear European suits or talk politics, but he is indisputably a gentle man. A man of books and tentative caresses, and sideways glances. He isn't afraid to say "I love you." I want to change this gentleness. Mold him into a father who will take hold of me, discipline me, command my respect, and make me shut up.

He does none of those things, although he occasionally goes hunting, which confuses me, for I know that a gentleman hunts. But does a gentle man?

One afternoon he brings a pheasant home from a hunting expedition. The body hangs limply in his hand, a malleable lump of feathers and a pretty, iridescent severed head. When I go over to examine it, the enormity of its death hits me. I grab the head and run into my bedroom. "How . . .

could . . . he . . . kill . . . it?" I blubber. Later I emerge to get a glass of water for the head. I dip its beak in. Then just to make sure, I dunk the entire head. The sunlight scatters its plumage across my room. I exhort it to drink and come alive again for my sake. Then I go on a Not Talking to Baba strike.

As a child, I'd reversed their heritages—calling my Iranian mother Mom and my American father Baba. They mandated that. But by the time we'd moved to Iran, I'd switched his name to Dad.

It is the spring of 1974 when we leave Philadelphia for Shiraz—a live-and-let-sleep city 6,578 miles east of the Liberty Bell. Rising low on the horizon, Shiraz's chief source of drama is the Zagros mountain range that corsets it, and also its name: the City of Wine and Roses—so named by the poet Hafez. Overall I remember yellow: the yellow bricks of our house, the thatched mud walls of a nearby village, and the sun, the raging sun that sends the entire city to bed between the hours of one and three because it is too, *too* hot to do anything else.

We had arrived in Shiraz four years after the Shah's anniversary cele-bration at Persepolis, that famous flaunting of Persian monarchy that the liberal press later derided as excessive, but which my mother considered appropriate. *Two thousand five hundred years deserves more than fireworks and a parade.* The Shah thought so, too. He invited five hundred heads of state to the party. The festivities took place in an elaborate tent city that sprung up like a mirage in the Persian desert—fifty white air-conditioned tents arranged in a star, accented by gardens of rosebush and cypress where every branch and bloom was tended by a Versailles florist.

But this was no mirage. The Shah's guests confronted a menu of quail eggs brimming with Caspian caviar, crayfish mousse with Nantua sauce, roast saddle of lamb with truffles, champagne sorbet, fifty roast peacocks stuffed with foie gras, truffle and nut salad, fresh figs and cream, and raspberry champagne sorbet—all tendered on Limoges china, and topped off with five thousand bottles of wine, speeches, a parade, and a *son et lumière* show. It was not the party of the year. It was the international social event of twenty-five centuries, and it colored my dreams more than any Grimm's fairy tale. Press accounts estimated that the party cost $15 million, money that might have been spent on social services. A pesky ayatollah known as Khomeini had a field day, madly denouncing the "evil celebrations" and making outlandish threats to the Shah. "I say these things because an even darker future, God forbid, lies ahead of you." But the Shah was oblivious— and truthfully so were we. Who could have known that the sun would soon set on twenty-five hundred years? When we arrived, Shiraz was midway between anniversary and anarchy, wine and roses, history and his- trionics.

Life here takes getting used to. The milk comes in glass bottles, never quite cold enough, with a thick dollop of cream afloat. There are no special surprises in cereal boxes. Weekends are Thursday and Friday. And when you ask, "How far till we get there?" you'll get your answer in kilometers instead of miles.

For a month we've been living at the Kourosh Hotel, with a swimming pool and waiters who brought seconds of café glacé, but my parents say we've just rented a home at the foot of the mountains! My younger sister Katayoun wonders if we can take one of the hotel maids and I wonder, our house is very close to the mountains: Are there scorpions? My parents say, no, we cannot take a maid and the probability of scorpions is small, so we move in. In our new house there are two bathrooms: American, with a shower, toilet, sink. And Iranian, with a ceramic hole in the floor. There's also a watering can to clean yourself, and a basin of water above, released by a pull string.

"Where is the toilet paper?" Katayoun asks.

"No toilet paper," my father says. "Just a watering can. You scrub your bottom with your hand."

I never heard of such tomfoolery. "Won't your hands get dirty?"

"Eeewww," Katayoun squeals and runs out.

Only three months here, and already I'm beginning to miss America. Also, it turns out there *are* scorpions. One night shortly after moving in, I'm doing homework when I notice one, holding his tail up and doing the lambada across my bedroom.

"Scorpion!" I shout. "There's a scorpion in my room!"

My mother grabs a can of insecticide.

"Pif Paf? You're going to kill it with Pif Paf?" I ask, incredulous.

But my parents head into the bedroom, armed with aerosol, and corner the scorpion. My mother sprays, and the scorpion runs toward my father, who catches the can and begins his line of attack. Back to my mom. Another pass, another burst. The scorpion is by now confused and congested and—judging from his jiggling tail—ready to unleash his deadly poison any second now. But the Pif Paf passes continue until we are all coughing in a cloud of aerosol and the scorpion has expired. My parents exchange glances—and abruptly break into high laughter. I could have died, I remind them.

I go closer to check: Dead. Covered in a thick layer of bug poison.

So's my room, my clothes, my hair. Good work, I tell them, even though everything smells like Pif Paf. At least there are no more scorpions doing the lambada.

WEEKENDS, my father loves sitting with bazaar merchants. They don't know what to make of him, a foreigner who doesn't buy, just wants to have tea, thank you, and has only a cursory knowledge of Farsi. It isn't for lack of trying, he just isn't good with languages—and Farsi is a particularly difficult language for the Western tongue. He makes up for it with curiosity and enthusiasm. Sitting there with a small tea glass, vapors rising, he sees all facets of Shiraz: the shoeshine urchins, the tea boys, the old men with glasses so thickly ground that they appear deranged but in reality just need help focusing on the rapidly changing world, and the tribal women shopping for new fabrics. How they love gaudy colors! Hot pink, radioactive green, sunshine yellow. Dusty-faced and loudly dressed, they stalk the bazaars kicking up their skirts in layered, discordant rainbows, and as they pass my father they look at him hesitantly. *"Salaam,"* my father says, and they nod. It is these exchanges, small and dimly lit, that give my father immense hope about life in Iran.

Above us the mountains are buzzing with their own ecosystems. Springtime, the poppies release their red brilliance into the sunshine alongside the brambles, lizards, scorpions, and other denizens of life on Zagros, and on such days my father rises like a man possessed. "Come," he says, to the chagrin of my sister and me, "today is a good day for mountain climbing." He leads us upward, on the lookout for life, up and up until we've reached no particular place, but my father's brought sandwiches, soft drinks, and fruit to enjoy, and we sit on a rock and look out over the Shiraz valley. Exhausted with scuffed knees, I wonder exactly what's so great about mountain climbing. "Look, a lizard," he says.

My father is a mystery to me.

Once, I notice he signs his checks *W.A.* instead of *Max*, which is what everybody calls him. When I ask why, he tells me, "I was born into difficult times. 1934. Lubbock, Texas. My parents didn't have a lot of money. They wanted to name me Max, but along comes my uncle who offers them good money to name me after him, Walter Albert. He doesn't have a son. My parents have a son but no groceries. That's how I got my name."

"Did it cost a lot to be a W.A.?"

"About two hundred dollars, I believe. Be grateful you have a name which is yours—no one's ego, no money, no bribe, no groceries attached. Your name is yours alone."

The alone part worries me. *Cyrus* sounds so responsible on the tongue. Dignified. So does *Cyrus the Great*, who, like all monarchs, was alone. And

I see how with two names, three if you include Dr. Copeland, my father is still alone in the world. His story blindsides me. It raises a million questions. But the only one I ask is how much did my grandparents get for naming him Walter Albert? I could ask if it hurt having your parents sell your naming rights. But I'm afraid of the answer. I do not want a lot of introspection. I do not want to hear platitudes about the little people. I do not want to be exposed—one more time—to Max's vulnerabilities. I want a father with no crevices or questions, who presents a united front to the world and doesn't look to his son for understanding.

A father with one clear name and no confusion.

It wouldn't hurt if he had a regular job either. Plumber, electrician, medical doctor, soldier, lawyer. Something concrete. But not Max. He's got a job with Hughes Aircraft and a black briefcase into which that part of his life fits—papers, numbers, pencils, all the instruments of my father's mind. Whenever he tries to explain his job, I think: "Dr. Copeland" is a trick, because there are no stethoscopes or prescriptions, and I wish he'd be something I can understand. At school if asked what he does, I say, "Hughes Aircraft employee," and, if pressed, "consultant."

I've heard him say this before and it sounds good.

He loves gardening. Inside my mother decorates, but outside he seeds, waters, and clips his way to contentment. Weekends when he's not in the bazaar or up in the mountains, he is planting roses and morning glories, tomatoes and cucumbers—beauty and utility, side by side. He loves working the earth. Even the barren Shirazi earth, which is tough and leathery as a tribal woman. "Come, plant with me," he says, surrounded by his Burpee seed packs, but I'm not one for dirtying my fingers. Maybe later?

My father's garden is his salvation, his one path to happiness, or at least out of sadness. I don't know what he's got to be sad about—and I don't want to know. When I see him alone in his garden, it reminds me how I don't have real friends, how potentially alone I can be, too. I feel reserves of sadness rising, but who can you tell? When I see him in the garden, happy alone, sweat beading on his forehead and staining his shirt, I wish he were someone else. Later I would understand: My father's garden equaled him. In its incandescent roses and quiet vegetables, he found the beauty and respect of his own private ecosystem. Entirely designed, cultivated, and nourished by him, reflective of him, available to him, the garden was insular and independent in its beauty.

Once, I find him on the living room floor trying to fix a radio. Transistor, batteries, wires, plugs: He is enclosed in a ring of disconnected, unworkable parts.

"Being electrocuted right now is about the best thing that could happen to me," he says.

I don't know why he's upset—and don't want to know. Instead of hugging him, I collect these moments and hold them against him, an inventory of shortcomings and vulnerabilities. "Remember the little people," he says. And I think: *Little?* Like he's Gulliver helping everyone else to build a better life, but really inside him is a vast loneliness because he's in Lilliput—with different customs, different language, no friends really, smart-alecky kids, and broken radios.

He isn't angry at the world, just himself. If Katayoun doesn't put the dishes away, or if I give him lip, or if he has a Discussion With Your Mother, he rages—but only with words. He swears, degrading his own life, his fatherhood. His rage turns to sorrow, then to quiet. Sadness opens up inside him, sharp and beautiful as his morning glories, spreading its petals around his heart—and on such days he will take long walks around the neighborhood and into the mountains, and when he returns you can try to approach him for forgiveness, say you're very sorry for giving him lip, and would he like an iced tea, here, but you will find him still hurt. He retires to bed with his Mary Renault novels, a shaft of light falling onto the pages, and he curls toward them embryonically, taking solace in history and a story that is not his.

Until, finally, he becomes a protagonist of his own invention.

Five years later in Tehran: My mother says he's off hunting at night. But the truth is far more exciting—and less troubling—to me. He is in prison.

The first really cool thing he's done. But this is more than I bargained for. Plumber, electrician, medical doctor, soldier, lawyer? Suddenly I have a coherent, precise definition of who my father is: Prisoner.

And for the first time I realize he isn't the quiet, unassuming man I'd thought.

SHAHIN

Sadegh Ghotbzadeh was once her suitor. They were enrolled in Georgetown's School of Foreign Service in 1957 and saw one another with some regularity. He was handsome, though not in the conventional sense. His nose and mouth were a bit too wide. His forearms were massive, their forest of hair suggesting a coursing, untamed virility. And he was always worked up about something, which gave his otherwise sensitive eyes the sheen of indignation, passion, and strength. The thing she remembered most was his black hair, which fell in a cavalier flip over his forehead, giving Sadegh a part movie star, part ruffian look—a welcome departure from the Georgetown boys with duck haircuts.

Imagine telling an Iranian you liked his hair. She'd sooner have died.

They saw each other mainly on the weekends, but their relationship was marred by a fundamental problem. While Shahin focused on her studies, Sadegh wanted to take down the man to whom she'd pledged undying loyalty—the Shah. This made for an awkward friendship. While she pored over St. Thomas Aquinas and hobnobbed with Georgetown's Jesuits, Sadegh led demonstrations through Washington's wide avenues. She hunkered down in the Library of Congress. He ditched classes and read Victor Hugo, Engels, and Orwell in Farsi. They argued over politics, religion, and everything else.

When they weren't arguing long enough to converse civilly, Sadegh spoke exultantly of his father—*"Agha,"** he called him. Shahin found that ironic. He was not some high government official. He was a bazaar merchant whose son never had enough money on dates. She bit her tongue. She was a Maleki. Her father was mayor of Meshad, governor of Khorassan province, and patron saint of the impoverished who frequently returned home coatless—having encountered someone in greater need of garments. A real *agha*. Still, Sadegh's reverence for his father touched her. At least he had one authority figure he did not want to burn in effigy or send to the gallows.

Rumors swirled about Sadegh. That he worked with the Libyan secret service. That he was CIA. That he had connections with the Communist parties in France and Italy. The last accusation was certainly false. Sadegh hated the Communists and took great strides to ferret them out of his own organization—the grandly titled Freedom Movement of Iran.

Once, the *Washington Post* published a photo of Sadegh, identifying him as an "Irate Student." The *Post* had no idea. A talented organizer and passionate orator, Sadegh was tireless in expressing his hatred of the Shah and organized a series of sit-ins and protests in front of the Iranian embassy, during which the demonstrators put paper bags over their heads and shouted, "Death to the Shah!"

Disparaging Sadegh for hiding under the bag, Shahin chided him. "Are you embarrassed? Then show your face like a man."

But Sadegh was a zealot, not a lunatic. He was aware of a constant threat that hung over the demonstrators: the Shah's secret police. "I would. Look at this face! But who knows how SAVAK would retaliate?"

Their courtship was doomed from the start. Doomed—because while she respected him, he was so punch-drunk with his heated beliefs that conversation was impossible. He was magnetic. Time moved faster when she was with him. But conversation was like a tennis match with no volleys,

---

*Honorific title for a man; e.g., "sir."

just one hard serve after another. And then there was the fact that made rapprochement with the Peacock King impossible. Sadegh had been imprisoned under the Shah. And if Sadegh's preoccupation with matters at home muted the development of a romantic relationship, it scuttled his academic career as well. When he skipped final exams to participate in his tenth demonstration of the semester, Georgetown had had enough. He was expelled.

So that was the story of Shahin and Sadegh. The courtship was brief and contentious. When it ended, Shahin never thought of Sadegh again.

Until twenty years later, when she did.

FEBRUARY 1, 1979: The ayatollah is triumphantly flying back to Iran after fifteen years in exile. Below, millions have gathered in anticipation, feverishly chanting "God is great" and "Khomeini is the imam." The country is mad with anticipation—awaiting the man who vanquished a monarchy with fiery underground cassettes and pamphlets, and now orbits like a lighthouse beacon. He is their new savior. In the streets, a helicopter has dropped thousands of flowers in preparation for the ayatollah's arrival. Soon the bloodshed will begin anew, but at least his return will be perfumed and pretty.

"How do you feel about coming home after all these years?" a reporter aboard the chartered 747 asks.

"Nothing. I feel nothing," Khomeini says, staring out the window impassively.

"Nothing?" his translator asks, surprised.

"Nothing."

Only, the translator knows a thing or two about public relations and says, "No comment," to the reporter.

As the scene plays out on TV, Shahin leans forward to see that the translator is quite handsome . . . and suited . . . and Sadegh.

Sadegh, who in the intervening years had thrown in his lot with the ayatollah, gained his confidence, and now returned victorious to Iran. *Mash'allah!* While she'd sworn fealty to a king now dying on another continent, Sadegh had befriended a lowly cleric who would become *Time's* Man of the Year, launch Islamic fundamentalism, and soon execute those with whom she'd socialized.

Game. Set. Match.

Sadegh had not only befriended the ayatollah. He had written his speeches, done his shopping, selected his cologne (Eau Sauvage by Dior, he told a journalist, "and why not, there's no law against smelling nice!"), and brokered the deal with Air France to fly him home. Within days of his return, Sadegh climbed to new heights of power. He assumed leadership of Iranian network TV, which he purged of leftists and royalists. He looked like a TV executive, too, always wearing a suit. His revolutionary brothers had chucked the necktie as a symbol of Western decadence, but Sadegh believed in insurgency *and* in style. Months later, in what must have been sweet remonstrance to Georgetown—the very institution that had turned him out for being too political—he was appointed foreign minister. No homecoming was ever more gratifying, no man more patient or prepared for success.

It is at just this point—the pinnacle of his life and the veritable pit of hers—that Shahin decides they should get reacquainted. And so the day after she confirmed her husband's disappearance, choked his driver, and admitted she'd lost all sense of direction in Iran, Shahin pays Sadegh a visit.

"TELL MR. GHOTBZADEH that Shahin Maleki wishes to see him," she announces to the desk clerk at the Ministry of Foreign Affairs, using her maiden name.

---

*"Well done!"

"You and a hundred other people," the man replies in observance of the growing crowd.

"Be quick about it, brother, I don't have time."

And she didn't. Max had been missing for forty-eight hours. There must have been something plaintive in her voice because the clerk looked up, clicked his tongue, and dialed Sadegh's office.

In the elevator, Shahin regards herself in the door's reflection and makes a few adjustments. Armed with a small canister of Chanel No. 5, she spritzes herself and pulls her headscarf back slightly—exposing a lock of freshly colored hair. If Islamic beauty was a suggestive art, Shahin knew the brushstroke. The exact angle beyond which a headscarf would fall straight off, the dab of lipstick that rouged the cheeks no more than a brisk breeze, the drape of a manteau that best accented her figure.

Stepping back to appraise herself, she remembers their first date. *Twenty years ago at Howard Johnson, Sadegh collapses in a booth, flush with the excitement of a successful sit-in at the embassy.* A succession of dates flit across memory. *Their first football game. The first time he concedes an argument. The night she tests his affections by dinner at an expensive restaurant—knowing he'll eat noodles for a week afterward.* Back then Shahin bore a strong similarity to Jackie Kennedy. More than once an awestruck debutante had asked her for an autograph. But now? There was no mistaking her for anything other than an anxious woman whose life was careening toward disaster. Naturally, the elevator doors open to a silver-templed, Italian-suited, even handsomer Sadegh than she remembered.

"You'd better behave," she tells him by way of hello, "or I'm going to give you a kiss in front of everyone."

"Oh, please don't," he laughs.

"There was a time you would have welcomed that."

"Times have changed, Shahin *khanoum*. What brings you here?" Given their distant history and his new appointment she'd half expected a brush-off, but he leads her into his office. "Please. What can I do for you?"

Seeing the tufts of hair curling from his cuffs, Shahin smiles imperceptibly. Sadegh is still a bear of a man. His cologne is different, musky, French
probably. He is a crossbreed of Islamic ideology and European flair—shot
through with brute masculinity. She finds this oddly comforting.

It will make her act of sedition that much easier.

MAX

Three months prior to his disappearance, Max is seated alone on the living room floor. It is his fofty-fifth birthday. He has just finished pan-frying himself a burger when the lights go off, as they always did at 8:30, plunging Shiraz into darkness. Max lights a dozen candles and settles back down with a groan. The floor is bare. Carpets. Furniture. Family. All evidence of their onetime life in Shiraz has been packed up and replaced by the boxed belongings of other Americans—and Gordon Hall's dog.

"Take care of him, he's a rescue," Gordon pleaded before leaving Shiraz.

Gordon Hall's dog is the bane of Max's existence. He pisses, barks, and craps everywhere, but until Max can figure out how to ship a dog through quarantine in England, then on to California where Gordon now lives, he's stuck with the mutt.

What a way to spend his birthday, Max thinks.

There are random acts of aggression. There are acts of kindness. During a revolution, it is easy to confuse the two. Earlier, Max was out washing the car when a woman in a chador approached. "Are you American?" she asked. "Go home!" Then she grabbed the bucket of soapy water, gripped her chador between her teeth, and began washing the car. Max was transfixed. The revolutionaries usually preceded "Go home" with a "Yankee"—not followed it with a scrubbing.

"Why?" Max asked.

"I have a son in Texas and the Americans are kind to him," she said, virtually pushing him away. "Please, go home! It is not safe for you."

It was the only birthday present he received that year, but it recalibrated his expectations and reminded him of the Iran he'd once known: the hospitable country that opened to Max like an exotic hothouse flower. Then clamped itself shut with him inside.

She was right. It wasn't safe. Martial law had been declared in the fall of 1978. There was a curfew from nine P.M. until six A.M. Soldiers manned strategic points throughout Shiraz, including Gas Circle, only three blocks from home and near the infantry training center where Max had taught English. In the center of Gas Circle stood a monument, maybe fifty feet high, erected by the Shah when oil prices had skyrocketed in 1972. A commemorative flame atop the column could be seen for miles around—a flickering reminder of Iran's petroleum path back to greatness.

During the curfew, the power is shut off from 8:30 until 10:30. There had been occasional power outages before the current political crisis, so residents have spare candles and lanterns on hand. But these new blackouts go on for months. And while they provide the cover of darkness in which revolutionary ambitions grow and spread, the hours of darkness are especially difficult for Max. Shahin and the kids left for Tehran weeks ago, after their school closed. As Max sits alone in the candlelight with Gordon Hall's dog—no family, no friends—his loneliness feeds on itself. He begins to suspect that this will not turn out well.

Outside, despite the curfew, the neighborhood churns with activity. Residents climb to the flat roofs of their houses. From the quiet comes the first cry: *Allah-o-akbar.* This is answered by another. And soon the calls come from numerous locations, young and old voices, predominantly from men and boys. This is the battle cry of the revolution.

Many nights, he climbs to the roof to listen to the growing chorus. Max recognizes more than a few voices. From across the street comes the cry of a wealthy bazaar merchant. He is answered by the chairman of the department of surgery at the university a block away. Soon others join in until the night rings with their voices—each house a minaret from which God's greatness is proclaimed and the fires of revolution stoked.

"I too have heard the voice of your revolution," the Shah said in his last televised address to the nation, months ago. "I promise the previous mistakes, unlawful acts, and injustice will not be repeated."

But it was too late. The revolution had sparked and the coming fire could not be extinguished—and each death, each cry, each shared story of repression (true or not) was fuel on a flame that already burned brightly. Iran would rise like a phoenix yet again! Islam would fight the corruption of the West! A thousand times brighter than the fire atop Gas Circle, these twin flames would be so bright, so powerful, as to be seen the world over. The revolution was on.

Where did that leave the Americans?

Most left at the first signs of unrest. Hughes Aircraft, Westinghouse, Bell Helicopter, Xerox, and many other Fortune 500 firms had long since set up outposts here, which meant that by 1979, fifty thousand people had to be evacuated. Airplanes were full of fleeing Americans. They left behind luxurious homes, unpaid bills, houseplants, dogs they'd rescued from ditches, rooms stuffed with brand-name furniture, and thirty-six million Iranians who looked upon the fleeing Americans with a mix of sadness, contempt, and envy. Max wished they were leaving also and had discussed this many times with Shahin.

Generally their conversations were quiet. They treated each other with respect and affection. But discussions of nationalism struck an emotional chord. When an acquaintance disparages a relative and the whole family rushes to the relative's defense—whether he deserves it or not—wise men scratch their chins and mutter, "Blood is thicker than water." Well, the Copelands were Shahin's family, but so was Iran. And the Copelands were Max's family, but so was America. When Max suggested that the best policy might be to pull up stakes and go because Iran was not safe, Shahin reacted as though she had been personally insulted. Refinement and gentility were no longer the order of the day. Max had thrown down the gauntlet, and one proud daughter of Iran leaped to her homeland's defense.

SHAHIN: Surely you're not afraid of a few hoodlums?
MAX: The banks are closing. Electricity is rationed. There's no kerosene. There are gunshots at night. Everyone is leaving. They've declared martial law, for God's sake.
SHAHIN: Everyone? C'mon.
MAX: The Saravchis . . .
SHAHIN: Saravchi is CIA. Of course he's leaving.
MAX: . . . the Johnsons, the Farmers, the Pascals, the Kendricks . . .
SHAHIN: I hear from the developer our new apartment will be ready in a few months. If we left now we would lose that. And my family is here! I can't just leave them behind, can I?
MAX: I'm telling you, I have a bad feeling about this.
SHAHIN: What's back in the U.S.? So a few revolutionaries are causing problems. It's nothing. Our life is here. Let's stay a few more months, see what happens.

So what happens? The Shah leaves. The schools close. The banks close. The ninth circle of hell breaks loose. Shahin and the kids move to Tehran to set up a new life in the capital.

And Max stays behind in Shiraz.

Nightly he sits by candlelight—cursing and daydreaming about a life back in America. He makes lists of all the animals on the farm he'll buy if they ever return (chickens: 12, roosters: 1, pigs: 2, horses: 4). He writes his inventory on the backs of envelopes, on napkins, on scraps, anywhere but on the pages of books, which are sacrosanct to him. Some nights he just listens. He wants to commit all this to memory, for his life has finally converged with the history books he reads. It turns out he is more than an eyewitness. Unexpectedly, Max is a *player*.

A bit player at first. When Westinghouse approaches him to help shut down its operations, Max says yes. Westinghouse had hundreds of employees in Shiraz, and he is tasked with closing their homes, shipping or selling their possessions, and paying off their debts. A tough task in any climate, but in revolutionary Iran the difficulties of getting around, doing business, and communicating with his (admittedly atrocious) Farsi are magnified.

Still, he swings into action. After months of unemployment, that feels good.

More than three hundred people line up for his first sale at the home of the Kendricks, an American family who'd returned to Falls Church. Hoping to test a small bit of the market, Max had posted notices at two food stores in the city, and the market now overwhelms him. Inside the apartment, women clad head-to-toe in chadors avidly negotiate better prices while the men hurry from room to room to examine every bit of merchandise. Bargaining is the rule of the day. Every article of furniture, cooking utensil, plant, and decoration has been priced, but that is no deterrent to negotiation. It is a fire sale, bazaar-style, in an American home.

"Death to America, but long live her appliances," Max jokes.

"I like this," Dr. Deghan says, pausing before a chest of drawers for perhaps the fifth time, "but it's overpriced."

"It's only six hundred *tomans*," Max replies—about ninety dollars—"and the other discounts I've given you far exceed that." It isn't as though he can't afford it. Dr. Deghan is not only the Kendricks's landlord but also a physician who owns and operates his own clinic.

"Let me have it for three hundred."

"We're selling the furnishings of all the Westinghouse families to meet their obligations for rent, utility bills, and other financial obligations. Would you give the Kendricks a three-hundred-*toman* reduction in rent?"

"It's different. Anyway, you will see—by the end of the day you will not be offered even three hundred *tomans* for this piece of furniture. Then you will ask me to kindly take it off your hands. I may not be interested in it later."

By the end of the day the only unsold items are a fly swatter and a jaundiced houseplant. Max takes the proceeds—about ten thousand dollars—and pays off the help, the landlord (whose wife eventually bought the dresser with her own money), and the electric company, then mails a check for the balance directly to the Kendricks in Falls Church.

So it goes. He develops a routine: Advertise the week before (food stores were perfect—reliable traffic by all cross sections), three sales a day, Fridays off. He hires a beefy man named Almas to guard the door, while three others price and sell. They greet the multitudes joyously.

Selling hundreds of pieces of furniture every day, Max begins to fixate on things—one or two items per household—and invent histories. This bed? It was from here that insomniac Randy Budsman had watched the waiters and shopkeepers trudge home after their shifts. This sofa? On it the Farmer kids had sleepovers, built forts, and taught each other sign language by the light of the Shiraz moon filtering through window slats. Later he'd realize these were stories he'd brought forward from his own childhood, cut and pasted over other American identities in solidarity. In this way Max keeps the spirit of Americans alive after they leave—and his loneliness in a harness. He regains traction. Life has purpose. He turns away from his garden's paltry offerings toward sturdier life forms—woods, plastics, metals—and in their commerce discovers what all great entrepreneurs know: There is joy in a good sale.

AT THE END OF THE SIXTH WEEK, he receives a call. The line crackles and echoes with a three-second delay—indicating an overseas caller. "Max? Max Copeland? George Demougeot here. I understand you've been doing a good job for us. How're things in Shiraz? What time is it there?"

"Good. Who are you?"

"George Demougeot. Westinghouse. I've been getting calls from a lot of people asking me to thank you. Including a Gordon Hall. Did you ship a mutt from Tehran all the way to Encino?"

"I did."

"A dog? Hundreds of things to rescue, sell, the country is falling apart, and you ship a dog back? Damned thing cost us six hundred dollars for quarantine alone."

"I rescued everything *and* shipped a dog back," Max says edgily.

"A dog." Demougeot chuckles softly. "Listen, Max, you've been a great help to us. Now we need you to do something else—essentially, the same thing in Tehran, only with more responsibility. Hello?"

"I'm listening," Max says.

"Westinghouse had a couple hundred employees in Tehran. We need you to sell their leftovers, send back the proceeds just like you've done. And something else. Do you know what our business is in Iran, Max? There is some material we need sent back. Electronic systems. Anti-aircraft weaponry. Tracking systems. That kind of thing. We had a contract with the Iranian air force, but it looks like that's gone the way of sanity in that country, and we'd like our stuff back. Equipment, manuals, spare parts, consoles, technical data, everything. Of course, we'd remunerate you handsomely. This is a matter of some—sensitivity."

"How handsomely?"

"How does thirty thousand dollars sound for a couple months' work? The money will be deposited in a U.S. bank account under your name. But. The assets, inventory, shipments, it has to be clandestine. You get me? Under no circumstances can anyone know about this—including your wife."

"Why?"

"Because that's the way it is."

"Shall we give our operation a name?" Max jokes.

"Operation Westward," Demougeot says. "And it's already in motion. You are to finish up Shiraz within the week. When you get to Tehran, go to our warehouse and take an inventory of everything there. Hire another guard. I want it under lock and twenty-four-hour surveillance. No one has access but you, understand? I'm going to give you a number to call in case you need to reach me—got a pen? Listen, Max, the company really appreciates your help. You're the only guy on the ground we trust. Any lingering doubts I had disappeared when you shipped back a mutt. That kind of dedication? It's priceless, frankly. You get back to the States and I'll take you out for a steak and offer you a permanent job. You need anything, anything at all, call me up, hear? Never know who's listening, though, so careful. Here's the number . . ."

The following week, Max received a letter from Demougeot. News of Max's activities in Iran had apparently traveled all the way up to the State Department, for alongside Demougeot's letter was an official certification, stamped with a bright red seal and graced by U.S. Secretary of State Cyrus Vance's signature. It gave Max power of attorney for Westinghouse's affairs in Iran. Officially this allowed Max to sell five jeeps belonging to Westinghouse. Unofficially, it allowed him to sell or ship everything else. Max would never see Demougeot—but true to his word, thirty grand appeared in his bank account.

A month later, Max went missing and the following headline appeared in the *Tehran Times*: CIA AGENT SMUGGLING RADAR EQUIP-MENT CAUGHT.

SHAHIN

Shahin had never taken Sadegh seriously.

Soapbox politicos weren't exactly her type. But standing in the foreign minister's office with its brocaded curtains framing the garden below, its richly hued Persian carpets, and elegant, Louis-Something armchairs that reminded her of her own childhood, Shahin swallows her pride and thinks: *How lucky we met twenty years ago.*

If anyone can locate Max, Sadegh can.

Sadegh had his own problems, of course—sixty-six of them, bound and blindfolded in the U.S. embassy. And the existence of those problems had turned Sadegh into a media star. A frequent guest on *Nightline*, he is defiant but gracious in insisting America's problems are self-inflicted—the result of its meddling and imperialistic ways. But that is for public consumption. Behind the scenes he is a pragmatic politician, constantly lobbying to have the hostages released. He knows the longer the hostages are held, the less likely the provisional government will win the trust of other nations—not to mention their investments.

Shahin does not care about the day-to-day travails of the New Iranian Order. Her problem is personal. But before she can broach the subject of Max, Sadegh leans forward conspiratorially and says, "You'll never guess whom I've got upstairs."

"Who?"

"Three more American hostages."

"Hostages?"

"Yes, Bruce Laingen was here the morning of November fourth, so we detained him and his colleagues. We couldn't return the chargé d'affaires to the student radicals, could we? So they sleep on the sofas upstairs like guests!"

Hostages at the Foreign Ministry? Shahin is dumbfounded.

"Don't be alarmed, they're treated with deference. They have their run of the entire third floor. You hear that thumping? Mr. Laingen is jumping rope. And frankly with all the chocolates the Swiss diplomats are bringing him—good." Sadegh pats his belly. "Some of us don't have time for exercise."

Shahin seems interested as Sadegh recounts the achievements of the revolution. She seems impressed as he recalls his role in it. She knows she cannot simply barge in on a former suitor, inform him of her marriage—to an American of all things—and ask his help in freeing her husband from the arms of revolutionary justice without a *little* small talk. And when the time is finally right, she tells Sadegh about Max, about his job with Westinghouse, and about his disappearance.

"Westinghouse. Didn't they manufacture military hardware?"

"Maybe. But Max was in charge of furniture, not weaponry."

"And he's done nothing to invite any unfortunate—developments?"

"He's an academic, Sadegh. He doesn't concern himself with political matters." She nearly adds, *It's beneath him*, when she remembers her audience.

Unbidden, Sadegh picks up the phone and dials the Central Komiteh—the communications hub for all branches of local government. "Find Dr. Max Copeland," he instructs. (Dr. Max Copeland: a small gesture that gives her hope this might be resolved amicably.) While on hold he pivots toward her and covers the receiver.

"I overheard Mr. Laingen this morning. There are a few roaches crawling around the building—it's Tehran—but do you know what Mr. Laingen and his Americans did? They named the roaches: The smaller ones are mullahs, the larger ones are ayatollahs. And they take great happiness in squashing them! Americans. It's like their heads are filled with hamburger meat. Who says things like this? Who takes these kinds of stupid risks?"

The answer becomes evident in short order.

"They've located Dr. Copeland," Sadegh says after a minute on hold. "He's been arrested for spying."

He's been arrested for spying.

The words loop around—reverberating from Shahin's head into her heart, where they land with a thud. Surely it is the latest in a long line of idiotic mistakes by a rogue government. Max is an academic. He butchers Farsi. At six-foot-three he's not exactly inconspicuous. And he has zero capacity for subterfuge. (Although he was awfully fond of *reading* spy novels.) This is the replay in her head. But in her heart? In her heart, she feels the tentacles of fear wrap her ventricles and squeeze—hard. The heart knows. The heart *constricts.* That is its job.

Suddenly the absurdity of it all—the hostages above, Shahin with her onetime suitor, now foreign minister, below, and Max somewhere in custody for impersonating 007—hits her. She leans forward and laughs as though she and Sadegh are at a cocktail party. As if Sadegh had told a joke.

As if it is all just a big *joke.*

"This is serious, Shahin, and it couldn't have come at a worse time," he says, arching his eyebrow toward the upstairs guests. By now the thumping from Bruce Laingen's physical fitness regimen has become intolerable. Jumping rope in the Foreign Ministry? What's next, basketball?

"Max—is not a spy. That's ridiculous."

"There will probably be a trial . . ."

"Sadegh, he's not a spy!"

"Maybe, maybe not. Doesn't matter."

"We've been married for twenty years; I would know if my husband was a spy. What do you mean, doesn't matter?"

"Recognition of America's sins and the Shah's return to stand trial, that's what people want. Two things. They won't get it, of course; Rockefeller and Kissinger won't allow that. But Dr. Copeland? He's not a hostage, he has no leverage. He is not here in an official capacity. And he's been found with evidence of plotting against the revolution. Your husband, I'm sorry to say, is an enemy of the state."

"Max loves Iran, knows Iran better than most Iranians! He's an Irani-ologist."

Sadegh cocks his head and looks at Shahin intently—almost wantonly. "I'm not going to argue with you."

"He is not a spy, Sadegh, I know my husband."

"You asked me to find Dr. Copeland—"

"And you did! You helped beyond my expectations with a single phone call—*mash'allah*. But . . ."

"—but I cannot get involved. Will not. There are sixty-six other Americans whose destiny hangs by a thread thinner than a mullah's eyelash! Would you have me jeopardize their fates, our revolution, international relations—to say nothing of my job—by intervening in a matter in which I have no jurisdiction? It's difficult enough fighting the hostage battle on several fronts, Shahin. No, I'm sorry. Too much is at stake."

"The hostages—some of the hostages are accused of espionage. What about them?"

But on that count, Sadegh is silent.

"May I ask: Does Westinghouse know he has been detained?" he asks.

"No."

"Have you alerted the State Department?"

"I thought I should come to you first."

"You've done well to do so. Now please respect the position *I* am in. And do not repeat what I've said. If you do I will deny it."

She has been dismissed. Sadegh is not going to provide any more help. Sidelined and alone, Shahin finds that her breath grows shallow. Her chest tightens. She feels a tear begin to form in the corner of her eye. And she realizes that she has to change tactics. She does not want to play the helpless female card, but she uses what weapons she has. She lets her eyes well up. She blinks out a tear. She trembles slightly. She turns away from Sadegh, defeated. He notices.

"Shahin . . ."

"Sadegh, I know we've had political differences, but if you cared for me—"

"Don't. Don't ask me this."

"Sadegh, let me tell you something you might not know, that I could never tell you before. Do you know at Georgetown when the Jesuits wanted to kick you out, who went to them to ask forbearance? Even though you were a terrible student who cared only for politics? Being the only Iranians there, I thought we should help each other. I did. Allah forgive me! And now you've destroyed a twenty-five-hundred-year lineage of kings, and gotten everything—more than—you dreamt of. I have two children and a husband in jail. Will you not help?"

"That was you? They told me someone had pleaded—"

He takes out a piece of official stationery, scribbles a couple of sentences, then balls it up and deposits it in the trash. He holds his head a bit. His mood seems to shift.

"Tell me something else," he says, fixing the full weight of his gaze on her. "Do you think of us as equals, Shahin?"

It is the most nakedly confrontational thing he has ever said to her.

Or perhaps the most honest? Sadegh settles back into his chair and watches Shahin's eyes widen, fleetingly. So it had come down to this? She has played her last card. Yet she will not lie to Sadegh. The most she will do is what a politician of Sadegh's stature might expect: Pivot.

"I think of us as even, Sadegh."

He smiles imperceptibly. "One last thing, then. I will instruct them to release Dr. Copeland to your custody. He'll be under house arrest until his trial. Understand? Home means prison. If he leaves the house at any time, tries to escape, steps out to sniff a rose, he will be taken back to prison and that's the end."

She does not understand—not any of it—but nods.

"Start looking for a lawyer," he advises. Sadegh looks at her intently—with a gaze that reflects the new reality; he is not beneath her anymore, far from it—and adds, "Shahin, you must understand that the Iran you knew no longer exists. Frankly, you should have left long ago. Now excuse me, I have real business to attend to. A press conference. Back in Washington I couldn't get anyone to pay attention and now look, they're all clamoring for time. The beasts."

With that, Sadegh bows slightly and he shows her out.

LATER THAT NIGHT, she sees his interview.

"Are you a hardliner?" a reporter asks.

"No, I'm a nice guy," Sadegh responds with brio.

History will bear him out. Sadegh will spend the rest of his career trying to free the hostages. He will fail. Standing in the path of a revolutionary wave, the early supporter of the usurper Khomeini will be swept aside.

And the world will never learn of the American he helped to free.

PART 2

THE FORGOTTEN HOSTAGE

MAX

O utside Tehran, a huge interconnected web of warehouses named the Turquoise Palace housed the unopened components of the world's most advanced radar system—$48 million worth of equipment, not yet delivered to the air force. The equipment was state-of-the-art, reflecting the Shah's intentions to turn his military into a muscular fighting machine. By 1974, he'd spent a cool $10 billion on weaponry, giving Iran a supersonic fighter force second only to that of the United States. His fleet included 528 helicopters, 398 self-propelled howitzers, over 10,000 anti-tank missiles, 80 Grumman F-14 fighter jets with the latest Phoenix missiles, and four Spruance-class destroyers that were more modern than those in the U.S. Navy. By the mid-1970s, Iran was awash with 70,000 American engineers, mechanics, technicians, and military advisors intent on delivering the Shah's dream army.

Among the companies bidding for contracts, Westinghouse was particularly aggressive. One of the products they pitched to the Iranian air force was a solid-state radar system known as ADS-4—a state-of-the-art technology with civilian applications. The system could both monitor Iran's border and land planes at Tehran's Mehrabad Airport. It was also the first radar with a height finder, meaning it could identify the coordinates of air traffic as well as the altitude at which planes were flying. It was the first of its kind, and it gave Iran an immense advantage in protecting its borders. Should the Russians invade from the north, the ADS-4 would give Iranians enough time to launch a counteroffensive.

Contracts were signed and letters of credit extended for eight ADS-4 sites. Soon the country was home to several hundred Westinghouse employees. The air force had a cutting-edge air defense system and Westinghouse a roughly $20 million payday.

All told, Iran ordered eight ADS-4 radar systems at a cost of $64 million.

By September 1978, a wave of social unrest washed across Iran. Against a background of power outages, demonstrations, and traffic disruptions, work on the ADS-4 program ground to a halt. Only one of the promised eight sites had become operational, and even that one had begun to deteriorate before the air force agreed to commission it fully.

Telling the air force its employees were "leaving for Christmas vacation," Westinghouse sent three Pan Am 707s to collect their employees. They never returned.

AS WESTINGHOUSE'S CLEANUP MAN, it is Max's job to empty the Turquoise Palace, and he routinely spends twelve to fourteen hours a day here. Logging. Packing. Loading. Dispatching. There is a small fridge in the back stocked with leftover commissary goods, and a cot for when he gets tired, but that is where the palatial luxury ends. This is a half-lit, twenty-thousand-square-foot stockroom crammed with sensitive military equipment. Often the warehouse is plunged into total darkness by power outages, and even then Max continues working by the light of candles and kerosene lanterns. Surrounded by high-tech gadgetry and low-level lighting, Max lets his thoughts wander. How had it come to this? All this military might—only to watch the country fall to an ayatollah with a tape recorder? Maybe Iran wasn't ready for modernization after all.

On November 24, Max is standing outside the Turquoise Palace enjoying the last few rays of wintry sunshine, when a car pulls up and two men bound out.

"Are you Coop-land," one asks.

"I am."

"Come with us," the taller one says, brandishing a gun. He is a youth of maybe twenty-five dressed in military gear. He grabs Max's briefcase.

"Call Mrs. Copeland," Max yells to his driver, Javad.

The revolutionaries walk Max to their Wagoneer. They cuff and blindfold him, and for what seems like an hour or so they drive—the steady volume of traffic indicating they are still somewhere in Tehran. Occasionally one of the gunmen strikes up a conversation, but after the second or third attempt, the other loses his temper and tells his companion to shut up. The car reeks of sweat. Max wonders: Is it the residual funk of fearful men, or him? He is afraid. His thoughts turn to his briefcase. He cannot recall its contents. After a while he senses the thick, warm taste of blood and realizes he's gnawed a hole on the inside of his mouth.

When the car comes to a stop, Max hears the sharp click of heels from a military salute. A metal gate swings open. He is yanked from the car and walked a distance.

When his blindfold is removed, Max finds himself in a holding room. The walls are covered in blue paint that has chipped away in places. A buzzing neon light burns overhead. A soldier asks him for his personal possessions—including a tiny Quran Shahin gave him for protection—and fingerprints him. He orders Max to change into dull green prison garb. Then he blindfolds him again and leads him to a cell.

Max removes the blindfold. He is alone. A cursory glance around reveals a cot, a squat toilet, and a bookshelf on which rests a Quran. There is unreadable graffiti on the walls. About twenty feet up one wall, Max sees a window facing the western sky. The sun has begun its track toward Mount Damavand and the horizon.

Max lies down on the cot. The blankets reek of the smell of unclean men. Eventually he sleeps.

Some hours later he wakes to a sandwich wrapped in plastic and a cup of tea resting on the floor of the dimly lit cell. Outside it is dark. He thinks about Shahin. How will she explain his absence to the kids?

More sleep.

Max awakens. What had he left in the briefcase? The thought haunts him for hours and fills him with fear. In the half-light, the graffiti in his cell assumes fantastical shapes—causing his imagination to run wild. He eyes the sandwich on the floor.

That briefcase. Damnation.

And then another thought. Will he be interrogated? Max has heard stomach-turning stories about prison interrogations in Iran. In the seventies, stories circulated about SAVAK's brutalities: Nail and teeth extractions. Rape. Near drownings. Snakes inserted into cavities. Acid dripped into nostrils. One particularly gruesome tool—the Apollo—was a conical device named after the NASA space capsule. Placed over the head, it was designed to muffle screams, while amplifying them for the victim. SAVAK earned its reputation as one of the most barbaric underground police forces in the Middle East. SAVAK is now gone, replaced by another band of enforcers who learned the art of torture because it had been practiced on them.

Eventually Max sleeps again. His dreams are populated by American belongings scattered across the plateau of Iran—sleeper sofas and washing machines, beseeching him to do something.

Waking, he sees the moon—a crescent through the window, luminous and exacerbating every fiber of loneliness within him.

Sleep. Wake. Sleep. Wake. In prison, this is how time passes.

That night Max curses his judgment, and bad luck, and Westinghouse. He did not think it was possible to feel lonelier than on those God-cursed nights when he sat in his home with nothing but a candle and his personal demons for company, but life has shifted again. He's in solitary confinement—a fitting conclusion to life here. Max knows Iran's history and geography better than his boyhood Oklahoma, but he never understood the mercurial, mystical Iranian soul. No American did. That is why just a few months after President Carter pronounced Iran an island of stability in the Middle East, the country descended into the maelstrom. And Max found himself pulled into the turmoil, his quiet expatriate life a memory. Where once he fought valiantly to find his place in Iran, now he recalls the shouts on the street of "Yankee, go home." And he thinks, *Gladly.*

In another corner of Tehran his countrymen are paraded before cameras—the world tuned to their fates—while he lies in a creaky bed, whereabouts unknown, waiting, waiting, waiting for destiny to unveil herself.

At exactly 4:30 A.M., the first round of predawn executions begins. Followed by birdsong.

CYRUS

I am just beginning to get used to a new school, a new language, and the metric system when the larger questions of existence are deposited in my trembling, ten-year-old hands. *The Glorious Quran*, it says in gold lettering. "A special place in heaven is reserved for those who read and memorize the Quran," my mother says, handing me the volume. "Happy Birthday!"

Already I can feel the weight of it alone makes me a better boy. That night I remove the red silk cover and kiss the book, touch it to my forehead as I've seen her do, then turn to the first page. To my surprise, I already know this page by heart—it is the prayer my mother taught me five years before. So I turn to the second page.

> *Alif, Lam, Meem*

> *This is the Book about which there is no doubt, a guidance for those conscious of Allah.*

As I read on, I discover that the Quran is full of direct commands—"Say unto them," "Do," "Do not do"—most of which are addressed to the Prophet. The language is quite ripe, a lot of *forsooths* and *verilys*, and it doesn't really read like a book. I recognize some of the characters—Adam, Eve, Mohammad—but there is no beginning, no plot, and no apparent method to its organization. It jumps back and forth in time and subject, apparently on the instruction of the archangel Gabriel, who told Mohammad what belonged where. Scattered throughout is advice on practical matters—fasting, pilgrimage, commerce, marriage, even financial matters. The Quran is the Word of God, yet I understand very little of it. And this realization drives me to confusion, and ultimately, to despair. It's been reported that whenever Mohammad received revelations, he suffered real physical consequences. He would fall silent, his face would become flushed, his body grew limp, and sweat beaded upon his brow—even in the winter. I knew how he felt. As I read the words, I feel an anxiety attack coming on. How can I make it to heaven if I can't even understand God's words, much less memorize them?

In my nightly study, I come across an army of biblical prophets: Adam, Ishmael, Noah, Isaac, Jacob, Joseph, Solomon, Jonah, Lot, Aaron, Moses, John the Baptist—and wonder if the Christians have hatched an insidious plot to infiltrate Islam. The Christians have Bible study. They have pet mice. And they have Cathy Payne, a freckle-faced classmate who routinely beats me to top spot on the honor roll, and who is reading *The Grapes of Wrath* while the rest of us are still thumbing through Archie comics. Cathy is the daughter of Church of England missionaries. Often she brings picture books to class for show-and-tell. For five minutes, she puts John Steinbeck aside and regales us with stories of Jesus cavorting with lambs, angels, and small children. Cathy herself is on such good terms with the book's protagonist that she speaks on his behalf. "Jesus loves you," she reminds me. "Well, I'm sorry, but he does!"

No one ever says, "Mohammad loves you."

"Be careful about the missionaries," my mother says. "If they start talking religion, tell them you're a Moslem and proud of it. Then walk away."

"But you went to Georgetown," I point out. "Wasn't that a Christian school?"

"Those missionaries are different," she says. "They encourage intellectual debate. They have respect for other religions."

None of which helps me in my quest to be a good Moslem. By the end of the year, I've come to the end of the Quran and still have no idea what it all means. So I turn back to page one and start all over again. Soon I begin to feel my age-old jealousy of Christians come creeping back. The Christians have church barbecues. They have Christmas. They have the son of God, for God's sake. Plus, everyone uses the name of Jesus. *Jesus H. Christ. What would Jesus do? Jesus loves you.* I didn't even know what Mohammad's last name was.

Even the Quran mentions Jesus more frequently than Mohammad. And apparently it mentions Mary, the mother of Jesus, more frequently than the Bible does. The Bible!

Kayhan Books is one of the few English-language bookstores in Shiraz, and it's where I go for my Hardy Boys or Enid Blyton mysteries. The store is managed by Mrs. Golli, who has a giant mole on her cheek.

"*Salaam, khanoum* Golli. Do you have a biography of Mohammad— preferably with pictures?"

"Are you a good Moslem?" she asks.

"Yes," I lie.

"Pray for me."

At first I think she wants me to mention her to God that night, but it becomes apparent that she expects a recital, right there in the middle of Kayhan Books.

"*Bismillah-eh-rahman-eh-rahim,*" I begin. "*Alhamdolellah-el-rabel alameen . . .*"

When I'm through, she smiles—her estimation of me rising a notch, alongside her mole. "*Borkallah!*"* she says, "but it's forbidden to depict the Prophet. Do you read the Quran?"

"Every night," I answer, leaving out that I found the Quran far more mysterious than the mysteries she sells. "Perhaps you have a biography of Mohammad without pictures?"

She goes into the back, returning a couple of minutes later with bad news: Mohammad's biographies are all sold out.

---

*"Well done!"

I leave with another Hardy Boys, full price, no discount for prayers offered.

AND THEN THREE YEARS LATER Mohammad walks right into my life.

The summer of 1978, our parents deposit Katayoun and me at Camp Evin, at the foothills of the Alborz mountains. On our first day I notice him standing off to the side—the only counselor with a beard. Mohammad is a head taller than everyone else, and generally keeps his distance from the other *morabis*,* perhaps out of mistrust for their Western clothes and carefree ways. He has an aquiline nose, kindly eyes, and black helmet hair. He kind of looks like a prophet, or maybe a CEO.

One day, Mohammad approaches me in the cafeteria and asks if I want to join him for prayers. I'd mentioned I was Moslem the day before, and so the following day at five A.M., he shakes me awake and together we pad down the hall for *voozoo*.† Then we make our way to a small, lit room at the end of the dormitory, where Mohammad has procured an extra prayer carpet for me. We stand tall upon our respective rugs and for the next ten minutes, he teaches me the easy risings and fallings of Islam, set to prayer.

It is the first time I've prayed alongside anyone.

Also the first time I've prayed at dawn.

Because we pray in Arabic, the word-by-word translations are lost on me, but the feeling? Standing alongside him, I have the sense of being plucked from a sleeping throng of campers for an extraordinary audience with God. There we are greeting Him as the first light spills over Mount Damavand, crests the campus pines, and casts its rays on our upturned faces. There are holy moments in life, moments when the universe splits itself open and reveals its beating heart to you. I'm only fourteen, but I'm pretty sure this is one. Night is transitioning to morning, peace is all around

---

*Counselors.
†Ritual ablutions before prayer.

us, and a fellow Moslem has taken me underwing and taught me the simple choreography of greeting God.

Unfortunately, Ramadan arrives the following day and Mohammad wants to know if I fast.

"Oh yes, fasting—I love it!"

This is an out-and-out lie. I can imagine no worse agony than hunger. But the truth is: I want to impress Mohammad with my devoutness. So I fib.

"Good. Tomorrow after prayers, we will begin the holy fast together."

The thought of an entire day without food is a misery I have not fully assessed. By noon, the mere whiff of salted lunch meats is enough to set me salivating. By midafternoon, I begin to feel faint and take to bed. By nightfall, I have come down with symptoms approximating the flu—fever, chills, the works. At the infirmary, they pronounce me dehydrated and attach me to a drip.

Allah is keeping me busy. This must be what martyrs feel like.

That night, Mohammad visits and expounds on the glories of the fast. Through deprivation, we learn not only to become closer to God, but also feel the pain of our fellow man. Fasting imbues us with a sense of patience and selflessness. It contributes to a lighter body and clearer mind. As I lie attached to my drip, spent and hungry, I am not certain I've learned these things. Is he congratulating me or admonishing me? Later, I hear my name echoing throughout the campus and assume that this too is an effect of fasting. Hallucinations are a rare side effect, so perhaps I am on the accelerated track? Then I see a head appear in my window, lighting fast, every couple of seconds.

This is how it all begins, I remember. *Limp body. Sweat beading on the brow. Visions. I am being called!*

Turns out, yes . . . but not by God. Katayoun had tried to visit me in the infirmary but was turned away, and now stands beneath my first-floor window, jumping up and down and shouting my name.

The following day, I am instructed to stop fasting by the nurses, but my appetite to know God continues unabated and in days following, I continue to rise at an ungodly hour and pray alongside Mohammad. It is my first experience with the brotherhood of Islam. There are a billion Moslems in the world, but I've never prayed alongside a single one, until now. In Islam, one professes one's faith by saying, "There is no God but one God, and Mohammad is His messenger"—and the summer of 1978, I see the truth of that.

THE CAMP CLOSES. Summer turns to fall and the revolution begins its slow burn. On August 19, 1978, an arsonist sets fire to the Cinema Rex in Abadan, and 450 people burn to death. The royalists blame the revolutionaries. The revolutionaries blame SAVAK. Liquor stores burn. Restaurants close. The bazaar shuts down in protest. Hotels and restaurants decree a four-day prohibition on alcohol. The whole country is in mourning.

And men begin growing out their beards.

Just like Mohammad, I realize.

My mother hates the bearded men—*reeshoo,** she calls them—and routinely takes them to task on personal grooming. The truth is, their beards are themselves beards, hiding their newfound politics. Revolution is in the air and a beard is the surest way to distinguish royalist from revolutionary.

That winter the curfew is on, the electricity is out, and cries of *Allah-o-akbar* punctuate the night silence. Rooftop to rooftop, our neighborhood is awash with declarations of God's greatness. After a few nights of this, I begin to understand this has nothing to do with God, that it is really a cry of protest against the Shah. And we are on the wrong side of things. I don't know how I know this, but I do.

God *is* great. But He also sounds a bit terrifying—borne on a hundred indistinguishable voices in the darkness. Islam is a religion of brotherhood, but can you be a true Moslem if you deny your brethren? I ask because I am

*Derogatory term for men with facial hair.

afraid of being jostled, lost, trampled, or shot. In days following, my brethren grow in number, take to the streets, and are dispersed—and when they return, they are mowed down by the army. Forty days later, mourners gather to memorialize the dead. They too are shot. On the fortieth day of their deaths, more crowds, more deaths. And so on until the cocktail of death, God, bloodshed, and religion is too much for anyone to fight—and the Shah leaves.

My idea about God begins to transmute. God and anger. God and injustice. God and the downtrodden. Hearing the thousand voices above and around us, the indignation and anger, I have a distinct feeling that the peaceful God I'd discovered at Camp Evin has ceased to exist. In my head, this new God looked like the ayatollah everyone was talking about, commanding and judgmental and exceedingly powerful—with not a drop of mercy for my fifteen-year-old soul. His name is Khomeini.

Sensing I'd been locked out of a great and powerful movement, I redouble my efforts and increase my prayers from twice to four times a day, one short of the prescribed number. I invoke God's name before meals, before leaving the apartment, before tests and gym class. God is everywhere—even my homework. I write *In the Name of God* very small, in the upper right-hand corner, on everything I hand in. Algebra, Farsi, English Lit, in the dizzying array of ninth-grade subjects, God's name is the one constant—leading to yet another problem: Because I've written His name on everything, I cannot throw away my homework afterward. So in addition to my prayer problems, I have a spiritual waste management situation on my hands. The stack of God-stamped homework grows.

"Listen up, everyone," my algebra teacher says one day, "just because there's a revolution going on doesn't mean you should toss God's name around like a dandelion. It's very disrespectful putting it on your homework, tests, and every little thing. God is not a study aid."

Everyone? So I am not the only one calling on God to help me solve for x?

I stop obsessively writing God's name on every little thing, but there remains the pile of God-stamped homework. I've heard that the proper technique for disposing of an old Quran is to burn it, or set the pages into a stream. "Absolutely not," my mother says when I approach her with the idea of a small homework bonfire on the veranda. And the only running water in Tehran is in the ditches coursing with mountain water—as well as Coke bottles, cigarette butts, plastic wrappers, and other city filth in which I'd sooner bathe than deposit my holy homework, so that's also out. But watching a small cyclone of autumn leaves in the yard, I hit upon it. *Wind.* That night I leave the pile of homework on the ledge outside my window. The next morning I awake to a clean ledge. My homework has dispersed all over northern Tehran—and with it, all evidence of my conflicted relationship to God.

Yet in my heart, I remain a God-tortured boy. I read the Quran. I get *voozoo.* I pray. I have studiously avoided all attempts to convert me. But my mind is in such a state. Every time I step onto my prayer rug, I start to think bad things about the saints—things that are just wrong. Soon, I'm afraid to step on the rug because of the thoughts, and my prayers become a race to the end, so fast that the syllables aren't even distinguishable, lest they be overtaken by those *other* words and thoughts. Holy Arabic and unholy English. My mom says that God loves me. She says a boy who reads the Quran and is blessed by his parents will go to heaven sooner than anyone.

"Yes, but does God know what I'm thinking?" I ask.

"Yes, God hears you. Especially you."

Uh-oh.

Katayoun doesn't pray—except for one night when she asks God for curly hair. The following morning, a cry of delight emanates from her bedroom. On approach, I discover the latest evidence that God is listening, cascading around her face, teasing her cheeks, and taunting my very soul. Curls! It's the first time Katayoun has ever prayed, and not even formally on the rug, more like a spontaneous conversation before bedtime. Luckily, the following morning her hair is flat and there are no other miracles occurring in her room overnight, and I am relieved.

At night, I begin to have a recurring dream: My dream self comes upon a door to the attic. It requires only the mildest effort to push it open—and there they are: a room of birds I'd purchased and neglected over the years. Thousands of them. Teetering on the edge of death. The stench of it nearly knocks me over. Dust motes and feathers drifting, poop everywhere. I realize that even without food or water, they've managed to procreate in the privacy of this forgotten chamber. So I go to work separating the dead from the dying, the dying from the salvageable, and it's the first chance I get to really hold these birds in the palm of my hand without them flying away. Time is running out, has been for years—but somehow they've held on until this moment to die in my hands. From bird to bird I go, holding cups of water to their tiny beaks, but they all expire. Everything I touch. I wake crying. It's the worst dream I've ever had, but who can you tell? I know the attic is my soul—contaminated and beyond salvation.

Countless times, I found myself on the other side of that door, and when I open it, there they still are—waiting for me to watch them die all over again.

WE HAVE JUST EXITED a bakery on Roosevelt Avenue, the major north-south artery that runs against the eastern wall of the American embassy, when I see a group of maybe fifty people gathering across the street. The banners and signs they hoist indicate yet another demonstration is in the works. Nearly a year into the revolution, the people have lost none of their fervor.

"Cyrus, is that you?"

At first I can't see who is calling me.

"Cyrus? *Beyah eenjah!*"*

And then I see him emerge from the crowd, holding a banner at his side. Mohammad. He strides over and puts out his hand. "How are you, *janam*?"†

I am in shock, that's how I am. A year has passed since I've last seen him and now here he is, calm and happy, like this was all so *natural*. My mother is also shocked, chiefly at the realization that this *reeshoo* knows her son. She looks from Mohammad to me, back to him. I'd shown her a picture of Mohammad once, a group shot of the camp counselors, and immediately she'd singled him out—the sole bearded *morabi*. Instinctively, I knew not to mention that we'd prayed together. But now here he is, beard and all, and I don't know how I should feel about this.

To my mother, Mohammad simply bows with his hand on his heart.

"What are you demonstrating for—or against?" she asks. "One never knows which way the wind is blowing."

"They've just admitted the Shah to America. They say it's to begin planning a counterrevolution. One never knows with America . . ."

"I see," my mother replies icily. "And this?"

He unfolds his banner. *Death to Carter* it says in broad, elegant strokes.

"Don't you think there's been enough talk of death?" she inquires.

Mohammad will not meet her gaze.

"You've raised a good son, a religious boy," he says, patting my shoulder and looking me in the eye. Then he bows again toward my mother, says, "With your permission," and rejoins the demonstrators.

Days later, a group of students who call themselves Moslem Student Followers of the Imam's Line scale the walls of the American embassy, take sixty-six people hostage, and put an end to Iranian-American relations. I don't know if Mohammad is a member of that group; I doubt it. I prefer not to think about him as one of the angry masses. Whenever the chants

---

*"Come here!"
†Term of endearment: "my dear."

and bloodshed and anger threaten to overwhelm me, I think back to that pre-dawn moment at summer camp. I owe Mohammad many things, among which is a reminder that God wasn't born on the wind of a thousand angry voices—but on the breath of two that greeted him quietly in a dimly lit dormitory in the foothills of the Alborz mountains.

SHAHIN

After leaving Sadegh's office, Shahin sits in her car, puts her head on the steering wheel, and cries for a half hour. When passersby knock on her window, she waves them away. Then, having given her emotions uncharacteristically free rein, she revs the car and heads home, cooks *chello khoresht ghormeh sabzi*—Max's favorite stew of kidney beans and dried lime—and ladles it into a Tupperware container. From the bedroom she fetches several pairs of his underwear and socks, a gold ring, and a handful of carefully chosen books: Churchill for the mind, Michener to entertain, Mary Renault because that's what Max reads when he's upset (something to do with history putting things into perspective, he once said), and a Quran to impress the guards.

And if the books themselves do not help Max relax, there are always the small white tablets she has pushed deep into the Michener lining at fifty-page intervals: Valiums.

WHEN MAX APPEARS in the holding room looking surprised, dazed, and angry, Shahin is the picture of calm—no longer the emotionally distraught woman who had left Sadegh's office. She does what she always does in ungovernable circumstances—acts like it's the most normal thing in the world to find Max in a prison uniform standing in a building that houses enemy combatants, national security risks, and prisoners of war. They might as well be meeting in the Georgetown cafeteria after a political science class.

"Max!" she says brightly. "I finally found you! Give me a hug."

"How did you find me?" Max says, astonished.

"A little birdie told me. Come. Sit," she says, pulling out a folding metal chair. "We've only got five minutes, but I've got some good news. You're going to be released in a couple days. And in the meantime . . ."

Shahin pops open the lid on the Tupperware and hands Max a fork. "Your favorite!"

But he waves the food away. "Oh, God—you're a sight for sore eyes. I was so worried about you, mouse. That first night when I didn't come home, I knew you'd be concerned. I kept thinking: Who's going to make the *korsi* in the front room and pick Cyrus up from school? And that Katayoun would miss her tutoring session in math. I started to write you a letter, then thought, you'd probably find me first. Are the kids okay? How did you find me?"

The words came out in a rush, but it is not Max's breathless speech that concerns her. In three days, he's lost a good ten pounds. She gives the Tupperware another nudge, then recounts the story of Sadegh and his rise through the Foreign Ministry. Telling a story is good. It clears her head and provides an air of normalcy to their precarious situation. She remembers that Max disliked Sadegh at Georgetown—finding him both pedantic and competitive, chiefly over Shahin. But as Shahin recounts the story, it is not Sadegh's courtship of Shahin that troubles Max. It is his courtship of Khomeini.

"Fuck Khomeini," Max says when she mentions Sadegh's relationship to the ayatollah.

Shahin is startled. But Max is just getting started.

"I'm serious. Fuck Khomeini. Fuck. Him."

Max may have forgotten where he is, but Shahin is painfully aware of their circumstances. She glances at the guard. He is preoccupied with a soccer game on TV. "No need to get upset. A little *parti bazi,*° well-placed friends, and you'll be out in no time. Now, would you please take a bite?"

"I'm on a hunger strike."

Shahin looks at him incredulously. She had expected trouble from government bureaucrats—maybe the prison guards. But she did not see this coming. "For God's sake," she cautions, "don't alienate these people."

"You need to do something for me. Call the State Department and tell them I'm locked up. Then call George Demougeot at Westinghouse. Then my parents. Will you remember that? Their numbers are in my address book."

"Call them yourself. Sadegh has promised you'll be released soon."

"Really?" Glancing inside the bag Shahin brought, Max sees a semester's worth of reading materials inside. "Then why did you bring me *The Second World War*? And *The Persian Boy*? And . . . a Quran?"

For the second time in as many hours, Shahin finds herself fighting back tears. Here she'd been maneuvering behind the scenes, working the angles, and negotiating like a *bazaari*, when Max was hunger-striking and demanding she reach out to the State Department. He had no idea how to solve problems in Iran.

And after all these years, he still harbors resentment of Sadegh.

"Would you trust the word of a man who courted your spouse?"

"Would you please trust *me*?" she says.

She pulls the rest of the books from the satchel. "Give James Michener a good shake. You'll find a few presents to help calm your nerves." Suddenly she is worried that she's been *too* liberal with the pills. Max was in a strange mood.

"Demougeot. State Department. Parents." Max says.

When the guard clicks his tongue, indicating her visit is finished, Shahin turns over the food, laundry, and books. "Take good care of my little jewel," she says to the guard, casually slipping the gold ring into his palm.

°Pulling strings behind the scenes.

OUTSIDE THE PRISON it has begun to snow. When Shahin turns the key in the ignition, her car sputters and dies. So she sets off on foot toward the nearest intersection and is soon lost in thought: She and Max have been married for twenty years. They had met in the fall of 1957, the first day after their respective arrivals in Washington, D.C., in the Hotel Harrington's dining room. "Do you always enjoy the luxury of a late breakfast?" he inquired, his voice brimming with a brazen, friendly confidence. In days following, she enrolled in Georgetown's School of Foreign Service while Max pursued graduate studies at George Washington. There were other suitors, including the rabble-rousing Sadegh, but somehow Max was always there. She saw him on Mondays for lunch. Every night they spoke for a half hour. On Saturdays, Max drove her to her job at Voice of America, then to the movies or dancing. Sundays they studied together at the Library of Congress. She came to know him as a thoughtful, outspoken, dependable man—stubborn too. But in all the years they've been together, she has never known him to be an irrational man.

"Fuck Khomeini?" Where had that come from? What kind of person says that—out loud? And why had he failed to acknowledge her cleverness in finding him and doubted her ability to free him? Instead he asked her to call others for help. Americans. As if they had any leverage.

The snow was coming down thickly now. When Shahin looks up from the creeping tundra, she realizes she's been walking in the wrong direction. Shaking the snow from her headscarf, she beats her arms and reverses course.

But a half hour later, the maze of side streets has not led her to the main road. There's not a car in sight. By now Shahin can barely see twenty feet in front of her, but she is propelled by a sense of righteous rage. The snow has seeped into her shoes. Her extremities are numb, her face caked in ice. But the fire of anger burns inside.

Curse this revolution, Shahin thinks. *Curse Carter. Curse these revolutionaries.*

Just then a pair of headlights illuminates the street, but Shahin's relief turns to dismay when the car disgorges two soldiers.

"Can we be of assistance, *khanoum?*"

"Na, merci."

"We are heading back into central Tehran. Are you certain we can't give you a ride?"

"May your shadow never grow short," she says, turning away. "Please go your way and let me go mine."

The soldier sweeps his arm across the white landscape. "*Khanoum,* you will surely freeze. We are members of the government, allow us to help you. It is our job to protect you! Come, get in the car."

"I don't trust you," she says, in a considerable breach of etiquette.

She can see she'd insulted them. Good. Accepting a ride would mean accepting their authority—and she is not prepared to do that. As the soldiers drive away and Shahin's heart sinks, she sees how in blind anger, we turn away from our rational selves.

MAX

The next day, after the call to prayer rings through the cells, Max folds up his blankets and begins: Forty push-ups. A jog to exhaustion. Forty more push-ups. Then an hour of meditation—or what Max assumes is meditation. He's never done it before, and so he sits pretzel-legged, breathes in and out, and tries to defocus. Time is tricky in prison. Without markers, answers, a release date, time stretches before Max like an ocean.

Usually reading is Max's meditation. It clears his mind and returns him to a place of deep stillness, but each time he cracks open Winston Churchill or Mary Renault, the words begin to blur. He pops a Valium, takes a deep breath, and tries to go within.

But his thoughts keep returning home.

He must take precautions. He must be smart about this—lay the foundation.

Asking the guard for a pen, Max composes a letter to his wife.

My dear Shahin, I thought it might be interesting to record my thoughts on recent events. Not that they are world-shaking, but they are somewhat unique for me, and the usual sedentary life which I am normally accustomed to leading . . .

But the letter is not for Shahin. Max doesn't expect the letter to be mailed—rather, to be read by the prison authorities—and so couched in the letter, which is a true expression of his fatherly and husbandly love, reminders to lock the windows and take Katayoun to her math tutor, is a cleverly planted explanation of his incarceration. He describes his arrest, the detained shipments, the guard who "has kindly brought me water whenever I wanted it, and one small glass of tea with lots of *ghand,* which I ate for lunch," and a step-by-step account of events leading to today. It is a thoughtful letter. It is also a strategic one, intended to set the stage for any legal complications that follow. And it is almost breezy in tone, for an innocent prisoner has nothing to fear. Toward the end, he turns wistful. Who knows, maybe the letter will make it to Shahin after all . . .

> *I guess I'm not really cut out for this sort of thing because my mind wanders and all I can think of is a garden, fireplace, nice flowers, going hunting and fishing, getting the children to school and having you happy and carefree once again. That seems like a lot to desire, and if so I suppose I'm greedy. Maybe I'm also shortsighted because I can think of only one place in the world where the above can be attained. At any rate, with respect to this experience, what is one more story to be told to friends, past and future. I'm sure in time, it will take its rightful place. Love + Kisses + I hope you got to color your hair today. Max.*

His thoughts turn to Westinghouse. What are they doing to secure his freedom? A year ago Ross Perot had hired a small army to rescue two of his stranded employees in Iran, then spirited them out in a risky border crossing into Turkey. Westinghouse has far more resources, not to mention incentive. By his estimate, forty-eight million dollars' worth of equipment lay in the Turquoise Palace, waiting—and Max was their only man on the ground. By now they'd have sounded the alarm up and down the Beltway. The Department of Defense. The CIA. Certainly the State Department.

---

*Sugar cubes.

By now, surely his name was on dozens of Washington memos flying about the capital.

Somewhere, somebody is formulating a plan.

"You are Dr. Copeland, yes? I am Hassan. Please sit."

Hassan appears to be about forty-five. Jet-black hair with features that arrange themselves pleasantly, with the exception of one of his eyes—which is slightly off center. Unsure which eye to look in, Max glances around for something else to look at, but the room is bare. Two chairs. A small desk. A neon light overhead. He folds himself into a metal chair with a writing arm.

"Please tell me why you are here."

"I want to see a lawyer."

"You know why you are here. Say it and it will be easier for both of us."

"I would like to see a lawyer," Max repeats.

"What is your date of birth?"

He waits, pen hovering, and Max thinks: A little information might grease the path to counsel. "August 21, 1934," Max says.

"Where were you born?"

"Lubbock, Texas."

"Eh-slowly. Where?"

Like most Iranians, Hassan cannot begin a word with *s* followed by a consonant cluster. *Slowly* becomes "eh-slowly." What did Max study in eh-school? How did he meet his wife? What brought him to Iran? Before he knows it, Max's life is unspooling as Hassan sips tea and transcribes his responses in a notebook—occasionally stopping to clarify a word or phrase. It seems innocuous enough, but this is how it begins. Slowly. Innocuously. Trust-buildingly.

When he gets to Max's job at the University of Pennsylvania, Hassan lingers. "So—you brought Iranian professors back to Iran, yes?"

In 1964, Max was hired to oversee an exchange program between the

University of Pennsylvania and Pahlavi University. The program had been jointly administered by the Shah and the U.S. Agency for International Development (USAID), an arm of the State Department. Max's mission was to recruit Iranian professors from institutions as exalted as George Washington, Stanford, Princeton, and Harvard with a carefully honed pitch. Pahlavi University was the first American-based university in Iran—and the second in the Middle East. By the end of the following year, he'd sent seventy professors back to Iran, prompting the World Bank to call it "the most successful program of its kind in reversing the brain drain."

"So you were working for the monarchy *and* the State Department?" Hassan asks.

"I was working for the future of Iran," Max says.

"Let me tell you what I think. With your Ph.D. in Iranian education and your trafficking of Iranian professionals, you were a good candidate for the CIA. Yes, CIA, don't look so surprised. When did they approach you?"

Max scoffs. "Do I look like a CIA agent to you?"

"Exactly. No one would suspect a respected doctor." Hassan regards Max coolly. "After you brought seventy professors here, you didn't go to work for the universities yourself. Did you? You sent so many Iranian professors back from America—but you? You went to work for companies with *other* interests. Hughes Aircraft. Iran Electronics Industries. Westinghouse. Tell me, why is a Ph.D. working for defense companies?"

The realization hits Max. This was just a formality. Hassan already knows Max's dossier.

"If I could have gotten a university job, I would have. I don't like corporations. They don't like me much either. But I wasn't doing anything particularly sensitive for them."

Hassan leans forward and smiles thinly. "You don't consider radar sensitive? Or did you forget? A week ago eight boxes of radar were intercepted at Mehrabad Airport, sent by you. Tell me, why is a respectable academic man—an Iraniologist—trafficking in radar?"

"Radar? Listen, the warehouse is stocked with thousands of boxes, thousands, most prepacked, and I can hardly be expected to know the contents of each. I'm not even sure I'd know what radar looked like. So I sent out radar. What's the problem?"

"The problem," Hassan counters, lighting a cigarette, "is the radar belongs to the Iranian air force. Number two, it was smuggled inside personal possessions—books, clothes, pots and pans—and shipped to a civilian address. And three, the problem is without this radar that belongs to Iran, our borders are vulnerable to anyone wishing to undermine our revolution. Which makes you guilty of smuggling, espionage, and theft. These are big problems, *agha* Doctor. Do you know what the punishment is for thieves?"

Hassan draws a quick line across his wrist.

"And for spies?"

Another line across the neck.

"But let us not speak of such unpleasant things. I am a reasonable man." He pushes his pad toward Max. "Write down the names of your CIA contacts."

"I told you, I'm not a CIA agent."

"Shall I help? I will write the first one," Hassan says, scribbling a name. *ARTHUR CALLAHAN.*

How did he know? As CIA station chief, Callahan had presided over the Agency's intelligence efforts in Iran in the 1970s. When he left the CIA, Callahan went to work for Westinghouse. He returned to Iran last December to visit the Shah, and finding an ailing, deeply ambivalent man in Niavaran Palace and a country on the edge of revolution, Callahan recommended that Westinghouse close shop—immediately. He had met briefly with Max to discuss "closeout options." But that meeting had been almost a year ago. *Which meant the revolutionaries had had their eye on Max for at least that long.*

There is another reason the new guard thinks Max is CIA. Before the revolution, SAVAK had shown up at Max's doorstep for an "interview." The plain-clothed officers had been respectful, almost deferential, in their questions about Westinghouse and why its employees had fled Iran so rapidly. Shahin had been absent that night, but Katayoun translated their questions and Max's answers. A twelve-year-old girl. With pigtails. Translating for the secret police. Max had asked her instead of Cyrus because, frankly, her Farsi was better and he didn't want anything mistranslated. Afterward he caught flak from Shahin, who was furious—but what choice did he have? You didn't send SAVAK agents home and ask them to return when it was convenient, did you? *Excuse me, could y'all come back Monday?* It was a relatively benign interrogation with none of the techniques for which SAVAK was known—by current comparison, it was a Riviera vacation—but it alerted Max that he was on their radar. They'd asked about Art Callahan that night. Had Hassan somehow gained access to those files?

"Arthur who?"

"Ca-lla-han," Hassan says, biting each syllable.

"Oh—yes. We met to discuss the logistics of evacuating Westinghouse."

"So you admit to meeting with the CIA?"

"He might have been CIA. I'm not. I don't have a secret name; I don't send coded messages or wait in train stations to exchange identical bags with strangers. I don't have a dart gun disguised as an umbrella. I've never killed anyone for government secrets, or toppled a regime, manipulated an election, or whatever it is eh-spies do. The radar was a mistake."

Hassan lights another cigarette and glares at Max. "My countrymen have been slaughtered and tortured by the SAVAK butchers. We have lost our independence, our hope, our oil, our lives—all because of Western greed. I myself lost a brother to SAVAK. Are you not embarrassed before the eyes of God?"

Then: "Come, let's be civilized, shall we, Dr. Copeland? Or W.A.? Or is it Max Copeland? Or Miles, the name by which you're best known?"

Looking at his interrogator, Max blinks. A wave of nausea washes over him.

Miles Copeland. Max Copeland. It was an unfortunate coincidence. Max had been a freshman in college when Miles Copeland had flown into

Tehran, rented a mob, mounted the CIA's first coup, and imprisoned the popular prime minister, Mohammad Mossadegh, who was threatening to nationalize Iranian oil to the detriment of American and British interests. A college dropout with an Alabama drawl that fluency in nine languages had done nothing to dilute, Miles Copeland would go down in CIA history, best known for an operation that had never been attempted before. The CIA-sponsored Operation Ajax was a stunning success and it cost the American taxpayers less than a million dollars.

In Iran, Miles Copeland was a hated man. For years afterward, anytime anything consequential happened in Iran, it was assumed that the CIA was behind it.

Twenty years later, the whispers followed Max around like a ghost. Social functions. Dinner parties. And denying it only brought further suspicion. Miles Copeland. Max Copeland. Both from the South. Both six foot three. Both experts in Middle Eastern affairs. In Iran, any association with the CIA was bad news. But to be confused with their number one spy, the man who'd taken down Iran's beacon, stripped her political system of integrity, and redelivered her oil into the hands of the British and Americans? God have mercy.

Hassan pushes the pad toward Max. "Write down your contacts."

"I'm not Miles Copeland," Max says forcefully.

Hassan grins. "In 1953 you were barely old enough to have a whiskey—much less stage a coup. I am not an idiot. But my colleagues? When they find out I have the famous Miles Copeland they'll tear you *lat-o-pareh.* No mercy. And who's to say you're *not* Miles Copeland? Your passport? Right now at the U.S. embassy they have discovered several passports registered to another CIA agent. The facts speak loud enough: The lone American left in Iran to represent American defense interests. Smuggling radar. Working with CIA station chief."

*Limb from limb.

Each of Hassan's assertions is like a piranha bite—small but precise—and Max is starting to bleed.

"Even your government doesn't know you're here. You are the forgotten hostage!"

He pauses for the words to sink in. "You will assuredly be put on trial, Doctor. And the world will know about your misdeeds. I am offering you one last chance to cleanse yourself. Write down your contacts . . ."

OUTSIDE THE PRISON, tensions had ratcheted up considerably. In Washington, Carter's military advisors were presenting him with options ranging from mining the Persian Gulf to a full-scale invasion of Iran. The USS *Kitty Hawk* had just arrived in the gulf with a full battle group of warships, comprising the largest naval force in the area since World War II. Outside the embassy, crowds were driven to near hysteria by speakers so frenzied and demagogic that the hostages inside were reportedly more fearful of them than their captors. And in Qum, the ayatollah was consulting his advisors about how to keep the hostage crisis in play for *longer*, having found it a useful distraction from mounting economic problems. The Den of Spies! All around, the forces of nationalism were at work, and the crisis between America and Iran grew darker and deeper. Confrontation was imminent.

In prison, Max is blithely unaware of the forces at play.

CIA Agent Smuggling Radar Equipment Caught

November 27, 1979

TEHRAN—The Revolutionary Guards here arrested a CIA agent who was trying to smuggle eight console radar machines to the United States.

Max Copeland, whose nationality was not identified yet, had booked eight boxes of radar equipment belonging to the Iranian Air Force at Mehrabad customs destined for the United States.

Airport custom officials said that the radar equipment was booked and cleared before the prosecutor at the Mehrabad Airport became suspicious and ordered the boxes be opened.

The investigations revealed that the radar instruments belonging to the Iranian Air Force were being smuggled by Copeland, who was working for the CIA.

Copeland was arrested from his office in Shemiran by the Revolutionary Guards who cordoned off his company for three days. A case of smuggling has been registered against Copeland and a thorough probe has been ordered to find other facts about the activities of Copeland in Iran, the officials said.

According to the Revolutionary Guards and airport officials, Copeland had also remitted about $90,000 to a foreign country.

Airport officials further said that the radar equipment, packed in separate boxes, was sent to the airport by a cargo booking company and the customs officials were told that the instruments were not used in Iran and were now being returned to the United States.

The officials, when convinced, gave the clearance but the prosecutor was suspicious and ordered the boxes opened for a thorough examination.

The Revolutionary Guards were also reported to have seized all the important documents present in Copeland's office in Shemiran to find out further facts about CIA activities and the role of Copeland in Iran.

Meanwhile the government authorities have directed the airport custom officials to be vigilant and examine each and every item being carried by foreigners as well as their luggage.

The matter had also been reported to the Air Force and a thorough probe is likely to be taken by the Air Force authorities to determine how the radar instruments were made available to Copeland the CIA agent.

—Reprinted from the *Tehran Times*

CYRUS

I was forty-eight when I discovered Max's Radar Affair and fell down the rabbit hole of my father's life. I had the pieces of his file taped to the wall, like clues from an unsolved mystery. Shipping records. Letters. Affidavits. Telexes to State. Newspaper articles. I'd heard that detectives find this a useful technique—suddenly a piece of the puzzle might jump out at you, showing how the other pieces fit.

The newspaper article in the *Tehran Times* was curious, mostly for the fact that the story died on page two. Why hadn't any of the American papers picked it up? Any news story out of Iran was big—oceans of ink had been spilled about the hostages—so why had an imprisoned "CIA agent" gone unnoticed? Briefly I found myself wondering if Westinghouse had somehow covered it up.

Over the past weeks, I'd written to all the Westinghouse veterans I could find. Most were retired. Many were dead. That was the trouble with trying to unearth details of a thirty-five-year-old case. Reliable witnesses were scarce. As one former Westinghouse executive wrote me: "I never heard of the radar problem . . . it was likely a well-kept secret within W, with only a few people informed. The people 'in the know' that I could direct you to have all passed away."

Jack Tyman had been president of Westinghouse International in Iran.

He didn't remember my father either. But he knew a lot about the consoles—"the best radar consoles in the world." As president of Westinghouse's business development team, Tyman had sold Iran the ADS-4 radar consoles that my father tried to "smuggle" out.

"The console is the screen on which the images show up," he said. "So if a neighboring country invaded Iran, this was where they'd see that. Each console was about three by three by four feet and weighed about a hundred pounds. You'd need a full-sized truck to ship them. A set of consoles might have cost, say, a million dollars."

Any idea why they were being shipped back to Westinghouse?

"The Iranian air force had made progress payments on the consoles," Tyman said, "but they hadn't paid the final payment—the final ten percent, which was where the profit margin was. Possession didn't take place until final payment. Maybe that's why. But that was Demougeot's bailiwick."

George Demougeot had been president of Westinghouse Iran, and was now deceased.

Further investigation showed that the entire ADS-4 program was riddled with problems. The Foreign Military Sales program required the Department of Defense (DOD) to oversee all Westinghouse matters related to procurement, storage, and delivery—a bid to keep suppliers honest. But the ADS-4 contract was done with the air force using an agent, not DOD, and when President Carter signed the Foreign Corrupt Practices Act prohibiting bribery, it created a huge problem for Westinghouse. Suddenly their $64 million sale was illegal. Both Westinghouse and the Iranian air force pretended that an agent hadn't been used—and that tens of thousands of dollars in bribes hadn't been paid. "You don't do business in those countries unless you have a friend, and a friend gets a piece of the action," one Westinghouse executive told me.

From there the problems snowballed. The air force chose Karaj mountain—a high, rugged, and barren tract near Tehran's Mehrabad Airport—for the first ADS-4 site. But heavy snows and violent winds caused delays. Westinghouse accused the air force of not providing adequate work or storage facilities. The air force accused Westinghouse of not providing detailed specs for equipment—chiefly, it suspected, because it wasn't familiar with the ADS-4 technology in the first place. Bills went unpaid. The violent weather persisted. One night, the winds bent the radome tower in on itself. But eventually the site was declared operational and work began on a second installation at Gonow mountain. From there the Iranians could monitor activity in the Persian Gulf.

By the fall of '78, the unrest sweeping Iran brought work on the ADS-4 program to a halt. With no work and rising instability, Westinghouse pulled its employees from the country. Suddenly Max found himself in charge of a giant warehouse full of high-grade military equipment.

Without DOD's supervision, Westinghouse could ship—"smuggle"—back the radar, then repackage and resell it. Did Max realize this? I knew him to be an ethical man but harbored no such illusions about Westinghouse—a defense contractor building highly sensitive radar systems. Iran was on a critical border, and their systems were monitoring the airport and the Persian Gulf. With a new regime in place that didn't appear friendly, maybe you don't want that stuff to be working? Maybe you want to repatriate, repackage, and resell those consoles, collect another cool million?

The question of ownership bothered me. Did Westinghouse really own the radar until the final 10 percent was paid? Years later, Westinghouse filed suit against the Iranian air force in the World Court. I plowed through the 150-page court opinion and its mind-numbingly detailed descriptions of uncollected monies owed Westinghouse. At the trial, Westinghouse trotted out nineteen witnesses, including George Demougeot. Not once was the ADS-4 radar mentioned. It seemed to me that if Westinghouse had been owed money on those systems, this would be the place to ask for it. They'd asked for everything else—down to the cost of electric adapters for circuit boards.

Westinghouse, it seemed, had pulled a fast one.

BUT THE BIG QUESTION, of course—the one that fueled my life and
upended the décor on my walls—was this: Was my father a CIA agent?
Thirty-five years later I was determined to get to the truth of the matter. In
this regard I was aided by David Smallman—an old-fashioned, politically
liberal lawyer who'd agreed to take me on as a pro bono client. I didn't expect the CIA to cough up my father's personnel files. But Smallman had
gone toe to toe with the CIA before, when the government brought the full
force of its judicial weight against outed spy Valerie Plame. I knew I was in
good hands.

"Things between Iran and America are just getting worse," Smallman
told me over lunch. "You have to understand, there are a lot of ops being
run. Two major wars being fought. Three if you count the war on terrorism. But Iran? That is a catastrophe looming, and the CIA will be disin-
clined to give you any information about anything pertaining to Iran.
There would also be possible blowback to filing a FOIA request."

Blowback? Interesting word choice. The term had originated with Miles
Copeland's Operation Ajax.

"Given all that, the CIA would never release anything suggesting we
spy on Iran. Of course we do. In the past we used multinationals like
Westinghouse to cover our tracks. But the CIA will never admit to this—
and any request which confirms it, especially as it pertains to Iran, will be
denied. Categorically. Filing a FOIA request is useless. Some bureaucrat
will walk it up to the seventh floor of Langley, where it will be summarily
rejected. They won't tell you why. They will neither confirm nor deny what
you're looking for. And it's going to raise a red flag."

So?

"So we're going to need another way in."

I took a bite of my niçoise salad—then flashed on something. "I don't
know if this is useful, but I have an affidavit from the State Department."
I fished it out of my bag and handed it to him. It had been signed by

Demougeot, then went up the chain of command to Cyrus Vance's desk in a matter of days. Effectively it gave power of attorney to my father in Iran.

David looked it over for a bit.

"You sure you want to know about your father? Sometimes it's best to let the past be the past. Take it from someone who's spent twenty years unearthing information."

Oddly, my dad had said something like that a couple of weeks before he died. It was the last thing I remember him saying to me, actually. But I was in too deep to pull back now.

"I want to know as much of the truth as can be known," I said.

David told me it was unusual that my father had been given such a trusted position in Iran—broad power of attorney in a crumbling country— unless maybe he was working for the Bureau of Intelligence and Research (INR), a small but insular division of the State Department tasked with analyzing sensitive subjects. INR was State's own internal, mini CIA. "But there was—and is—a lot of discord between INR and CIA. Your father might've gotten stuck in the middle."

"You can tell all that from an affidavit?"

"Call it a hunch. Look, it's quite possible your father might've been working with State and the Agency. But State is loath to identify itself with the CIA. It's their thing; they like to do things legitimately. My impression is that your father had conflicting loyalties. That he was a principled man of decency and courage caught in very difficult circumstances. Throw Westinghouse into the mix, a million dollars of radar, the hostages . . . Somewhere along the way there was an eruptive moment that made it impossible to act in principled ways. And rather than take the hit, someone hung your father out to dry. That affidavit is fascinating. It was done in a very public, non-Agency way. He may have been set up by his own people."

"Who?" I said, suddenly feeling like I'd been drawn into a game of cloak and dagger. "Westinghouse? The Agency? State?"

"We'll see," David said enigmatically. "We're not going in through the CIA. We're going in through the State Department."

THAT NIGHT I DREAMT of Max. He looked much younger—maybe thirty, with a full head of hair—and I nearly didn't recognize him. He was handsome and happy, and I almost felt as if it were actually him, dropping in from the afterlife. I'd once had a similar dream about Marilyn Monroe. At the time, I was editing a book of eulogies. In my dream she was absolutely radiant—ruby red lips, flawlessly milky skin, flirty eyes. Then the fax machine went off and Marilyn retreated into the ether. The next morning I went to the fax machine, cursing whoever had sent one through at four A.M.—and saw that it was a permission slip to reprint her eulogy.

So here was Max, young, radiant, happier than I ever recalled—appearing while I was knee-deep in his life. And laconic as ever. In my dream he spoke two words: "Follow me."

Oddly, this was the very thing that struck terror into my heart as a kid—the prospect that I'd follow in his footsteps. He seemed sad, excessively intellectual, and perhaps unknown to the world—the exact opposite of my mother. She was the solar-powered light toward whom we all turned, while my father hung distant and lunar in the night sky of my childhood. There's no question he struggled with depression. At two A.M., I'd wake to pee and see the band of light from under his door, behind which he was curled into his books—his chief source of solace. It would have been easy enough to knock, give him a hug, some recognition that he wasn't alone in this world—but did I do that? Did I take one step toward the bedroom?

Every child fears the dark, but to me it was that band of light that struck terror in my heart.

In Max's times of greatest need, I avoided him because I didn't wish to become infected with his sadness or fear or doubt—not knowing that these qualities already lived inside me, and that no matter how much I overcorrected and turned toward Shahin, I could not deny the other half of my blood.

Follow him? It was the last thing I'd wanted to do.

Yet here I am thirty-five years later with the pieces of Max's Radar Affair taped to my walls. Here I am the same age as Max, forty-eight, and awake at two A.M., gripped by the fear that life is passing me by. It occurs to me I might be having a midlife crisis and that the answer lies not in a reevaluation of my own life, but that of my father, who has already set the stage for all this.

Awake, I obsess about him.

Asleep, I dream of him.

Follow me? Where exactly does he intend to take me?

SHAHIN

TEHRAN, 1979

One evening the doorbell rings and there he stands.

Silent and unshowered, Max clutches the family to his chest and holds them tightly for a good, uncomfortable half minute. He has been gone for less than a week, but it might as well have been a decade. Max looks almost spectral, definitely thinner, and his eyes are slightly hollowed. But for now Max holds the entire family—perhaps for the first time—in his arms. Locked down tightly. Like a vise grip.

That night Shahin prepares a feast of lamb stew and rice, Shirazi salad, iced Pepsis, and *naan sangak** so fresh that the steam still rises. She sends out for Max's favorite éclairs. But he picks listlessly at his food and makes jokes about a prison diet—how he is finally at his goal weight.

"Are you going to tell us about prison?" Katayoun asks.

"No," he says, pushing his glasses up. "I'd rather not."

Fine. Sadegh had called earlier reminding Shahin that Max was under strict house arrest and would be watched. The weeks ahead would be difficult enough. For tonight at least, it was best to get back to some semblance of normalcy.

And so for the next few days, the Copelands bake chocolate cakes from

---

*A bread traditionally oven-baked on a bed of river stones.

the dwindling supply of Betty Crocker mixes. Rearrange the living room furniture. Polish the stainless steel counter in the kitchen until it fairly gleams. Max rereads his library of thrillers, mysteries, and history books, while the kids thumb through the Sears catalog and reimagine their lives in America for the gazillionth time. On TV, Ayatollah Khomeini thunders against the Great Satan, and a few miles away on Taleghani Avenue, the crowds outside the embassy grow louder—calling for death to the Shah, death to America, death to Israel.

Apropos of this, Max admits to scrawling *Death to Khomeini* on the prison walls—the first tidbit of his prison life that he coughs up.

"You what?" Shahin says, "*Ya hazrat Ali!*" Max! In pencil?"

"Pen."

"You better pray they don't see it."

"I don't care if they do find it. I hope they do. I wrote it nice and large."

"Oh God, are you crazy?" Shahin says, holding her head. "Do you have a death wish?"

Predictably, Max refuses to answer any more questions. Shut down, shut out, shut up, that is his way. He retreats to the bedroom with a book.

In the Islamic Republic, women stay home while men do battle in the real world, but in days following the Copelands get it backward. While Max polishes, waters the plants, reads, cleans, and cooks—usually spaghetti or mac 'n' cheese plucked from a stash of leftover commissary products—Shahin is out tending to business. The day after Max's arrival a letter from the Iranian Ministry of Justice arrives. She doesn't tell Max, but his trial is slated for December 21. Three weeks away.

Every day Shahin leaves at first light and begins scouting for a lawyer, but attorney-hunting is depressing these days. Their offices are bare. Their fancy diplomas gone. They sit like beaten-down divorcees. It seems the only attorneys left in Iran are here not to carry the banner of justice for-

---

*Expression of astonishment: "Oh, Saint Ali!"

ward, but to scavenge from its sad remains. *Mashghoolam*, they say after hearing Max's predicament. *I'm busy.* Shahin is no fool. She knows it's because Max is American. Recently, there have been whisperings about trying the hostages as spies, and just yesterday an article in the *Etela-at* questioned the professional reputation of any lawyer who'd dare represent them.

Finally, after a dozen such meetings—tea, feigned concern—her sister Mahin puts her in touch with one of Tehran's power brokers. "If anyone can help Max, it's Sharifi." But the vision Shahin encounters in Mr. Sharifi's office does nothing to boost her confidence. There he sits, a cigarette dangling from his chapped lips, as defeated as all the others. Where is his lawyerly feistiness? He looks like an aged cat waiting for death. His office is cold—it's a bad sign when even lawyers can't afford heating.

"*Khanoum*, unlike my countrymen, I don't believe in painting a beautiful picture. The clerics are trying to establish *Velayateh Faghih*, rule by Islamic jurisprudence, and are encountering resistance from the secular forces. It's coming up for a vote. In this regard the hostages have been a great gift to the clerics. Surely you can see how a trial against the U.S. will ensure its passage? How it plays brilliantly as a high-profile act of nationalism?"

"What's that got to do with Max?"

"For all their bravado, they cannot put the hostages on trial. But they can and will put your husband on trial. And if someone at the judiciary hasn't figured out the benefits of this, it's just a matter of time. Do they have proof of his crimes?"

"Of course not. My husband is not a spy."

"Well, that won't matter. They won't need proof. Imagine the prosecutor's news conference: *The Americans are already undermining our new government—just as they did in 1953! What should we do? What must we do as Iranians? As Moslems?*"

Unbeknownst to Shahin or Sharifi, this was true. Years later, in his autobiography, Miles Copeland would boast he had been dispatched back to Iran—again—by President Carter to explore the possibility of yet another coup. A quarter century after Operation Ajax, Max's CIA doppelgänger would not let Iran well enough alone.

"So what am I to do?" Shahin asks.

"Make certain the press doesn't write anything more on your husband. If they come for interviews, turn them away. Keep a low profile. And you must postpone the case as long as possible—at least until after the council has scheduled the vote for the constitution. Even if it goes to court afterward, he will not receive a fair trial. But if it goes to court before? Mr. Copeland will likely be found guilty and receive the harshest sentence under the law."

That was her cue. "Mr. Sharifi, I only wish the other lawyers had your cast-iron spine! My sister has told me of your many gallant feats and love of impossible cases. Naturally, a lawyer of your prodigious talents must be handsomely remunerated." Here Shahin opens her purse, fishes out an envelope bundled with several hundred thousand *tomans*, and slides it toward him.

"'Impossible' is the word, *khanoum*. Regrettably I cannot help."

"Come now, I am not ashamed to say that we need you. What is to become of justice in this country? Surely you are not afraid of these bullies . . ."

"Hah. Do you think it's the bullies I'm afraid of? It's the law. Justice means nothing. Do you know what that idiot Khalkhali said?" A roly-poly man who presided over revolutionary tribunals, Chief Justice Khalkhali was said to be personally responsible for the executions of eight thousand men and women—and reputed to take great pleasure in strangling cats. "He said, 'There is no room in the Revolutionary Courts for defense lawyers because they keep quoting laws to play for time, and this tries the patience of the people.' Can you imagine? I'm trying *their* patience!

"These days, trials are frequently held at midnight, last for a half hour, and conclude with a round of gunfire. Do you know how long they permit lawyers to meet with clients? Sometimes not even five minutes. And lawyers who defend political dissidents are themselves targeted by the regime. I'm sorry, but my hands are tied."

Shahin is about to launch into a fresh volley of pleas, but Sharifi holds up his hand. "How well do you know the Quran?"

"I studied it many, many years ago as a schoolgirl. Why?"

"Good. I suggest you represent your husband. At the very least, you'll have more than five minutes to prepare his case."

"Are you mocking me? As his lawyer? If you haven't noticed, women aren't doing too well in Iran today. Covered. Retired. Segregated. The age of marriage has been lowered to nine, for God's sake. *Nine.* I understand that in court a woman's word is worth half a man's. Is this the court you'd send me into to fight for my husband?"

"God bless the Shah," Sharifi says. "His record on human rights might not have been stellar—but his record on at least half those humans was damn good. Find a way to make that work in your favor. You're a resourceful woman. Turn your weakness into a strength. But if you're going to represent your husband, see that your flirtations are only through the eyes, *khanoum* Copeland. Please adjust your headscarf. And flattery—it won't work in a court of law."

At this, Sharifi abruptly stands up. "Remember, no press. I'm surprised the Iranian papers haven't followed up on your case yet. Make certain it stays that way."

Shahin leans forward. "Why should I trust you about this?"

"You shouldn't. Trust no one, *khanoum*. Not the lawyers in search of a backbone. Not the judge who wants to make a name for himself. Perhaps not even your husband—an American who has yet to explain himself. Trust God."

SHAHIN IS NOT RELIGIOUS BY NATURE. The last time she cracked open the Quran was the Persian New Year, when she traditionally read a prayer to the family. But she had grown up the daughter of a revered and religious man and was well schooled in its verses. "The Quran is a light that responds to the quest for meaning," her father had once told her. Tonight for Shahin, the holy book is not a book of light. It is Defense 101—a legal code to be consulted, underlined, and memorized in defense of Max. With the trial only two weeks away, she's got to make it through 6,200 verses (twenty of which pertain to judicial matters and testimony—but which twenty?) and six hundred pages, memorize it, and build her case. That night, Shahin takes the family Quran down from the shelf, kisses the book, touches it to her forehead, and begins what will become a nightly ritual. Out comes her pencil. Up go her feet on the ottoman. And for the next several hours as the city slumbers, she casts through the word of God looking for possible defense strategies. *Here is a passage on false accusation. Another on bearing false witness. And another passage on forgiveness.*

"Your trial is coming up and we should talk about your defense," she says to Max at breakfast the next morning.

"Yes—I've been talking with the State Department about that . . ."

"The State Department?"

"Yes—they should know I'm in a shitload of trouble. Why didn't you call them like I asked you to?"

"I did. I practically *begged* them to get you out of Iran—but . . ."

She flashes back on the conversation she'd had with a sympathetic but ultimately useless official on the Iran desk. *We are doing everything we can*—which Shahin understood to mean nothing at all. "You're the U.S. State Department, God help us, can't you, I don't know, get him a passport from another country and fly him out that way?"

"I know this is a very difficult situation, ma'am. We are not in the passport doctoring business. If you'll be patient . . ."

Goddamn useless bureaucrats. Max had even worked for the State Department in the sixties—was this how they treated their veterans in an hour of need?

"But?" Max says. "You begged them to help get me out of the country, but . . ."

What could she say? That for all practical purposes, his country has hung him out to dry?

"Max, listen. There will be a trial. That is definite. I can't pull any strings to have it delayed or postponed. It's going to be soon. And like it or not, I'm your best bet. Have you forgotten what a stubborn woman you married?"

"I don't understand. Are you proposing . . ."

". . . that I represent you. Yes. And you can be sure I'll do a good job of it."

"What? No. Absolutely not. There are hundreds of lawyers out there—why in the world would you do this? What do you know about the law?"

"Remember how quickly I picked up Spanish? French? English? The law is just another language, Max—a religious language. I've studied the Quran since I was a girl."

"But why shouldn't I hire a professional? Westinghouse would pay for it."

"Because the professionals aren't professionals. Because *sharia* is the new law of the land—which means you will be tried according to the standards specified in the Quran and in the traditions set by the Prophet. And because right now, every lawyer in Tehran knows just about as much as I do—not a lot. But if you want to be tried in an Islamic court by a secular lawyer, be my guest."

"I do, thanks."

"Goddammit! I've been interviewing every last lawyer in Tehran. And none of them will take your case. They're all worried about taking an American client. Sorry, but you're stuck with me."

Max blew out a stream of air. "Is that why you've been studying the Quran all night?"

Shahin nods.

"Jesus. I was worried. I thought . . ."

"That I was becoming . . . religious?"

"Yes," he laughs.

"Max, exactly how did you land in this mess?"

"Shahin, there's no way I will allow you to represent me. I'm not bringing you into this."

CYRUS

One year earlier: We move to Tehran into a third-floor apartment in the north quarter—a sad place with a dark kitchen, small rooms, and humongous heaters that burp and guzzle. Kerosene is rationed and when we run out, my mom stands in line for five or six hours. Afterward Katayoun and I lug the vat of kerosene up three flights, spilling a steady stream of it on each floor so that long afterward our hallways smell of kerosene, and anyone looking to incinerate the royalists on the third floor need only light a match. But sometimes there is no kerosene. On those chilly nights, we sleep under the *korsi*—a low table with an electric coil underneath and blankets thrown over the top. The *korsi* is a stuffy, overheated thing and somehow the temperature is never quite right; your exposed half is shivering, your covered half sweating. It is a sad, cold, hot, weird winter during which I study, write bad poetry, pop pimples, and style my hair endlessly.

And occasionally make crank "long live the Shah" phone calls. My mother has warned us—repeatedly—about talking politics at school, but she never said anything about anonymous calls at home. We are royalists. Whenever things subside a bit, my mother says, "It's the calm before the storm; the Shah will come back soon." But he doesn't, and so one day I take matters into my own hands. I dial an old camp counselor.

MITRA: Allo?
ME (DISGUISING VOICE): Long live the Shah!
MITRA: OK—and?

Crap! It hadn't occurred to me that there were other royalists left in Iran. But at this point I can't really introduce myself because what kind of idiot begins a conversation with *Javid Shah*? I slam down the receiver. Then realize: *What if our calls are monitored?* For the next several hours I hide by the corner of the window, convinced a jeep will soon pull up and disgorge a band of raggedy *komiteh* men who will arrest me for being an enemy of the revolution, age fifteen.

Other times, I spend hours making up nicknames for my sister—much to my mother's chagrin. "Katayoun means 'queen of the world,'" she informs me. "I spent nine months coming up with the perfect name. Use it."

"How about 'Buzby'? Brilliant, no?"

"Brainless."

"Or just 'Buzz'? You don't like *any* of the names I've come up with?"

"No, love. Is that the kind of inventive mind you have? Honestly, which mother would put up with such garbage with a revolution going on?"

My sister has a different response. Typically a sweet and mild-mannered girl, Katayoun has a secret side that, prodded, turns her into Wonder Woman. Once she chased a bully off our school bus because he was threatening to kick my ass. Weeks later, she openly defied the Revolutionary Guards at the Hilton Hotel who stormed in with their AK-47s and ordered all the women out of the pool. "No mixing of the sexes," they said. "That includes you, little girl." So what does my sister do? Swims farther into the deep end—knowing they won't shoot her or get their fatigues wet by jumping in after her.

Suffice it to say, you don't want to get on Katayoun's bad side—which is exactly what happens when I invent one nickname too many. Suddenly she comes after me, fists blazing, and I flee behind closed doors. *Thwack!* Her fist comes through the door. Astonished, I open the door and for a silent minute, we both marvel at her brute strength. She's twelve. She's just put her fist through a wooden door. Thin wood—but still. Only now we have two new problems: The apple-sized hole means we're not getting our security deposit back. And: How are we gonna hide the hole from our mother?

When she comes home that night, a poster of *PUPPIES DO THE DARNEDEST THINGS!* adorns the door to the family room, and a kitten-in-a-tree poster (*HANG IN THERE!*) graces the other side.

"Do you like our new decoration?" Katayoun inquires enthusiastically.

My mother, who has no wish to stifle our creative impulses, nods weakly.

"No more nicknames," Katayoun whispers.

My mother has her own nickname for us: *Seh Teflaneh Moslem*. The Three Islamic Orphans—since Max is still in Shiraz selling American stuff. As the revolution surges forward and we hibernate in our dreary apartment, my mother draws us ever closer to her orbit. She distracts us from the boredom of revolution with promises, none kept, that she will buy us a monkey, send us to Switzerland, find me a dime store like Woolworths. Sensing she had a hormonal adolescent on her hands, she takes to reading me *The Life Cycle Library*. I tolerate these readings with an air of disaffected, mild interest, but as soon as she puts the book down, I hunt for it, anxious to devour any news about my changing body. Alas, *The Life Cycle Library* is a terrible manual, full of practical advice and pastel drawings, with no hint of the excitement and compulsive desires that electrify my every waking hour.

It isn't until my father joins us that spring, trailing boxes of unsold American booty, that I find deliverance from my frustrations. There it lies at the bottom of one of the many cartons—a "gourmet guide" with 1970s graphic drawings of a couple who from all appearances don't spend too much time on personal grooming. The man has a full beard (he looks like a revolutionary, in fact) and the woman hasn't bothered to shave her armpits. I stuff *The Joy of Sex* into my shirt and make a beeline for the bathroom.

And that is, as they say, that.

"Are you picking at your pimples again?" my mother inquires after I've been in there too long—proving that where the innocence of childhood ends, the innocence of parenthood begins. Outside, the ayatollah has unleashed an extraordinary revolution onto the world. Inside, my revolution is led by a musky couple who, I'm guessing, don't use deodorant. Afterward I return the book to its box, swearing to God to never touch it (or myself) again.

That winter I break every promise to God that I make, vaulting between holiness and filth with no apparent irony. Every night I read a page from the Quran. I also read *The Hardy Boys. The Count of Monte Cristo.* And I read a slew of World War II books; the suffering of the Jews fascinates me, maybe because they put my own pathetic life into perspective, survived, and managed to write a book about it. I plow through *The Diary of Anne Frank* and weep copiously. At fifteen, I am in collusion with the most persecuted race on earth.

THE FOLLOWING SPRING we move to a sprawling three-bedroom off Jordan Avenue that is a bit closer to civilization—by which I mean Kentucky Fried Chicken, Pizzeria, and Disco Fever, a darkly lit music store where I spend every last *toman* of my allowance. Along with the books, Dad has carted in leftover Americana of all kinds. Potpourri. A Flying Nun doll. Records. Lava lamps. A particular source of happiness is the Sears and Roebuck catalog, through which I page in anticipation of our return to America. I dog-ear the pages and carefully consider the side-by-side refrigerators, oven ranges, tube socks, and tank tops that will constitute our next life.

Outside the calls for death multiply: Carter. Israel. The Shah.

Inside I reflexively crank up Karen Carpenter.

I look upon the American belongings as artifacts of a golden time. Just a few short years ago, radio advertisements trumpeted made-in-America appliances. *"Amreekaee! Amreekaee! AMREEKAEE!"* the announcer said, bumped by an echo so that "American" sounded impressive but a bit hollow. The commissaries hawked Pixy Stix and Skippy peanut butter. On TV, *Little House on the Prairie* and *The Six Million Dollar Man* and *Family Affair* were staples. In 1976, my parents signed me up for Little League at Farah Stadium, where Gatorade poured like wine and crowds cheered as young Joe Budsock rounded the bases in his cleats. That was the year Lee Majors blew into town with Farrah Fawcett-Majors.

"Can you believe it?" my friend Ali Reza asked. "The Six Million Dollar Man? In Shiraz?" Shiraz wasn't exactly a cosmopolitan city—the films we got were at least a year old—but here was Lee Majors, *the* action star, coming to Shiraz, and wasn't life grand?

That week our teacher took us to an electricity exhibit, a colossally boring collection of lightbulbs, conductors, and instruments designed to showcase the benefits of electrical current. But as we piled into the strobe room, suddenly, magically, us sixth-grade boys were transformed into Six Million Dollar boys. Lit at the half second, we moved in slow-motion staccato, tossing punches and jousting like our hero. *Eh-eh-eh-eh-eh-eh.* To me, Lee Majors with his arched eyebrow and Washington-crossing-the-Delaware dependability represented the best of America.

"Hey, you and the Shah are both married to Farrahs!"

"Yeah, and I'll bet the Shah's Farah doesn't hyphenate *her* name," Lee might say. "Or use half as much hair spray."

Oh, the conversations that tumbled through my head! Lee's brother was stationed at an air base near Shiraz—the occasion for his visit—and I thought I might have a chat with Lee about recent events. There were twenty-four thousand American soldiers stationed in Iran and they weren't exactly behaving themselves. Perhaps a quick word from Lee might put all that to rest?

Basically there were two types of Americans in Iran: adventurers and corporate (or army) transplants. The adventurers had either married Iranians or come for a more colorful life abroad, venturing deep into Iran's bazaars and learning introductory Farsi. They learned to cook Persian food and mingled freely with the locals. Rarely did they shop at the commissary. I recall a particularly lovely American, Mrs. Jurabchi—blue-eyed and pretty as a catalog model—who'd married an Iranian physician. She was charming and fluent, and at my mother's cocktail parties she always made a point of asking me about my favorite subjects. At school, teacher Wyn Tunnicliff lit us with a love of literature. Chris Bock scrawled history's narrative onto the blackboard. Jeanne Pascale taught biology by pointing to me and announcing, "Cyrus Copeland, I see your epidermis!" The American teachers at the Shiraz International Community School were inventive in their approach to education.

Then there was the other kind, the—I hate this term—*ugly* American who'd come for a paycheck. They only shopped at the commissary and pronounced Iran "Eye-ran" and lived in gated compounds furnished with floral sleeper sofas, God's eyes, and macramé plant holders. They preferred shag rugs to Persian, obviously. Cassie and Mike were the latter sort. By then I was no longer the sole American in my class. Cassie and Mike came from "broken families" and read books like *The Other Side of Midnight*, which according to Cassie had fantastic sex passages. Sullen and blond, Cassie had a half brother who'd allegedly tried to have sex with her. She dropped these tidbits casually, as if she were secretly amused. How can I put it? The new Americans exuded a sense of *danger*. One time I remember Cassie brought her collection of halter tops to school. That morning the sixth-grade girls paraded into the bathroom and came out minutes later, belly buttons and shoulders exposed, strutting and chattering in that flip, slightly cruel way young girls have about them—what are *you* looking at?

Did I mention it was Ramadan?

All across Iran, Americans were making waves. Recurrent episodes of public drunkenness and violence were widely reported. In Isfahan, a couple of women clad in skimpy shorts and halter tops (again with the halters!) strolled through the Friday mosque, chatting and laughing while Moslems prayed. A teenager drove his motorcycle through the royal mosque. Several women overturned a table in a crowded restaurant because of slow service. Another American shot a taxi driver in the head in a dispute over the fare. And almost all the culprits went unpunished because the twenty-four thousand members of the American military enjoyed diplomatic immunity under the Status of Forces Agreement, and the balance had U.S. passports backed by their powerful embassy in Tehran.

"I can understand why people would be appalled at American behavior," Sandy Mendyk would later say. As the U.S. vice consul, Sandy had seen everything. "The drunkenness in Isfahan. There were rumors some of the wives were running a prostitution ring. Companies had slots to fill and had to go scrounging for people. Sometimes they didn't end up with the best sort."

Then in 1979—overnight, it seems—they disappear. Iran's avowed ally becomes its staunchest enemy, leaving fifty thousand Americans no choice but to flee. They take what they can carry. The commissaries close. Wonder Bread? These days there's not even the unleavened kind, wrapped in newspaper with hot pebbles clinging. At Mehrabad Airport, there is an exodus of blue-eyeds and their Samsonites rushing toward the gate, clutching their tickets. We are half Iranian. We stay. Things will get better, my mother says. But they get steadily worse and every day I feel the weight of being American on my puny fifteen-year-old shoulders.

Later I would come to understand that I am the by-product of two of the most ethnocentric cultures on the face of the earth. Cultures tend to perceive the world through their own unique lens, of course, but Iran and America are fairly exceptional in this regard. Still, my parents worked hard to cultivate a sense of duality in us. We fasted for Ramadan. Had barbecues on the Fourth. Learned to crack *tokhmeh* seeds, curse in Farsi (sex, death, prostitutes, the more colorful the cuss the better), and haggle in the bazaar. "Kids of mixed marriages are often smarter, better," my mother said. I'm not sure that's true—but I do know that it never seemed an either-or choice. Until now. The crack between my two worlds has grown into a chasm, and I am falling headlong into the abyss.

One of my last memories of the American presence in Iran was this: My father took us to see the IEI* school production of *The Wizard of Oz*. It was an excellent show, very polished, with good production values and rousing numbers. Dorothy was a tall blond American girl with a crystalline voice that cracked with sweet sorrow at just the right moment. Two of my friends, Babak and Bijan, played Munchkins. When the wicked witch appeared, it was in a blaze of dry ice that elicited *ooh*s and *aah*s. The production was testament to everything good about America—its excellence, its sense of wonder and theatricality and hope. It was *outsized*. Soon the cast would sail out of Iran on leased 707s, having discovered that although they could create little Americas all over Iran, there was no place like home.

And now here I am surrounded by their artifacts—books, records, posters of John Travolta—while they're back in the States enjoying hamburgers and strawberry milkshakes. One afternoon on the way home from school, I am accosted by a couple of university students. "Where are you from?" they ask. But they have a gleam in their eye and by now, I know American is a dangerous thing to be. I sprint home and proceed, for the umpteenth time, to rearrange our furniture. I corral Katayoun into this effort, and together we heave all the furniture into the middle, a nucleus of soft fabrics and dark woods, then spin it outward again in fashions that emulate the Sears catalog—the fount of my inspirations.

"What is this, school?" my aunt Mahin inquires when she visits that night. "Everything is lined up so precisely."

It is. My right angles are a stab at some measure of order in our messy and ungovernable lives.

It is about to get a whole lot messier, too. It makes me laugh—those halcyon days when I looked forward to Lee Majors's arrival. A spy in Iran! I'd begged my dad to get me his autograph before Lee and Farrah decamped in a flurry of blond curls and limousine exhaust. The following

---

*Iran Electronics Industries.

day, he handed me a cocktail napkin. The message on it looked suspiciously like Max's chicken scrawl.

Dear Cyrus, be a good boy. Love, Lee Majors

It was a final memento of my father's curious sense of humor. Here I'd been worshipping a TV spy when possibly a real one had been right under my nose all this time. Drilling me on homework. Making pancakes. Planting morning glories. Subverting the revolution.

PART 3

TRIAL AND TRIBULATION

SHAHIN

O ne Friday morning, Shahin is rummaging through some old files
when a card slips out and lands at her feet.

On the occasion of the Coronation of Their Imperial Majesties
The Shahanshah Aryamehr and The Shahbanou of Iran
coinciding with the Forty-Eighth Anniversary of the Birthday of
His Imperial Majesty
Mohammad Reza Pahlavi Aryamehr of Iran
The Ambassador of Iran and Mrs. Ansary
request the honour of your company
at a Reception
on Thursday, October 26, 1967
from seven to nine o'clock.

R.S.V.P.
Regrets only   *3005 Massachusetts Ave. N.W.*

The black ink still glitters. Printed on the finest stock, it is so slick and
sturdy that twelve years later it looks new. Shahin remembers the ambassador's party. She had worn a floor-length Valentino gown—a keepsake

from her days as a model in London during the 1950s. Back then, she had paraded the newest continental fashions before London society—duchesses, ladies, marquesses, anyone with a deep purse and a taste for colorful fashions from Paris. Shahin had acquired a few dresses herself, as well as a sartorial flair that has stood her in good stead ever since.

The Washington party was a wildly extravagant affair—luscious thickets of kebab, jeweled rice, chilled vodka martinis, and rivers of French champagne. The guest list was studded with Iranian and American captains of industry, artists, professors, and politicians. Richard Helms, the director of the CIA, was there. So was politico Henry Kissinger and television host David Frost. It was rumored Elizabeth Taylor might show up. Max recognized a few of the professors he'd recruited for Pahlavi University, all of whom shook his hand warmly.

Ambassador Ansary himself seemed to be channeling Jay Gatsby, as he regaled Max with his recipe for a successful party—champagne, caviar, and violins. A master linguist and inveterate social climber, Ansary was heir apparent to the Washington social whirl. No one doubted it was his wife, Maryam, whose impeccable taste was behind the affair, but that did not dissuade Ansary from freely offering his advice on drinking and entertaining: Nurse a single scotch, he told Max. Never mix wine and whiskey. Change menus frequently. Mix Eastern and Western cuisine for a convivial atmosphere.

It was the Shah who fascinated Max. He cut a handsome figure but was perhaps a bit shy. For much of the evening, the Shah had stood off to the side, letting his third wife, Farah Diba, greet well-wishers. Meanwhile, Shahin had been speaking with the ambassador's wife when she was informed that the Empress wanted to meet her—causing Shahin to spill her strawberry compote down her décolletage.

"Dear God, you certainly can't greet the Empress like *that*," Maryam said.

"Take me to her," Shahin replied. "Quickly, before I lose my nerve."

In retrospect, the red stain struck her as a terrible omen, a sign of bloody times to come. But that night, Shahin joked about it.

"Look how nervous Your Majesty makes her subjects," Shahin said, pointing to the stream of red juice staining her bone-white gown. They shared a laugh.

She found Farah to be lovely—educated, gracious, and quite beautiful. Also curious: Where had Shahin grown up? What did she study? Had she met His Majesty before? Eventually Shahin concluded that the Empress was not only putting her at ease, but also doing due diligence. The Shah's second wife, Soraya, had been a classmate of Shahin's. Perhaps Farah thought Shahin was one of her husband's former girlfriends?

Seeing Max chatting with the Shah, Shahin brought the Empress over. For a few minutes they stood conversing with the royal couple. It was autumn and a light breeze came in through the French windows.

"I am familiar with your work on behalf of Pahlavi University," the Shah addressed Max. "Education is vital to Iran's advancement in the world, and it's my intention to make Pahlavi the finest university in Iran. Perhaps even the Middle East. Tell me, Dr. Copeland, do you believe this is possible?"

Max, who had written his Ph.D. on higher education in Iran, coughed up a few tidbits on the challenges ahead.

The Shah regarded him thoughtfully. "I would like to extend a formal invitation for you to come and continue your work in Iran."

Max smiled and bowed slightly, as Shahin had taught him. "How kind."

"I am not being kind. Iran needs men like you, Doctor—men who might marry Western education and curriculum to the changing needs of a modernizing nation. Men of cultural sensitivity. I hope you won't take my invitation lightly. Promise me you'll think about it?"

The Empress had made a similar proposal to Shahin earlier that night. And so it was that on the Shah's forty-eighth birthday, Shahin and Max found themselves contemplating an alternative future in Iran. For who could turn down the call of royalty? Shahin had never been more proud of Max as he stood speaking with the Shah about the educational needs of Iran. And he looked so dashing in his tuxedo.

Twelve years later, holding the invitation to that magical night, Shahin finds herself wondering how everything could have gone so drastically wrong so quickly. The Shah on the run, Max under house arrest, and Pahlavi University shut down for "cultural re-education" and purged of every bit of Western influence Max and his professors had introduced. His new hires had long since fled to America.

HER REVERIE IS INTERRUPTED by a sharp knock at the front door. "Open up on orders of the Ministry of Justice."

"I'm alone," Shahin says. "I won't open the door without my husband here."

"You won't open the door *because* your husband is there," comes the reply. "We just spoke with the landlady. We have a warrant to take him downtown."

"Slide it under the door," Shahin says. Seconds later a slightly rumpled document appears at her feet, embossed with the ministry's logo and signed by Ayatollah Beheshti himself. It had gone straight to the top.

"How do I know this is authentic?"

"Khanoum," warns the guard, menacingly.

"You can have your document," she says, sliding it back, "but not my husband. Now go away, and be ashamed that you have disturbed a family this early."

Sadegh had promised Max his freedom—at least until the trial ended. Had someone in the government roused a judge from his weekend slumber and gotten Sadegh's word overturned? There had been a well-publicized argument within the new regime involving the Foreign Ministry, mostly over the hostages, and it had grown increasingly rancorous. Had Max become a pawn in a power struggle? Shahin knows one thing for sure: If she gives up Max, she is not likely to get him back.

Drawn by the commotion, Max and the kids—still in their pajamas—walk into the living room. She puts a finger to her lips. Outside, the men are whispering.

"*Khanoum*, believe us, we just want to talk with him. We will return him tonight."

"What do you take me for? Sell it somewhere else, brother."

"You've left us no choice."

More whispering. Seconds later the door reverberates with a thunderous crash. Then another. *They are knocking down the door.*

"Okay, okay, wait," Shahin says. "Give us a minute." She disappears into the kitchen. When she returns she is wielding a carving knife. "I'm holding a knife to my chest," she cries. "You force open this door and my blood is on your hands."

It's as if a lioness has burst forth—a terrified and powerful and semi-suicidal lioness.

"Okay, calm down," the man says, which brings a sour smile to Shahin's face. Hysteria, men were so reliably afraid of it. "*Khanoum*, please. Open the door. I just want to talk."

"Just talk?"

"You have my word."

"Swear to God?"

"I swear."

"Go downstairs in the street where I can see you."

As the men descend, Shahin turns to Max. Scattered throughout the apartment is a treasure trove of things indicating the Copelands are not exactly Islamic Republic enthusiasts. The invitation she held only moments before. Photos with the Shah. Commendations. Invitations to royal court. And, rolled up under the armoire, a woven portrait of the Shah and Shahbanou. Aware that more men might be lurking behind the door, Shahin silently points out a few things to Max, hoping he will use this time wisely and conceal the evidence, for she does not know how long she can keep these hooligans at bay. Then, donning a headscarf and a coat over her nightgown, she descends to meet the revolutionaries.

Outside it is an improbably sunny day, almost too bright. It is the middle of winter, but Shahin has already broken into a sweat.

"See here," the smaller guard says. "We have a warrant . . ."

"Your names?"

"With deference, Saiid," the taller one replies. He is a bear of a man, but quiet, with a straggly beard. It's clear his smaller, wiry friend is in charge. "This is my colleague Akbar."

"I've told you what I think of your warrant. My husband is to be held under house arrest—call the Foreign Ministry."

"The Foreign Ministry has no business with the Ministry of Justice," Akbar says.

"So the left hand doesn't know what the right is up to? How convenient. But until you clear up these inconsistencies, my husband stays put. And doesn't it strike you as the height of arrogance to overturn the word of Khomeini's right-hand man? Sadegh Ghotbzadeh himself decreed my husband stay under house arrest. When I find out who is behind this, he will face the full wrath of Mr. Ghotbzadeh *and* the Imam—and I wouldn't want to be standing in the path of *that* hurricane."

Years ago, Shahin had been principal of a school in Shiraz. In that capacity, she had learned how to handle everyone from disgruntled parents to imperious board members, usually with a combination of intimidation and Aristotelian logic. These armed guards were no more than wayward students, probably eighteen or nineteen, barely out of school, probably assigned to their position as small thanks for their participation in the revolution. A title and a gun. It took so little to make today's youth happy.

Glancing up, Shahin sees their landlord looking down from her first-floor window, clearly displeased at all the attention this was attracting. In the adjacent window, another face. All across the neighborhood, Shahin realizes, a sea of faces in windows and behind curtains are watching her with bated breath—perhaps wondering how long a woman might hold two armed guards at bay. She wonders that herself.

"We are only doing our duty . . ."

"Duty? It's your duty to terrorize people on a Friday morning, dragging them from their warm beds? Is this the Islamic Republic? You have only five duties as Moslems, none of which include harassing innocent foreigners."

"*Khanoum*, that is for the courts to determine, and—"

"And they shall, when he appears for trial and not a moment sooner. Where are the two goons who usually guard our house?"

"I gave them a break," Akbar says.

"I suppose you told them to return tonight, when you said you would bring my husband home?"

"Of course."

"Do you know what the Quran says about liars?"

In this fashion—over a sustained volley of small insults and Quranic quotes—a couple hours pass. Shahin is dimly aware of passersby, all of whom keep their chins tucked and eyes averted. Even the *koocheh* boys* who normally co-opt the adjacent street have taken their soccer game elsewhere. When her mouth goes dry she excuses herself to get a sip of water from a neighbor, then returns and lays into them anew. The object is to keep talking, keep them engaged and distracted until either they leave or someone intervenes.

Or until Akbar loses his patience, which is eventually what happens.

"*Basteh!*† Saiid, go fetch the doctor. Go! *Khanoum* has made donkeys of us."

The next few seconds pass in whirlwind slow motion.

When Saiid makes a break for the front door, Shahin sprints after him. "Do not answer the door," Shahin yells when the landlord answers the in-

---

*Street boys.
†"Enough!"

tercom. "There is a minor misunderstanding to be sorted out." The silence that follows is interminable, then, *click*, the building door swings open. The three of them race up the stairs to the second-floor landing, where Saiid pounds on the apartment door.

"You gave me your word! If you are a proper soldier of Islam, you cannot enter this house. Can-not."

Saiid pauses, and then, with the full force of his ungainly body, hurls himself against the door again.

"Truly, Allah guides not one who transgresses and lies," Shahin shouts, which appears to temporarily stun the men. "You swore to God. Saiid, I can see from your gentle demeanor you are a good man. A kind man. Your name indicates you have the blood of the Prophet. *Transgression against God is a sin for which there is no atonement.*"

Saiid takes a step back and looks at Akbar. For a second it appears he might cry.

"This is your fault," he says to Akbar angrily. "You shouldn't have promised."

"Me?" Akbar says incredulously.

"Let's just say he wasn't home."

"The entire neighborhood has seen us belittled by a woman, fool. He's under house arrest—of course he's inside." Spinning around, he pounds on the door: *tagh-tagh-tagh*.

For a moment, there is only silence.

"*Surah* 24: If ye find no one in the house, enter not until permission is given to you: if ye are asked to go back, go back."

Silence and a zillion dust motes hold the three in perfect abeyance. For the past hour, Shahin's quotation of scripture has appeared on her tongue almost intuitively—proof that her nighttime preparations have paid off. Each quote, each verse perfectly timed.

Suddenly Akbar raises his hand and, in a move that stuns Shahin, backhands Saiid, sharp and swift across the cheek. Then he turns to face the woman who has emasculated him.

"This is not the end, *khanoum*. When my superiors find out you have disobeyed our warrant, you'll be next. You will regret this."

Turning on his heels, Akbar leaves—almost pushing Saiid down the stairs.

INSIDE, Shahin collapses onto the floor, suddenly aware of an approaching migraine. The family gathers around. "Give me a second, I can't breathe. Give me an aspirin."

When Max returns with the aspirin, she downs it, then looks directly at him. "What did you do?

"Us? Don't worry, we hid everything—or flushed it. The apartment is clean."

"No, *what did you do*? I think I've earned the right to know. Kids, go to your rooms. Your father and I need to talk."

Increasingly Shahin suffers from migraines. When she feels one coming on, she retreats to the bedroom, draws the curtains, and wraps her head in a wet towel. And she feels one coming on now. But the wolf is at the door. And she wants to know why.

She has no intention of abandoning this line of questioning.

MAX

Max had once loved Iran. Once he had been so head-over-heels in love with the country that hearing anyone disparage it actually *hurt* him. He had written of this to Shahin's mother. "When people criticize America, I don't mind. I even join in. But I cannot bear to hear someone speak of Persia in even a derogatory tone. I love Shahin *joon's** country more than mine—so much more—because it is a part of her, and very, very dear to her heart."

In 1965, Max and Shahin and year-old Cyrus were living in Arlington, Virginia. Max was working for the State Department as a Fulbright Officer, recruiting university lecturers for such distant lands as Egypt, Greece, Afghanistan, Turkey, and Iran. Abroad, the Shah had just launched the White Revolution—a far-reaching set of political, social, and economic reforms aimed at transforming Iran into a modern industrial society. Fueled by $500 million in yearly oil revenues, the Shah's initiative was the fastest-growing, most ambitious development program in the Middle East.

Of particular concern to the Shah was education. In recent years, thousands of young Iranians had left the country to study abroad, and many failed to return when their studies were completed. And it was only getting worse. In the prior 140-year reign of the Qajar monarchs, 93 students were sent abroad. Shahin's father had been one of them. During Reza Shah's reign, the number grew to 278. But by 1965, more than 18,000 Iranians

---

*Jan or *joon*: "dear."

were studying abroad—and it was a tremendous drain of both money and talent. To combat this, the Shah envisioned a partnership with the University of Pennsylvania to bring American education to Iran.

He had announced the venture during a speech at Franklin Field on Penn's campus. "We are confident that the fruitful cooperation between this distinguished center of learning and our newly conceived university will strengthen the bonds of friendship between my people and the people of this great country," the Shah said.

When he learned of the program, Max wrote to the president of Penn, Gaylord Harnwell, with a proposition: Hire him to recruit professors for the new school. A month later, Shahin and Max were living on Philadelphia's Main Line in a sprawling three-bedroom house ringed with maple, oak, and apple trees. Max was only earning $6,500 per year, but he had meaningful work in education, and it brought him a step closer to his wife's country, culture, and heart.

Soon their home became a gathering place for expats, professors, even the Iranian ambassador. When Max's father arrived for a visit, he was impressed—although maybe a little out of place. "Shahin had a party one night and invited 38 people, including Max's boss and his wife, people from the State Department that do work similar to Max, people from the Egyptian, Turkish and Iranian embassies and the Voice of America," he wrote in a letter to his mother. "Voleta and I were hobnobbing with a lot of dignitaries but we behaved pretty well."

Work on the Pahlavi-Penn project was time-consuming and often inefficient, given the diverse interests and parties. In Iran, the locals resented pushy foreigners. And the Americans were frustrated by a culture where self-interest drove almost all decisions. The Shah saw two benefits to the program: It introduced Western education to Iran, and it shifted the focus away from Tehran University, which had become a hotbed of political activity. And the United States saw a benefit, too. The U.S. Agency for International Development (USAID), the State Department's sponsor of the program, wanted to use the project as a way to check Russian influence.

Against this backdrop, it took much fortitude and finesse to make progress, but Max was determined. He traveled across the United States, luring professors from Georgetown, Yale, Brown, and Stanford with a well-rehearsed pitch. To younger teachers, he casually mentioned they could avoid the draft in a city as lovely as Shiraz (which, by the way, had weather like Tuscon). To Iranian professors, he emphasized the opportunity to educate their own people at home and strengthen the intellectual infrastructure of the country.

A university pamphlet enumerated the benefits of life in Shiraz: "The lovely outlying gardens, the wide modern streets and boulevards, the modern medical and educational facilities, including an American Community School, have made this city one of the most attractive places to live in the whole Middle Eastern region. This is really where East and West meet. There is a European and American community of about 300, primarily composed of outstanding scholars, technologists and scientists. Their presence adds much to the cultural atmosphere of the city. English-speaking movies, social events, visiting lecturers and artists provide a busy calendar of events . . ."

One of the most gratifying parts of the job was the opportunity to build a library from scratch. Growing up on a ranch in Grove, Oklahoma, Max had attended a one-room schoolhouse alongside hillbillies and Indians who barely knew how to read. The first time he laid eyes on a library, he thought his mind had died and gone to heaven, and soon found himself contentedly adrift in a sea of literature and history. Books were his refuge from a dusty life of herding cattle and clearing brush. So twenty years later when the opportunity to help build a library on the other side of the world came up, he jumped at it.

The Pahlavi library was to house forty thousand volumes in English. Max met with Penn's librarian to help build a basic list, which he supplemented with a study of the Harvard catalog. He then began contacting publishers, other libraries, and university presses, asking for books at a discount or for free. Soon, nearly a ton of books a week was being shipped to Shiraz, where another American librarian cataloged them.

Books and professors. It thrilled Max to tilt America's trade balance ever so slightly. So many of America's efforts to build foreign influence had failed—Vietnam being the latest—but at Pahlavi University, East met West with considerably better results. By 1968, the university was turning out students with a higher GPA than any other university in Iran. One thousand students were living on a modern campus designed by a young architect named Minoru Yamasaki, who would later design the World Trade Center. Most of these students got in on their own merits, not their family connections.

When the USAID contract with the State Department ended as a matter of policy, Max orchestrated a contract directly with Pahlavi University, prompting the president of Penn to write Max and personally express his gratitude. "The success achieved under your direction was a major factor in the establishment of a direct contract between Pahlavi and Pennsylvania. I believe that this is a unique development in the field of international cooperation between universities. As the chief architect of this innovative step and director of subsequent operations, you can be justifiably pleased."

He was. Max had never been happier. In Pahlavi-Penn, he'd found a bridge between his homeland and Shahin's. His love for Iranian culture grew deeper. But he couldn't help feeling he was on the wrong side of the bridge.

ONE DAY a note from Arthur Upham Pope crossed Max's desk.

Pope had established the Asia Institute four decades earlier in New York City—but the institute had fallen on hard times, and the Shah invited him to relocate it at Pahlavi University. So Pope picked up his life, his cats, and his wife and moved to Iran at the ripe age of eighty. Pope wrote to Max and advised him that he wanted to purchase the Maleki library for Pahlavi

University. At fifteen thousand volumes it was "by far the most important library assembled in Iran in modern times (and) would really attract great scholars from abroad." Pope was quite the scholar himself, having published a three-thousand-page *Survey of Persian Art* showcasing the art of Iran from prehistoric times through the present.

Pope's note put an idea in Max's head. He wanted for himself the kind of life Pope had—a life that crossed cultures and brought the peoples of the world closer together. Pope was old and frail and dabbling with Shahin's family's library. But he was living Max's dream. Max was young, working for Iran and the university, but at a great distance.

And so it was that on November 25, 1965, Max found himself en route to Iran for the first time—ostensibly to negotiate some university contracts, but really to test an idea of an alternate future. Stepping off the plane at Mehrabad Airport with Shahin, he found himself in a real-life Oz. An only child and something of a loner, Max was swept up into a vortex of love and enthusiasm by Shahin's family, who took up one-third of the arrivals lounge. *"Vay, beya bebeenamet!" Mash'allah!"* The Malekis descended on the couple like a blanket and enveloped them. Shahin's brothers pumped Max's hand for a good twenty seconds. Her youngest brother, Mosoul, kissed him on both cheeks, while Shahin disappeared under an avalanche of kisses.

The following days were a whirlwind. The bazaar. Tea houses. Each night a different party in their honor. Daytimes, Max explored Tehran's tree-lined avenues or hiked in the mountains. "Don't think I need to tell you what a wonderful time we're having on our trip," Max wrote his parents. "Iran is a beautiful country, and a varied one too, with deserts, mountains and forests. I went hunting three times. Got a partridge—my first—on a very, very high mountain outside Tehran."

He learned the art of taking public taxis. Standing at an intersection with his arm out, Max waited until an unmarked car, often already full of passengers, slowed down long enough for Max to shout out his destination.

---

*"Let me take a look at you!"

If the car was headed that direction, it stopped and Max got in and made small talk with his fellow passengers—who reassembled themselves to accommodate his six-foot-three frame.

He also learned the fine art of *taorof.* An intricate code of behavior that reminded Max of the Japanese code of honor, *taorof* was an elegant *pas de deux* where everyone knew what to do with grace at any given moment—resulting in a harmonious society where one placed concern for everyone else's welfare above one's own. Or at least seemed to. The "you first—no, *you* first" scene often held Max up at the doorway for a good ten seconds. Basically, *taorof* was a fight for the lower hand. "Manners are everything in Iran," Shahin explained. "For a dinner party, you can't simply show up with a dainty box of napoleons. You have to bring a whole kilo."

One day, he and Shahin were invited to a wedding. Kazem was Shahin's second cousin and onetime suitor who had since gotten engaged to an Afghan princess. A handsome fellow with a mustache and eyelashes so thick his eyes seem to struggle under their weight, Kazem challenged Max to a shooting match. But this was no *taorof.* Turns out Kazem was a little miffed at Shahin for turning down his marriage proposal at age fifteen, and so, donned in their wedding finery, the two took out their guns and took aim at a pebble winged into the air. Then at plates resting on the far wall of the garden. When Kazem offered Max a cigarette, he interpreted it as a peace offering—but no, Kazem wanted to shoot it out of Max's mouth.

"Enough," Shahin cried. "Stop this tomfoolery! I don't want to become a widow at your wedding, Kazem!"

But Max wasn't one to stand down from a challenge. Not in front of Shahin's family, of whom he had become inordinately fond. Taking thirty paces, Max turned to face his new nemesis.

"Bazham boro," Kazem insisted. Farther back!

Finally Max stood at the far wall surrounded by shards of china. This was not good. The distance between him and Kazem spread before him like the Sahara. A thought skipped across his brain: He had not told Shahin how he'd like his remains handled. A shot rang out. The cigarette was demolished. And Max could taste the faint, sour kick of gunpowder on his lips.

Out came mounds of Caspian beluga. Jeweled rice. Freshly slaughtered lamb. Tubs of rosewater ice cream, all served up by waiters in braided gold uniforms. An Iranian pop star serenaded Max—"our special American guest"—with his current hit song. In the days that followed, Max came to love this country of turquoise minarets and poets, where people shot cigarettes from his lips, serenaded him, and treated him as their long-lost son. Everywhere he went, people opened up to Max's genial, curious approach. Villagers. Nomads. *Bazaaris.* Everyone was taken by the amiable American whose knowledge of Iran often exceeded theirs.

Chief among Max's delights were the Persian carpets. In the Orient, carpets were man's constant companion, adorning the sacred areas where he said his prayers, and decorating his house. But in Iran Persian carpets were an oasis of color and light. For hours, Max watched as bazaar salesmen unfurled them—here was a Kashan, or might he be interested in a Tabrizi? "All the paintings of the Renaissance aren't worth one Persian carpet," Max wrote his parents. In a week, he could spot the difference between a Jozan, a Balooch, and a Tehran. In two, he could tell you the ratio of wool to silk, the knots per centimeter, and the type of knot used. He became a devotee of *joojeh kebab*† and rosewater ice cream. Of poets— Hafez, Rumi, Saadi, Omar Khayyam, and the most Persian of all poets, Ferdowsi, whose *Shahnameh* was a national epic of 50,000 dazzling verses. "I know of no other country except maybe Japan that has produced as many poets as Iran," he wrote. "Did you know that the word 'paradise' is a Persian word? Now I understand why."

But paradise was getting busy. Iran was buzzing with foreign investments and flush with capital from the sale of her oil. Outside Isfahan, surveyors scouted for the final location for a $285 million steel mill. A $450

*Bazaar merchants.
†Chicken kebab.

million pipeline under construction would carry natural gas from the oil fields, across the desert, and into the Soviet Union. At Bandar Shahpour, a $100 million petrochemical plant jointly owned by Iran and America's Allied Chemical Corporation prepared to open. Everywhere Max looked, something was being built. Oil refineries. Ports on the Persian Gulf. A new state-of-the-art dam. Tehran was a bustling, modern metropolis with more than a million cars, most of which seemed to be making U-turns at full speed.

Max stood at the vanguard of the White Revolution. Massive industrialization and social change were on the way, and his work in higher education was a critical part of the nation's move into the future. And so Max made a decision. The Copelands would move to Iran. The move was still a few years off, but it was definitely coming. Max would follow in Arthur Pope's footsteps.

"We came back from Meshad and then went to the Caspian Sea for four days," he wrote his parents. "It was a very pretty and impressive area, full of trees and water and vegetation—quite different from Tehran. We also went to Isfahan and Shiraz and stayed a day in each city. Both are quiet and beautiful. Pretty mosques, wide streets, and very colorful. So as you can see I've become a Persia fan! It sure is a pretty place and with so many warm brothers and sisters-in-law, why that's an unforgettable combination."

Several years later, at the Shah's invitation, the Copelands returned—this time as a family of four. And Max did a job he loved. And he lived the life he wanted. But somehow it had all gone wrong. Fifteen years to the day after he first came to Iran, he was arrested.

And he was now standing in their apartment facing an angry Shahin, who only wanted to know one thing.

"WHAT DID YOU DO?"

"Us? Don't worry, we hid everything—or flushed it. The apartment is clean."

"No, *what did you do?*" she says. "I think I've earned the right to know. Kids, go to your rooms. Your father and I need to talk."

By the time he's finished telling her about Operation Westward, Shahin is furious. "Why didn't you tell me?"

"That's . . . complicated. Demougeot insisted on secrecy, and I thought it a good idea, and he pointed out it would give you plausible deniability in case things went wrong. So."

"Demougeot is a snake," she says. "No, don't protect him. He's not protecting you, is he?"

It was true, he had been awfully difficult to get on the phone ever since the trouble started.

"Akh, akh." Shahin laments, shaking her head. "Turn the lights off, please."

"Okay. I have to tell you something else. Those men? They were the same guys who arrested me two weeks ago outside the warehouse."

"Are you certain? I mean, you only saw them from the window."

"Positive. It's obvious they're going to take me back into custody. It's also obvious I'm not going to get a fair trial. I'm sorry—are you sure you'd rather not discuss all this later?"

"No," she says vehemently.

"We both know I'll never get a fair trial here. They're going to make it look bad. I . . . I think I should leave the country, Shahin."

"And you will."

"No—I mean *now.*"

Max climbs onto a chair, pushes back the air-conditioning duct, and withdraws a map. Uncreasing it, Max points to a web of blue lines emanating from Tehran.

"There are several routes out of Iran. Pakistan's one possibility, but it's a thousand miles across desert terrain. To the north, good old Mother Russia. Afghanistan's to the east and Iraq to the west. None of these countries would assist a fleeing American. But . . . if I could make it down to the Persian Gulf, I just might be able to flee on a boat or a barge bound for

Kuwait. I hear you can rent a dinghy, and it's only fifty nautical miles across the gulf. But the Kuwaitis are cracking down. They're shipping escaped Iranians back on the very next flight, cuffed, and who knows if they'd be kinder to Americans crashing their borders?"

"I see you've done your homework," Shahin says calmly.

"There is one more possibility. Ross Perot did it for his employees. Just yesterday I was listening to a story on the BBC. This guy had hiked over the Zagros mountains into Turkey, bribed a border guard, and made his way to Ankara. It took almost a week. But it's doable."

"And you want me to lead the expedition?"

"I want you to get me a smuggler."

Shahin looks at him, dumbfounded. "You get caught smuggling radar. And you want me to find someone to smuggle *you* out?"

"I'm in good shape. I climb mountains. I just need someone who knows the terrain."

"Is that why you've been climbing the stairs?"

Recently Max had adopted a daily regimen of 100 flights—up and down the main stairway in the hall until he was soaked and breathless. Every afternoon at four o'clock, before the landlord's children turned the stairwell into an after-school playground littered with toys, Max ran the staircase until his lungs hurt and his knees ached.

"You think the stairs are the same as the Zagros mountains? In winter?"

"You're upset," Max says. "We should talk about this tomorrow."

"God forgive us! My husband smuggles radar out of the country, goes to prison—and now wants me to hire a smuggler? Max!"

"I need your help, Shahin."

"Let's say I get you a smuggler. You survive the trek across frozen mountains and don't fall off a cliff. Let's forget about your bad knee. The smugglers don't rob you and leave you dead. By some miracle you make it to Turkey. Let's say all this happens. Then what? What would happen to us, did you think about that?"

"The kids can fly out beforehand, and you and I . . ."

"No, Max. Stand trial. I will represent you. Then we will leave this country together—legally. Not like criminals."

"Listen! The other day Khomeini threatened to try the hostages as spies. Diplomats! Imagine what they'll do to me."

"By the time I'm through they'll give you a going-away party."

She gets up, takes two wobbly steps toward the bedroom. Her migraine is charting its course. Soon it will strike sudden and hard—a pillar of pain just behind her eyes.

"Tomorrow we'll talk about your defense. I want to know everything about Westinghouse's operations in Iran. Everything. But now I'm going to bed. Bring me a wet towel, please, and a belt."

Max folds up the map and shoves it back into the vent. Then he fetches Shahin a belt, a bucket of ice, and a towel. He knows the drill. For the next several hours she will shut herself away from the world, soak her face in a chilled towel, and pull a belt tight across her head.

SHAHIN

The mood of the country has darkened considerably.

Outside the embassy, angry followers of the ayatollah pump their fists and shout themselves hoarse. Inside, the fifty-two hostages are bound and blindfolded. Iran's deputy chief Islamic prosecutor Gharafpour has issued a challenge to the United States: Return the deposed Shah or the hostages will be tried as spies. Anyone convicted will be executed. The threat generates sufficient alarm in the White House for President Carter to respond, through Swiss intermediaries, that putting one hostage on trial is the same as trying the lot of them. The American response will be devastating.

"Why should we be afraid?" jeers Khomeini. "We consider martyrdom a great honor."

Standing in the eye of the storm is Shahin's old Georgetown friend, Sadegh Ghotbzadeh. He appears almost nightly on American television, trying to strike a note of genial aggression, while looking sufficiently blood-thirsty to the mob at home. It is an impossible balancing act. Sadegh thinks it is a mistake to hold the hostages (fourteen of whom have been released), but he must be circumspect in his dealings with the Americans and the radicals in the new regime. And now, on December 10, in the middle of the greatest challenge to Sadegh's new ministry and a few days before Max's trial, he must deal with Shahin.

"Shahin *khanoum*—this is the second time I'm honored in less than a month. Did you miss my handsome face?"

"I thought I'd pop in and say hello. Tell me, Sadegh, what kind of a Foreign Ministry are you running? It's noon, but the office isn't closed for prayers. Women are running around without a *hejab*—trying to get your attention, perhaps? And I nearly got trampled by the media outside. What's going on?"

"Oh, that," he says with a cavalier wave. "I've decided to run for president."

"*Mash'allah.* Not four weeks here and you're already tired of the Foreign Ministry. Perhaps the power has gone to your head?"

In fact, Sadegh no longer looks like the buoyant man who has become a network star in the United States. A mere three weeks after he's taken office, the hostage crisis has clearly taken its toll. He's lost weight. Puffy, bloodshot eyes. Sadegh is in daily secret contact with the State Department and the hostage takers, trying to find a solution to this vexing problem. But the crisis has electrified the country. And the increasingly populist movement in Iran is forming a wedge between him and the revolution's hard-liners.

But Sadegh still has hope. And he has faith his political star will continue to rise.

"I can do a better job as president. This office isn't for me. *Befarmaeed,*"* he says, motioning toward a chair.

"They came to get Max again—or at least they tried to. Does someone have a vendetta against you?"

"Me?" he smiles coyly. "Who doesn't? Tell me, how is the good doctor?"

"As you might expect. Worried. Depressed." She lowers her voice. "I haven't told him, but today I got notice he's to be tried before a revolutionary tribunal."

"Hmm. This is not good."

The revolutionary tribunals were sham trials. They had a single pur-

---

*"Be my guest."

pose: Get rid of the prior regime's loyalists. The trials were brief. Some lasted a few hours, others only a few minutes. To date, more than 630 people have been put to death by the tribunals—their sentences carried out within hours of the verdict. There was no opportunity for appeal.

"Can you help? Perhaps get him transferred to a different court?"

"Your faith in me is impressive, Shahin. But no, I'm afraid not."

"What use are friends in high places? You're Khomeini's right-hand man, *mash'allah*! I'm not asking for special dispensation—only to have him moved to a reputable court," Shahin says.

Had she known the true extent of Sadegh's power, she might have pushed even harder. Iran was run by the Revolutionary Council, a secret society of fifteen men who determined everything from nurses' salaries to bank nationalizations. The men were a mix of clerical and secular, all appointed by Khomeini. Sadegh was one of the fifteen. As a member of the council, Sadegh was also responsible for appointing both prosecutors and magistrates to the revolutionary tribunals—the ones who would prosecute Max *and* the ones who'd determine his guilt or innocence. All of these men owed their job, their position, their unparalleled power not to the God they'd sworn loyalty to—but Sadegh and his clandestine council.

But Shahin knows nothing about this. And Sadegh is far too wily to let on.

"You certainly don't suffer from shyness, do you?" he asks. "I have a dozen reporters outside, all sniffing for a hint of misconduct or corruption, and every night I'm on television explaining America's misdeeds to the world. The Islamists are always watching. They are waiting for me to make a misstep. The student militants are worse. What am I to tell them? Instead of prosecuting the spies, I'm going to help one—and the husband of a royalist at that?"

"Sadegh, *he's not a spy*. I know my husband."

"Are you sure? Forgive me, but you seemed awfully surprised when you heard of his activities."

"I have not come here to be insulted."

"Smuggling radar is a serious offense."

Shahin stops cold. She has not mentioned the radar to him. Has he been making inquiries? All this time, she assumes that someone else has been using Max as a pawn—but could that person be Sadegh? She remembers Sharifi's warning: *Trust no one.*

"Max didn't realize it was radar."

"Of course not," he says with a twinkle. "Still, I can't help."

"No. Anything pro-American, even if it's the right thing to do, won't sit well with the electorate, will it?"

Sadegh grimaces. "He's not the only American in trouble, you realize."

"Yes, I know all about the hostages and your houseguests upstairs."

"There are others," he says vaguely, then abruptly switches the subject. "Perhaps you should talk to Charlie Chaplin."

It was a derisive reference to Abolhassan Banisadr, the former foreign minister, who had a mustache that reminded people of the Little Tramp. Sadegh and Banisadr sat on the Revolutionary Council together. They were friends until Sadegh replaced him as foreign minister. Now, they were both candidates for president and in a matter of weeks they'd turned from chummy colleagues to bitter adversaries.

"Of course it won't do any good," Sadegh adds. "Banisadr is a laughing-stock—everyone knows Khomeini is *my* benefactor."

"I don't give a damn about the election, Sadegh. This trial is happening at the worst possible time; with all this anti-American sentiment I'm afraid Max will become a scapegoat. I have a bad feeling about this. Please. Won't you help an old friend?"

"There are larger things at stake, Shahin."

"The presidency? Or your hungry ego? I don't know which of your two faces to believe. At Georgetown, do you remember what you said? *I don't want the power, I've seen what it does to other people.* Good luck with your campaign. You're not the man I thought you were . . ."

In a flash of anger, Shahin gets up to leave—then, spying a copy of Ferdowsi's *Shahnameh* on the bookcase behind him, stops. A lush tale of national pride and politics, the *Shahnameh* is a distinctly Persian book and does not sit well with the Islamists. Shahin is surprised to see it on Sadegh's shelves, for it contrasts with the religious spirit of Khomeini's regime. Khomeini *hates* anything Persian.

She turns to Sadegh.

"Remember when you flew the ayatollah home? Someone asked how he felt about returning to Iran, and he said, 'Nothing.' You mistranslated his answer. You said he had no comment. But I saw the look on your face—the look of absolute disbelief. You lied to save face for him. I'm sorry to tell you this, Sadegh, but he cares only for Islam. Not you. Not Iran. Not the thirty-six million Iranians who are under his thumb. Beware, Sadegh, the father always kills the son."

"Excuse me?"

"Legend says the young must die to protect the power of the old. Are you so certain of Khomeini's patronage?"

"I brought Agha home. I wrote his speeches. He is a spiritual father to me. Of course Agha will support me. In a month's time, you'll be seeing me in a new role: president. And then you'll eat your words, Shahin."

THAT NIGHT, Shahin launches Plan B. She writes Banisadr a long, emotional letter—reminding him of the philanthropic contributions of the Maleki family and wishing him luck in his presidential campaign. She encloses a sizable contribution. She says nothing about Max.

THE NEXT DAY Shahin is wrapping up her Quranic studies when she catches sight of Sadegh on TV. An undisclosed number of the hostages will be put on trial by the revolutionary tribunals, he announces. Listening, Shahin realizes that he has been planning this move all along, and that she has underestimated her longtime friend. Yet again. These are the same courts that will try Max. A word from Sadegh would have forever linked Max to the hostages, but by staying silent he had given Max a small, fighting chance. Sadegh had helped by not helping.

Or . . . is she misreading the whole situation? Everything in Iran happens *poshteh pardeh*—behind the curtain—and she knows Sadegh well enough to know that she will never really know him, or glimpse the machinery behind his curtain. She and Max. Max and the hostages. She and Sadegh. Sadegh and Khomeini. Their fates seem strangely entwined in a way she will never quite understand. Buffeted by forces far beyond their control, what else can they do but play their part?

How shall a man escape from that which is written, Ferdowsi wrote. *How shall he flee from his destiny?*

The hostages will not be the first Americans to be tried by the tribunals. That distinction belongs to Max.

CYRUS

David Smallman, the lawyer I'd contacted to help locate my father's CIA file, had quit. I had placed several calls to him, and several e-mails, but none were answered. It was now January.

The last time I'd spoken to Smallman was July, and during that meeting he was enthusiastic. He'd been talking with a friend of his who, he implied, had connections with the CIA—and his friend wanted to know why I was looking into my father's past. Did I really think my father was a spy?

I suspected my father might have done some questionable things while he was in Iran—at least, questionable from an Iranian point of view. He was, after all, an American, and I could imagine him doing some things on behalf of the United States, things possibly in the interest of America's national security. But I never thought of him as a full-time CIA agent. And yet . . . he fit the profile, didn't he? Very knowledgeable about the country. Secretive. Low-profile job in the defense industry. High-level Iranian contacts through my mom. And quite a few people seemed to think he was—including my mother.

I never thought of myself as being paranoid. But the relationship between Iran and America seemed to be in a constant downward spiral. Saber-rattlers on both sides made almost casual references to war. And now David

Smallman, who was delving, perhaps, into national secrets on my behalf, had seemingly vanished. Had he been silenced by the government? Had he learned something about my father?

A friend warned me, "You may have stepped into something." My friend also announced he would not speak to me again until I saw *Three Days of the Condor*, a CIA-centered thriller that had Robert Redford walking around for two hours with his head on a spindle, trying to see who was going to shoot him from behind the bushes. So maybe I was getting a little paranoid. Or maybe I needed to find more grounded friends.

There was, though, that apparently cozy relationship between Washington and the spy agency. Just after the revolution, the radar equipment on Iran's northern border was mysteriously destroyed. By whom, no one knew. Possibly the Soviets. Possibly even Westinghouse, which had no desire to leave its best technology in the hands of a hostile state.

George Beck had headed Westinghouse's Iran program, and accompanied ex–CIA station chief Art Callahan to his meeting with the Shah. After that meeting, Westinghouse shut down operations and fled the country.

"The Iranians have been trying to buy spare parts for our systems for years," he told me. "Of course we wouldn't sell them the parts. They're not a friendly country."

I asked Beck if he knew whether the CIA had placed agents within Westinghouse.

"I knew we had CIA placements," he said, "but I never knew who they were. Non-official covers, that's what they were called. NOCs. But I stayed away from all that. I wanted to stay out of it. I didn't want to know much about it. I didn't think it was necessary to know."

Beck went into considerable detail about Westinghouse's departure from Iran. The 707s. The twenty-four-hour evacuation notice. The U.S. embassy's desire that Westinghouse keep its employees in place. Demougeot's daily updates. Yet he had never heard of Max—the guy left in charge of closing out the affairs of Westinghouse's employees. The guy tossed into prison for trying to move Westinghouse's very expensive and very strategic equipment back to the United States. Why had Demougeot failed to report Max's situation up the Westinghouse chain of command?

"Do you think Demougeot was CIA?" I asked.

Beck scoffed. "He was a nice guy. Smart. Good with people. Good manager. Nah, I don't think he was CIA."

Maybe Beck just didn't want to know. One thing was clear: If Westinghouse was housing CIA operatives, the feds certainly didn't want that advertised. Especially now. Westinghouse was now a purveyor of nuclear technologies—a hot button with Iran these days.

I wondered if I was making a mistake delving into my father's supposed CIA connections. Every American imprisoned in Iran is accused of espionage. The accusation is so frequent and so automatic that many people do not take the allegation seriously. But suppose the charges in my father's case were true? That would upset the State Department's messaging, and it would lend credibility to a regime the United States had been trying to discredit and destabilize for years.

I felt a surge of paranoia creeping up on me again.

AND THEN David Smallman surfaced.

"The news isn't good," he said. We were back at Nice Matin, the same restaurant as a year ago. Same booth. Same niçoise salad. "I had a conversation with the former director of national security. Apparently your father's files are no longer at the State Department. The CIA came in and took them. The technical term is 'clawback.' He believes that this period was a huge embarrassment and he thinks the files have been moved to the CIA."

As Smallman continued to speak, I began to feel like I was trapped in a game of three-card monte. Picking the right shell to look under for the real Max Copeland was becoming increasingly less likely.

"Of course it could be a lie," he continued. "It could be misinformation meant to dishearten you. But my sense is that it's gone. Between the international sensitivities and prevalence of leak investigations, I think we have to accept the inevitable: Any possibility of getting cooperation through official sources is foreclosed. We're going to have to find another way in."

The ways in were fast diminishing. President Carter had sent a note saying he didn't recall Max's predicament—and he reputedly had an excellent memory. (I noted how he'd not responded to my e-mails, but rather sent a handwritten note; later, I discovered this was because he didn't want his communications tracked by the intelligence community. I knew how he felt.) The FBI and Department of Defense had written back saying they knew nothing about my father. The Pahlavi-Penn program had been run by USAID, a division of the State Department. I had sifted through their archives and found no evidence of any covert connections. I did learn that Max earned the princely salary of $6,500/year, and wondered how he had managed to pay a mortgage and support a family on that, even in the 1960s, on Philadelphia's posh Main Line.

"You know, Fulbright and USAID were often State covers for INR," David said.

But if my father was connected to the intelligence community—and if he had managed to extract millions of dollars' worth of sensitive military equipment from under the ayatollah's nose—why didn't the CIA or INR help him? He was under house arrest, not detained under the watchful eye of the entire country like the hostages. It would have been relatively easy to extract him.

The more I thought about it, the more perplexed I became. Had Max been sacrificed to a larger game, or had he been caught in the middle of competing interests? President Carter's cabinet had been notoriously divided on Iran. Zbigniew Brzezinski and Cyrus Vance fought daily. Vance was a humanitarian who believed in diplomacy. Brzezinski was a hawk. Their schism had widened, and eventually Washington's entire Iran policy was paralyzed by infighting. And now a large part of the story was buried. No one at the Department of State was talking, and Vance's archives, which are housed in the library at Yale, had been "classified indefinitely by the Department of State," the librarian at Yale told me, adding, "You're the only one asking for them."

David took a bite of his niçoise salad.

"I'm increasingly aware that this is a somewhat complicated story, and that whatever happened this will become a political issue because of what's going on right now," he said. "The nukes. Israel. Drones. Elections. It's a very, very sensitive time. There are major disagreements in policy circles about how to handle this—so it's terrible timing."

He suggested a better place to look for answers would be in the transcript of my father's trial. If such a transcript existed, it was in Iran—and nosing around in the Islamic Republic for the files of an alleged CIA spy did not seem like the best idea. But there was another way. One person knew quite a lot about my father's trial. She rarely spoke of it. I knew what had happened before the trial, and I knew what happened afterward. But what occurred during the five hours when my father appeared before the tribunal was stored only in my mother's memory.

No need to go to Iran. No need to scour the archives in Washington. The answers were on Philadelphia's Main Line.

"MOM, we need to talk about Dad's trial," I said.

"The past is the past," she replied. "It's thirty-five years later. Let your poor mother enjoy her retirement, won't you?"

She refused to talk about the past for good reason, she said. "Your father was a spy. It's not a source of pride. And I don't want to revisit those hours. I just don't."

I had heard her say this before, but I didn't know how she was so sure Dad was a spy.

"I was there, wasn't I? I saw the evidence."

Maybe she was tired of my questions. Maybe she was upset by the family friend who'd asked her only that day, point-blank, if Max had been a spy. Whatever the reason, she decided to talk.

"I'm going to tell you this once," she said. "Only once. So pay attention."

SHAHIN

TEHRAN, 1979

December 21 is the longest and darkest night of the year. Iranians know the winter solstice as *Shabeh Yalda*—celebrated for centuries as the victory of the sun and goodness over darkness and evil. From the next day forward, the light grows longer and evil recedes. But on this night, the ancient forces of *ahriman*—evil—are said to be at their peak. All over Iran, candles are burned to chase away the darkness and ensure defeat over evil.

In the name of Allah, most compassionate, most merciful.

Like many other proceedings in Iran, Max's trial begins with a prayer. But compassion and mercy have long been absent in Iran's revolutionary trials. Since the first trial convened almost a year ago in a girls' school in southern Tehran, six hundred people have been sent to the firing squads— usually taken up to the roof, or out to the courtyard, and summarily shot. The trials were payback for Pahlavi leftovers, SAVAK officials, high-level royalists, or other traitors to the revolution. In this context Max was accorded a unique privilege: He would be the first—and last—American sent to the tribunals.

Good or evil. Light or dark. Perhaps that depended on your nationality.

Shortly before noon, Shahin and Max enter the courtroom. A sharp beam of light beats down on an empty table on the far side of the room. An assortment of people—some familiar, some not—sit in pews on the opposite side of the table. Shahin spots Javad, the driver, and Saiid and Akbar, the youthful Revolutionary Guards who had come to take Max away. There are several other bearded men she does not recognize. But the pews aren't full of spectators. Shahin had expected the place to be crawling with reporters. The defendant is an American and a suspected spy. But no one has a camera or a notebook.

On the far side of the room, the judge is sitting behind his desk and beckons them with a casual wave.

"Stay close to me," she whispers to Max, "and remember, I am going to do all the talking."

"Wouldn't have it any other way," Max replies.

"*Ba ejazeh,** I am Shahin Maleki Copeland, wife of Dr. Copeland and daughter of Abdul Hossein Maleki. We have been summoned here to address the charges against my husband."

The judge peers at her from under his eyebrows. "Does your husband need a translator?"

"That won't be necessary," she says. "I can translate. I am also here as his lawyer."

"Not possible," the judge replies. "This is an official undertaking. The results cannot be questioned, *khanoum.* Unfortunately you cannot represent your husband."

The prosecutor, a slight man by the name of Nayeri, rises to reinforce the judge's position. "The imam has been clear about this. *Sharia* law prescribes that there are to be no female lawyers in court—only witnesses. And even then we must discount their word by half."

When Shahin turns to address him, the prosecutor refuses to look at her.

Fighting the urge to respond to his show of disrespect, Shahin instead gently casts his insult aside. "Naturally I'm only a woman and a housewife, and cannot be expected to do as good a job as a trained lawyer. Think of

---

*"With your permission."

me not as his lawyer, but his wife—and a woman familiar with God's law." She turns to face the judge. "Of course, the Quranic passage referenced by the prosecutor, *Surah* 2:282, pertains to testimony about financial matters, not all testimony."

The judge casts a critical eye at Shahin. He's a salt-and-pepper-bearded man who is the presiding imam in a seemingly unfriendly environment. But Shahin has a sixth sense that tells her he is trustworthy.

"Come with me," the judge says.

A moment later, she is alone with him in his chamber—a modest room decorated with overlapping rugs and a photo of Ayatollah Khomeini. In the corner there is a samovar, from which he draws Shahin a cup of tea.

Has he brought her back to solicit a bribe? Shahin has no idea why the judge has summoned her to his private quarters. In Iran all business is done *poshteh pardeh*, behind the curtain, but Shahin doesn't wish to insult an upstanding judge by broaching the subject. So she says nothing. Finally, the judge breaks the silence.

"I have read your husband's file," he says. "It seems to me you might have a few questions. Is there anything you want to tell me in private?"

Ah, so he was giving her the chance to turn him in!

"Nothing that needs to be said privately, Your Honor. We have been married for twenty years. We have no secrets."

The judge stares at her for nearly a minute. Shahin begins to feel uncomfortable.

"As you wish," the imam says. "If you change your mind at any time, let me know."

Back in court, Shahin takes her seat next to Max behind the wooden table. The sun lands on the table so brightly, it's almost blinding—the distilled light of a hundred suns. The imam calls the court to order, reads a brief passage from the Quran, and the prosecutor rises.

"In the name of God, the most compassionate, the most merciful. The defendant, Dr. Copeland, is charged with the following crimes," Nayeri intones.

He proceeds to read a list of fourteen charges. Some have colorful names like "spreading corruption on earth" and "friendship toward the enemies of God." Three charges in particular give Shahin pause: smuggling military weapons, hindering the air force in its defense of Iran, and espionage for the Great Usurper. More than half of the charges Nayeri reads are not listed on the indictment Shahin received three days earlier.

"Your Honor, there is a small problem," Shahin says, rising to face the judge. "Many of these charges are Islamic in nature. We have only been an Islamic state a couple weeks now with the ratification of the Constitution. And as Your Honor is no doubt aware, the Quran explicitly says that Islamic law is not retroactive. I would therefore ask those portions of the charges that relate to Islamic law be set aside—and that our discussion be confined to nonreligious law."

The judge regards Shahin with cool respect. Emboldened, she continues.

"Also, I received a copy of the indictment a couple of days ago," she says, holding the piece of paper. "Seven of the charges are new! Collecting funds for the support of the United States? Expanding the influence of imperialism . . ."

The judge interrupts. "You will have a chance to address them."

"But I haven't had a chance to prepare."

"*Khanoum* Copeland, you will discover this sooner or later—best you know it now. This is not a Western court. We follow the spiritual law, and it is timeless in its application."

REZA NAYERI, the prosecutor, was also a cleric. He lacked charisma in the courtroom, but what he lacked in style he made up for with a dogged pursuit of what he perceived as justice in the new Islamic state. Already he'd racked up victories against several SAVAK agents, a Kurdish smuggling ring, a drug cartel, and one unfortunate cousin of the Shah who'd made the mistake of staying in Iran. All were buried in anonymous graves outside Tehran.

Now his sights are set on Max, and he rises to address the court.

"For years, Westinghouse has been a supporter of the corrupt Pahlavi regime. For years they have turned Iran into a market for foreign goods and lived off our oil—leaving us with a nonworking air defense system that we have paid millions of dollars for. This is a list of the incomplete projects, paid for and left dead when Westinghouse departed a year ago."

As Nayeri speaks, Shahin becomes aware of a critical piece of trial strategy. She cannot let the terms *Max Copeland* and *Westinghouse* become synonymous.

"Your Honor," she interjects, "my husband is not an employee of Westinghouse, merely a contractor, and cannot be held responsible for their lapses."

"*Lapses?*" Nayeri shouts. "*Thievery.* To date, we estimate he has sent over thirty million dollars in cash and merchandise back to America."

Turning to face the judge, Shahin tries to limit Max's role in the case.

"Permit me to respond to Mr. Nayeri's allegation. Dr. Copeland was engaged by Westinghouse to close down their operations in Shiraz and Tehran. The monies he accumulated were proceeds from the sales of household items left behind by Westinghouse employees. But my husband has always been mindful of his obligations to Iran. The American employees received what was left of their resources *after* Iranians received their due. My husband paid the landlords. He paid the household staffs. He satisfied any and all debts owed to Iranians. He even paid the utility companies. So please—whatever you accuse my husband of, let it not be the thievery of Westinghouse."

The judge casts a quizzical look at the prosecutor. But before Nayeri can speak, Shahin continues.

"I have with me a partial list of the landlords in Shiraz, which my husband has constructed from memory. The list of other debtors may be found in the Westinghouse warehouse. I am confident if you contact the people on those lists, you will find that the so-called 'stolen monies' are actually paid debts."

"Perhaps," Nayeri says, "but after Doctor moved to Tehran, he assumed responsibility for their *corporate* resources. Weaponry. Spare parts. All variety of military machinery. This equipment belongs to our military, yet Doctor began repatriating them to America. And this is where the real story begins. Lieutenant Colonel Aziz Gholampour, please step forward."

A middle-aged man rises and stiffly strides to the front—Nayeri's first witness.

For the next half hour, Col. Gholampour outlines the relationship between Westinghouse and the Iranian air force since 1971. That year, the parties entered into a series of contracts that were designed to provide Iran with an integrated electronics depot to handle the air force's increasingly diversified needs. After the depot became operational, a second set of contracts was signed. Then a third. The most lucrative of these concerned Westinghouse's proprietary radar systems. The company promised that the radar would help guard Iran from Soviet incursions and provide a window on Soviet military activity near the border.

By 1978, Westinghouse was knee-deep in a series of claims and counterclaims about the radar contracts. And then Westinghouse withdrew its employees from the country.

"And now we are stuck," Col. Gholampour says, "with radar systems that are semi-operational. Unusable equipment. Missing spare parts. They promised us a glorious technology that would make us the best air force in the Middle East! They left us without wings. I rue the day we signed those contracts."

"Surely you don't hold my husband accountable?" Shahin interjects.

But, clearly, he does.

"What happened to our radar?" the colonel snaps. "Why did he try to send it back?"

Nayeri tells the court eight boxes containing ADS-4 consoles belonging to the air force arrived at Mehrabad Airport on November 17. "And no one knows what was shipped before that date. The Record of Contents says nothing about 'radar.' The records do not identify Dr. Copeland as the shipper. Why? Because he *knew* he was doing something illegal."

"My husband knows nothing about weapons," Shahin scoffs.

Nayeri turns to face her directly for the first time. "Mrs. Copeland. You are trying the patience of this court. Do you expect anyone to believe that your husband is an innocent bystander when he works for a defense company?"

"You do not dispute his work in Shiraz. Given his efforts to pay back the debtors there, I would ask you to ascribe to him the same morality in Tehran. My husband is not a thief, merely the last man left to clean up Westinghouse's mess. The radar was a mistake—packed months before he arrived in Tehran."

"Millions of dollars of weaponry belonging to our air force—sent back to the United States, the great enemy of Iran? Would you have the Iranian people believe that such a secretive, important theft was a *mistake*? It is not a mistake. It was a deliberate act against the Islamic Republic ordered by President Carter."

"President Carter?" the judge repeats, surprised.

Emboldened by the court's interest, Nayeri continues. "On November fourteenth, President Carter ordered all our undelivered military equipment held as retaliation for the hostages. Then he froze our assets. This is why Doctor sent back our radar. He is acting in the interests of the United States!"

The judge looks at Gholampour.

"Tell me, what is the radar used for, Colonel?"

"To pick up intrusions into Iranian airspace," Gholampour responds. "Without radar, we cannot monitor the skies, leaving our planes vulnerable and ineffective."

"How much is it worth?" the judge asks.

"One radar console is approximately one hundred fifty thousand dollars," Gholampour responds.

The witness's testimony being complete, the judge recesses the proceedings and retreats to his chambers for tea.

SHAHIN KNOWS the prosecution's next witness. She remembers her last encounter with him.

Javad Shamshiri nervously places his hand on the Quran and affirms he will tell the truth. He then recounts a series of trips he made with Max during the last several months. The pair had made daily runs, he says, from the warehouse to the shipping office, always carrying a dozen boxes. Each was tightly bound and addressed to Westinghouse headquarters. Once he cut open a carton and, seeing highly technical equipment that "looked very dangerous and confusing," immediately closed it. Being a humble driver he wanted no trouble. "When the authorities came and arrested Doctor, I ran away. But last week, Agha Nayeri found me and offered me the chance to testify for my country."

"Did Dr. Copeland swear you to secrecy?" Nayeri continues.

"He told me to say nothing. He paid me well. Today, I tell the court and absolve myself of the responsibility."

Looking at Max's former driver, Shahin feels a brief pang of pity. Then fury. How quickly people switched allegiances.

But Javad is not finished. "I have something else to say. *Khanoum* threatened to kill me! She wrapped her hands around my neck like I was a chicken and squeezed. She said she would kill me!" Here his voice rose to a high-pitched cry, as though he were being strangled all over again.

Shahin freezes.

"Are you accusing *khanoum* of attempted murder?" the judge asks.

"She came to my house after midnight. She threatened to kill me if I didn't tell her where Doctor was. I still have nightmares. I swear, I still feel her nails digging into my neck."

Confronted with the accusation (which happens to be true), Shahin looks at the judge, an expression of pure exasperation on her face. "Strangling my husband's driver? God grant me patience!" Then she turns to her accuser: "Javad, I realize it's been a terribly difficult time for all of us. I know you must be under quite a bit of stress. But really."

"You know you did," Javad shouts.

"Did anyone else see this?" the judge asks.

"It was in a dark alley behind my house. It was after midnight. Everyone was asleep."

"Midnight. Your Honor, does this seem remotely believable? I'm a woman. He's a hundred kilos, *mash'allah*."

The focus of the trial has clearly shifted away from Max and the radar. But the judge has to ask, "Why would *khanoum* strangle you?"

"So I would tell her where Doctor was."

"And you wouldn't tell her otherwise?"

Here Javad breaks down completely. Pointing to two men in the back of the courtroom, he says, *"They* threatened to kill me if I did."

Shahin turns and sees Saiid and Akbar.

"Everyone wants to kill Javad," the ex-driver moans. "My life is woeful! *Beechareh shodam!*"*

"In any event, *khanoum* is not on trial here and you are still alive," the judge says. "Take your seat. You have given your testimony and we have heard it."

"But she tried to . . ."

"Enough!" the judge thunders. And the ex-driver finally closes his mouth.

AS SHE WALKS into the hallway with Max during a recess, Shahin is about to learn what lawyers from Cicero to John Adams to the local pub-

---

*"I am wretched!"

lic defender have already learned: Clients have a way of trying your patience.

"Who is that man who keeps on glaring at you? In the back?"

"My interrogator," Max says quietly.

"Your interrogator?" Shahin repeats, surprised. "You never said you were interrogated."

"A lot of things happened in prison."

"Did they—did they do anything to you?"

"No, no, it's nothing like that. But he knew about the radar. And he also knows about a few meetings I had with a man from the CIA. That might come up."

"You met with the CIA?" Shahin says, stunned.

"This guy Art Callahan, they sent him to meet with me to coordinate the departure of Westinghouse employees. He used to be a CIA employee; now he works for Westinghouse."

It seemed like only moments ago Shahin told the judge she and Max had no secrets.

"You met with a CIA agent?"

"No, it's nothing like that. I mean, yes he was the station chief in Iran. Then he came back to head a project for Westinghouse last November. Met with the Shah. But then the revolution happened and instead they pulled everything out. Callahan helped arrange the evacuation."

Shahin puts her head in her hands. "Jesus, Joseph, and Mary."

"What?"

"The CIA is involved, aren't they?"

"What? No. I just met with the man—once, twice. I haven't heard from him in months. He wasn't even CIA when we met. By then he'd quit the Agency."

Suddenly, a scene vaults across Shahin's memory. 1974: She was alone at a Holiday Inn in Texas when she realized she had lost her purse. It was one A.M. Max was in Iran, having just started work with Hughes Aircraft, but had left a number to call "in case any difficulties arise." Within an hour of the call, a man appeared at the hotel and handed her an envelope containing a thousand dollars in cash. At the time, she was grateful and thought no more of it. Until now. That amount of cash? From someone working in the defense industry? Delivered at one o'clock in the morning? She decides the transaction had *CIA* written all over it.

BACK IN COURT, Akbar and Saiid give their testimony. When the judge asks if they'd threatened to kill Javad, they deny it—prompting yet another outburst from the beleaguered driver. "'One word and you're dead,' that's what you said to me," Javad wails. "Everyone wants to kill Javad! Would that I were never born."

"Would that," the judge agrees under his breath. "Continue."

Akbar goes on to recount the day they went to take Max into custody— only to find themselves locked out in the cold by Shahin and subjected to three hours of ridicule in front of the entire neighborhood.

"I mocked you?" Shahin replies. "You mocked God. Does the Quran not say *'Enter not houses other than your own until you have asked permission and saluted those in them'*?"

"We showed you our warrant!"

Ignoring the youth, Shahin addresses the judge. "Your Honor, I'd heard about people posing as Revolutionary Guards coming into your home to steal from you. I didn't know what to believe. They were two arrogant youths with guns. I was scared. If they were truly guards sent by the court, I apologize."

"Lies!" he screams. "She threatened to commit suicide if we entered!"

The judge turns to Nayeri. "One says *khanoum* will kill herself, the other that *khanoum* would kill him. Does this sound rational? Looking at this lady, can you believe she is a suicidal murderess?"

"Did you even see Dr. Copeland?" he asks Akbar.

"She wouldn't allow us."

"Then this testimony is entirely about *khanoum*? Have we not already established that *khanoum* is not on trial here? I will not repeat myself."

BY THE TIME the last witness is called, it is five P.M. The trial has lasted long for a tribunal. Several other employees at the Westinghouse warehouse have testified about the secrecy of Dr. Copeland's operation. The prosecutor has trotted out postal records showing that Max sent more than six hundred crates of merchandise and $93,000 cash back to the United States. Estimating that each carton contained items worth $50,000, he concluded that Max had fleeced the Iranian air force out of $30 million worth of equipment.

"Let me repeat that," Nayeri tells the court. "*Dr. Copeland shipped back thirty million dollars' worth of equipment to America.* Ever since 1953, Americans have been meddling in the affairs of Iran. Stealing elections. Stealing our oil. And now stealing the very machinery that purportedly keeps Iran safe. There is little question, between his actions and long history of defense work—all while claiming to be an academic, a 'doctor'—that Dr. Copeland is truly a CIA spy."

"This is a careless and baseless allegation," Shahin cries. "My husband is neither a thief nor a spy. If you have evidence, then produce it!"

"He confessed to meeting with a known CIA station chief!"

"Ex–station chief. To plan the departure of Westinghouse employees," Shahin says.

"You've shown a surprising familiarity with the Quran, *khanoum*. Do you know what it says about espionage?"

"I do."

"Recite it for the court."

"I am his attorney, *agha*, not your witness."

"*'Avoid suspicion as much as possible, for suspicion is in some cases a sin. And spy not on each other, nor speak ill of each other behind their backs.'* I would advise you to be *more* suspicious. In fact, Doctor is *such* a good spy that even his wife was unaware of his activities. Or were you?"

Shahin leaps up. "Where is his confession? The law stipulates that a fact can be proved by oath, evidence, testimony, or a confession. So show it to me!"

"You want a confession?" Nayeri spits. He plucks a Polaroid from his files and presents it to the judge, then to Shahin. "Before he left prison, Doctor left a small memento for us."

Shahin does not need to see the picture to know its contents: There in large black letters are the three words that will undo her husband.

"How do you explain *this, khanoum* Copeland?"

"I also note that he ceased to sign this confession."

"Come—let us not play games any longer. Here is the final proof that Doctor is an enemy of the revolution!"

"Your Honor, when an innocent man is thrown in jail, taken from his wife and children and detained under secrecy, he vents. He says things he does not mean. He cannot be responsible for his anger."

"Death. To. Khomeini," the prosecutor says for effect. "The meaning is quite clear. And I note *khanoum* was well aware of it."

AND JUST AS QUICKLY as it began, the trial draws to a close. The judge has declared one last break before the trial concludes, during which Max and Shahin retire to the hallway. Outside it is getting cool. The sun has gone down and they sit alone in the semi-darkness.

Max smiles wanly. "It doesn't look good for old Max, does it?"

"Don't worry," Shahin replies. "I still have one or two tricks up my sleeve."

"Listen, I want you to know that I appreciate your efforts, Shahin. I will remember this to my dying day—which may arrive sooner than I'd planned."

Shahin looks at her husband. His face is ashen.

"Nonsense," she says. But in her heart she feels a spreading darkness.

"Did you really strangle Javad?" Max says after a bit.

Shahin smiles.

"Good. He was a coward and a snitch, and I never liked him much."

"THE REVOLUTIONARY TRIBUNALS were born out of the anger of the Iranian people, and these people will not accept any principles outside Islamic principles as set forth in the Quran and Qisas," the judge says. "Today Dr. Copeland stands accused of myriad sins. Does the defense have any witnesses?"

"Only me, Your Honor," Shahin says.

The prosecutor rises. "It appears *khanoum* wants to have it both ways, to be both lawyer and witness! Even the Western courts do not allow this."

"Your Honor, all of his friends and colleagues are gone," Shahin says. "His parents are in Texas. So yes, I am asking if I might say a few words in his defense."

Then without waiting for anyone's approval, Shahin takes a breath, steadies herself, and rises to address the court.

"A woman was the first to see the truth of Islam. When no one stood beside Mohammad, Khadija saw the truth about her husband and was his first witness. Today I stand before you, a woman in an Islamic court, knowing that my husband is innocent of these charges. It's true, Dr. Copeland has been caught in a very unusual predicament. His actions were not particularly wise. But were they evil?

"Because Doctor is the last American left at Westinghouse's office, you are holding him"—she was about to say *hostage*, but thought the better of it—"responsible. Is this fair? Let us not allow our prevailing anti-American sentiments from clouding the truth. *'Do not let your hatred for a group make you depart from justice,'* the Quran reminds us.

"Ever since he arrived in Iran six years ago, my husband adopted this land as his own. He converted to Islam. Years ago, he told me he wants to

Our last family portrait in Iran, November 1979, just before our lives spun out of control. It would be the last time we Copelands sat for a photographer.

August 1978: Katayoun and me at Camp Evin. That was the summer I met, fasted, and prayed alongside Mohammad.

My mother was principal of the Shiraz International Community School from 1976 to 1978, after which the revolution caught fire and we moved to Tehran. This was her official school portrait.

The Shah and President Carter in happier times. | *Getty*

January 16, 1979: Shah Mo-hammad Reza Pahlavi leaves Iran with Empress Farah Diba at his side. Officially, the Shah left for "vacation" and medi-cal treatment; unofficially, his departure marked the end of 2,500 years of Persian mon-archy. That day, we were trav-eling from Shiraz to Isfahan, and found our car engulfed in a throng of people shouting "Shah raft!"—"The Shah is gone!" | *AP*

Sadegh Ghotbzadeh, rising media star. He was known to American audiences as a regular guest on ABC's *Nightline*. | *AP*

February 1, 1979: After fifteen years in exile, Khomeini ventures into the crowds of Tehran. | *AP*

November 4, 1979: Students calling themselves "Moslem Student Followers of the Imam's Line" storm the American embassy and take sixty-six people hostage, leading to the total disintegration of relations between Iran and the United States. | *Getty*

The hostages in whose shadow my father's own "international incident" got lost. Left to right: Al Golacinski, unidentified Marine, Joe Subic, and Bill Belk. | *Corbis*

A couple weeks after the hostage crisis, this article appears in the *Tehran Times*—leading to "Max's Radar Affair" and the eventual dissolution of our lives in Iran.

January 21, 1959—Shahin Maleki married Max Copeland in Arlington's Mount Olivet Methodist Church. Attendees included Shahin's mother, Farokh Lagha Maleki, who came from Iran, and Max's parents, who ventured up from Grove, Oklahoma. Earlier that day, they got married in Washington, D.C.'s mosque.

The Malekis and Max on his first trip to Iran, 1965. Center row, left to right: Shahin, Max, Madar Joon (Shahin's mother and the family matriarch), Uncle Aziz, Aunt Parvin. Top row: Aunt Zari, Uncle Mosoul and his wife Aunt Mariam, Uncle Aziz's wife Aunt Mahin, Uncle Taghi. Bottom row: Taghi's wife Aunt Aghdas, my cousins Mohsen, Mahshid, Ali, Farshid, Shahla, and Mariam, all flanking Uncle Hooshang.

My beloved grandfather Abdol Hossen Maleki. He died before I was born, but I've always felt spiritually bonded to him.

Shahin was a model for DH Evans in London, circa 1949.

Me on the bleachers at Iranzamin School in Tehran. Weeks later the school was shut down by the Cultural Revolution Committee.

January 13, 1980: On the phantom flight to London— the only three passengers on board.

My family in happier times at the historic Eram Garden in Shiraz. I still recall the perfumed scent of about ten thousand roses from that day. Today, the classical Persian garden has been declared a World Heritage Site.

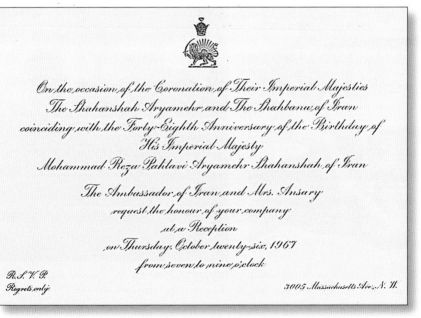

On the occasion of the Coronation of Their Imperial Majesties
The Shahanshah Aryamehr and The Shahbanu of Iran
coinciding with the Forty-Eighth Anniversary of the Birthday of
His Imperial Majesty
Mohammad Reza Pahlavi Aryamehr Shahanshah of Iran

The Ambassador of Iran and Mrs. Ansary
request the honour of your company
at a Reception
on Thursday, October twenty-six, 1967
from seven to nine o'clock

R.S.V.P.
Regrets only

3005 Massachusetts Ave., N.W.

The invitation to the Shah's birthday party, wherein the royal couple invited my parents to Iran.

Max in uniform at Oklahoma Military Academy, senior year (1952).

Percy Buchanan's yearbook photo at the University of Oklahoma, 1950. Often compared to Rudolph Valentino, Percy had a wonderful sense of humor, as evinced by the title of his unpublished memoir: *Autobiography of My Hero*.

The OU students in Asia on Percy's Experiment in Understanding tour, 1956. Top row, left to right: Max, three unidentified gentlemen; middle row: Owen Butler, Percy Buchanan; bottom row: Alberta Pennington, Kay Cochran, Katie Elliott, Martha Watson, and Ann Wilson.

The University of Oklahoma paper ran this front-page story the day after Max, Percy, and the Sooners left on their Experiment in Understanding. Photo, left to right: Max, Owen, Percy, and Alberta.

Max in Thailand, 1957, with military personnel from the Thai Army College.

The *New York Times* list of hostages. The fifth name makes me wonder about the veracity of media reports, especially when it comes to foreign policy.

| *New York Times*

Unofficial List of U.S. Hostages

By The Associated Press

Following is a list, compiled by unofficial sources, of the American hostages being held in Iran. Hometowns and ages are provided where available.

Thomas Ahern, 48, Falls Church, Va.
William Belk, 44, West Columbia, S.C.
Robert Blucker, 52, North Little Rock, Ark.
Donald Cooke, 25, Memphis, Tenn.
Max Copeland
William Daugherty, about 33
Robert Englemann, 33, Hurst, Tex.
William Gallegos, 22, Pueblo, Colo.
Bruce German, 43, Kensington, Md.
Duane Gillette, 24, Columbia, Pa.
Allan Golacinski, 29
John Graves, 53, Reston, Va.
Joseph Hall, 31, Elyria, Ohio.
Kevin Hermening, 20, Oak Creek, Wis.
Donald R. Hohman, 38, West Sacramento, Calif.
Leland Holland, 52, Laurel, Md.
Michael Howland
James Hughes, 30
Charles Jones, 40, Detroit
Malcom Kalp
Moorehead C. Kennedy Jr., 49, Washington, D.C.
William F. Keough Jr., 49, Waltham, Mass.
Steve Kirtley, 22, Little Rock, Ark.
Kathryn Koob, 43, Jesup, Iowa.
Frederick Lee Kupke, 33, Francesville, Ind.

L. Bruce Laingen, 57, Bethesda, Md.
Steven Lauterbach, 28, Dayton, Ohio.
Gary Lee, 37, Falls Church, Va.
Paul Lewis, 23, Homer, Ill.
John W. Limbert, 37, Washington, D.C.
James Michael Lopez, 22, Globe, Ariz.
Johnny McKeel Jr., 27, Balch Springs, Tex.
Michael J. Metrinko, 33, Olyphant, Pa.
Jerry Miele, 42, Mount Pleasant, Pa.
Michael Moeller, 29, Loup City, Neb.
Bert Moore, 44, Mount Vernon, Ohio.
Richard M. Morefield, 51, San Diego.
Paul M. Needham, 29, Bellevue, Neb.
Robert C. Ode, 64, Falls Church, Va.
Gregory A. Persinger, 22, Seaford, Del.
Jerry Plotkin, 47, Sherman Oaks, Calif.
Regis Ragan, 38, Johnstown, Pa.
David Roeder, 40, Alexandria, Va.
Barry Rosen, 36, Brooklyn, N.Y.
William B. Royer Jr., 49, Houston
Thomas Schaefer, 50, Tacoma, Wash.
Charles Scott, 48, Stone Mountain, Ga.
Rodney V. Sickmann, 22, Krakow, Mo.
Joseph Subic Jr., 23, Redford Township, Mich.
Elizabeth Ann Swift, 39, Washington, D.C.
Victor Tomseth, 39, Springfield, Ore.
Phillip R. Ward, 30

The New York Times
Published: November 3, 1980
Copyright © The New York Times

be buried here. Doctor has nothing but love in his heart for Iran, and he has demonstrated his devotion to Iran in myriad ways. He helped found a new university system, combining the best in Western education with Iran's needs. He brought back three hundred eighty professors to Iran. He taught English to the army. He raised our children with a love of this land. There is no Westerner with greater knowledge of Iran—or love. Can anyone in this court describe what this country was like under Cyrus the Great? Can anyone in this court trace its development from that era through the modern day? Can anyone in this court name all of Iran's rivers? Can anyone in this court describe the beauty of the sunrise from atop Alborz? Can anyone in this court name Persia's many contributions to world culture?"

She turns and points to Max.

"Doctor can," she says. "Does this sound like a traitor? A liar? A spy? A smuggler?

"There is a great mistrust of America these days, deservedly. For decades America has colonized Iran with its values, its employees, its weaponry while they themselves floated above the fray. I have watched with a heavy heart as Americans escaped our laws, because they were backed by a powerful embassy. That embassy is now closed and I am the only one representing Doctor's interests. His wife.

"But as good Moslems, we cannot confuse the government with its citizens. Cannot! Ayatollah Khomeini himself has said this is not a struggle between the United States and Iran, but between Islam and the infidel. My husband is an upstanding Moslem who converted to Islam twenty years ago.

"As for being in contact with the CIA? This is like being visited by SAVAK. Who *hasn't* been visited by SAVAK? Do we then accuse you of being SAVAKI-ee? Meeting with an ex-CIA is an alarmist, baseless charge.

"And what of his unfortunate writings in prison? It was a terrible thing to say. But I suspect the walls there are full of angry, pent-up emotions of innocent men. This was no transgression against Imam Khomeini. For that, two conditions must be met. Revolt against the imam and the use of force. What force is available to a prisoner? A pencil?

"All day the prosecution has paraded a succession of witnesses. Ask yourself if they are reliable men: An emotionally unhinged driver. A colonel with access to information usually available to a four-star general. A deceitful Revolutionary Guard who accuses me of suicidal tendencies. An interrogator without a confession. To these men I would say, *'Oh followers of Mohammad, do not preach what you do not practice.'* There is much talk about purifying our country these days, but by acting with such blatant disregard for the truth, we ourselves sow corruption on earth, do we not? Let us not be guilty of the very things we condemn, my brothers, but hew to the values prescribed by Islam: tolerance, peace, and forgiveness."

Here, Shahin wipes away a tear and turns to face the judge.

"If you find my husband guilty, you must find me guilty too! And my family. We shall all languish and die in prison rather than allow Doctor to suffer the miscarriage of justice in a land he loves as his own—and a religion in whose folds he once found comfort."

She tells Max to hand her his copy of the Quran, then takes the small volume and lays it on the desk in front of the judge.

"Upon this holy book I swear to his innocence," she says.

SHAHIN AWAITS the judge's verdict with a rising sense of anxiety. She has been permitted to defend Max. She has been allowed to testify on his behalf. She has also been allowed to cross-examine, even ridicule, some of the state's witnesses. Thinking back on the events of the last five hours, Shahin decides that she has done everything she can to help Max, but she remembers the words of the judge: *The revolutionary tribunals were born out of the anger of the Iranian people.* The anger directed at the United States is palpable in the streets. The anger directed at Westinghouse is palpable in the courtroom. The new regime has accused Max of being a spy—and though she has tried to plant a seed of doubt in the judge's mind, causing him to question the government's conclusion, she has been arguing before a revolutionary tribunal. And what revolutionary has ever been haunted by doubt?

Fifteen minutes later, the judge returns to the courtroom and announces his verdict without pause or ceremony.

"Dr. Copeland is guilty of all the charges against him. His sentence is twenty years. The equipment in the Westinghouse warehouse is the property of the Islamic Republic. This verdict is final and not subject to appeal."

As he turns to leave, the judge looks at Shahin and says, "Mrs. Copeland, may I see you in my office?"

Stunned by the verdict, Shahin collapses into the chair. She has lost the case. More importantly, she has lost her husband. Feeling a tight knot, she looks down and sees that her hand is tightly gripping the chair's armrest. On top of her hand, Max has placed his own.

"It's okay, honey," he says. "You tried your best."

Laconic and thoughtful. To the end. That is how Shahin would remember him.

But before she has a chance to process any of it, or say farewell, she must see the judge.

When she enters his chamber, the judge points wearily to a chair. *"Befarmaeed,"*[*] he says. "That was quite a performance. You look like an American. When they first brought you here, I thought I might assign you a translator. But not only do you speak Farsi, you recite the Quran in Arabic. *Mash'allah."*[†]

Shahin, her head bowed, is still too shocked to speak.

"An educated woman who knew the Quran better than my prosecutor," the judge muses, suppressing a slight laugh. He then turns deadly serious and fixes Shahin with a stare. "I believe you innocent of your husband's activities."

Shahin starts to speak, but the judge interrupts her.

"Last week I sentenced a man—an Iranian—to death on similar mea-

[*] "Please."
[†] "Impressive!"

sures. He was a consort of Mossad,* and like Doctor, he had a wife and two children. Their tears did not move me. He now lies in an anonymous grave like all other traitors. Yet I find myself being lenient on an American. Do you know why?"

Shahin gropes for an answer. "Your Honor, if I have impressed you in any way, consider that for these charges the Quran provides many possibilities—one of which is exile. I beg you to be merciful! Does the Quran not say 'Let them forgive . . .'?"

She is not allowed to finish.

"Stop," the judge says. "I have been merciful, more than you had a right to expect. I did not allow anyone in my courtroom to speak down to you. I did not allow any reporters to come in and cover the proceedings. But there is little I can do about the penalty. The penalty is fixed by Islamic law."

Shahin is beginning to feel dizzy. For five hours, she has held her ground in the courtroom—but now, after a few minutes in the judge's chambers, it is as if the ground has opened, and she is falling headlong into the chasm. A succession of visions rises before her. The call to Max's parents. The endless visits to dark prison cells. She sees Max's face retreating into the darkness, getting smaller and fainter.

The judge sits quietly and studies Shahin's face. Finally, he speaks.

"And then there is the matter of where he is to be imprisoned."

Shahin can feel the bile rise to the back of her throat. The judge means to send Max to Evin—the dark prison looming above Tehran where all convicted spies, traitors, and all other enemies of the revolution were sent. Evin was Tehran's Bastille. Few of its denizens were ever heard from again. Rising from her chair, Shahin approaches the judge and grasps the sleeve of his robe. This last act is strictly forbidden, but she is not above begging.

The judge gently unclasps her fingers.

"I see no reason why we cannot return Doctor to house arrest."

"Your Honor?"

---

*Israel's secret service.

"The bond is set at fourteen million *tomans*."*

"Fourteen million *tomans*," Shahin repeats, dumbfounded. It is more than Shahin has or will ever have. "Only yesterday I was standing in line for rationed oil and heaved a tank up three flights by myself. If I had fourteen million, I likely wouldn't be here right now. I'd be in Switzerland."

"Are you not a Maleki?"

"The money is gone," she says quietly. "Deeded to hospitals. Public parks. Orphanages."

"I note your possessions include a tract of land outside the city."

"If it pleases you, Malekabad is a small tract passed down through four generations to me. But it is the only inheritance I have of my father, and my only connection to Iran."

"Then this will be quite interesting," he says. "If Dr. Copeland remains under house arrest it won't be a problem, will it?"

Years from then, as Shahin looked back on the whole saga, she would admire the judge's instincts and terrible elegance of his solution. The scales of justice that balanced husband and homeland. Matrimony and patrimony. So what if the last of her Maleki fortune were posted to secure Max?

"Twenty years?" she says.

"Twenty years."

And because Shahin doesn't wish to sacrifice her dignity alongside her patrimony, she simply says, "I will bring you the deed."

"Should Doctor violate the terms of his arrest, the property will be forfeited and you will be responsible. A local prosecutor will visit from time to time. He will find your husband present."

---

*Roughly two million dollars.

CYRUS

Long before Shirin Ebadi, Esq., won her Nobel Prize, my mother became the first female lawyer of the Islamic Republic. Her career lasted
only five hours, and like much else in her life, her legal exploits would remain an unsung accomplishment. But how many lawyers could top her
résumé? A female royalist in the Islamic Republic of Iran. Representing an
alleged American spy. Using the Quran like a scalpel to slice the prosecution's case apart. John Grisham could not make this stuff up.

"The passage of time and freight of history," my mother scoffed when I
marveled at her accomplishment. "It was thirty-five years ago."

I understood now why revisiting those hours gives her a headache. If
she was convinced Max was CIA, that invited a whole host of follow-up
questions—none of which were pleasant. Were Max's allegiances to the
Agency, or his family? Had his activities put us in danger? Had Max used
his position as her husband to deliver information to the Agency and advance U.S. interests? In many ways, Max's Radar Affair was like an extra-
marital affair—worse, for Shahin was the one who had rolled the Trojan
horse into her homeland.

"And yet you swore on the Quran he was innocent."

"I'd do it again, too. He was the father of my children."

"But—it's the Quran."

"The Quran permits lying under two conditions. One, when you have to save your life. Or two, when you can save another person's life. I had to get him out of their hands, sweetheart."

"Did you ever ask Dad point-blank if he was CIA?

"You know your mother. What do you think?"

I think she would sooner ask Javad for a ride to the supermarket. *Besaz-o-besooz*, the saying goes. Make do, but burn within.

I recalled the night Max came home after being in military prison. There was a look in his eyes I'd never seen before. He pulled us all into a tight hug—too tight, as though he'd realized something and tried to pull all of us back from the brink, but it was too late. In CIA movies there is often a moment when the agent realizes his work has exacted a terrible price—a quiet scene where he's tucking his kid in, or watching his wife do the dishes. It is always a domestic scene. Often wordless. I think they have those scenes because those moments really happen. And when Max pulled us into that embrace, we were living that scene.

But while that scenario had a certain dramatic appeal, I still wasn't convinced Dad was in the CIA. What were the chances—two Copelands, Max and Miles, both Southern gents, unrelated, both Agency men dabbling in Iran's affairs? The probability was remote. And yet . . . what if the charges were true? My thoughts turned to Art Callahan, the CIA station chief in Iran. After Max's death I remembered seeing Art's name in Dad's address book. His time in Iran had dovetailed with Max's, and it now struck me that if the charges against Max were true, Art might have been his handler.

Handler. Such a cloak-and-dagger word—and yet . . . it all kind of fit.

"Art's knowledge of the Mideast and North Africa was amazing," a Westinghouse executive recalled. "After he left the CIA, Art and I took a few senior executives of Westinghouse back to Iran in August of 1978 for an audience with the Shah. It was obvious that the Shah was very ill and because of this, and other information, it was decided on the way home that we needed to plan the evacuation of all of our people."

I'd found an unmailed letter Max had written to someone named Art. The letter was dated 1966. In it, Max summarized his recruiting process for Pahlavi University in considerable detail—down to the pregnancy of some potential recruits and his assessments of their personalities, degrees, and whether they'd make good additions to the university. But was it for Art Callahan? If so, it meant that he'd been in contact with the CIA thirteen years before his trial.

The simplest way to solve the puzzle was to ask Art Callahan. Unfortunately, he had died just over a year ago. But I managed to track down his son Kevin, and we chatted a bit about life in Iran. Kevin recounted how everyone had thought he was CIA during his time there because his father was CIA station chief, and his professors at Pahlavi University either chided him for the connection or sought to curry favor with him because of it. Since then he'd delivered against their expectations. "I work for the Agency now," he told me matter-of-factly.

Instantly my heart went cold. "You work for the CIA?"

Somehow I knew this conversation was going to put me on the CIA's radar—assuming I was not already a blip on Langley's screen. "Listen, I just wanted to reconnect with my father's old friends," I said. "Did your dad ever mention Max?"

"My father rarely talked about his work. But—we should get together. Talk."

"About what?" I asked. I knew full well what.

"Iran. The old days . . ."

"Sure, sure," I said, doing a massive internal eye roll. It was the least smooth way of asking someone on an intelligence-gathering date I'd ever heard. Max might have been Art's asset, but I sure as hell didn't want to become Kevin's. I gave him an e-mail address I rarely used, then promptly deleted it.

In days following I noticed a strange clicking sound on my phone line. Was it the CIA—or my paranoia? David Smallman had told me about a secret program where the government was tracking our phone calls. *Yeah,* *right,* I thought, unable to fathom that the U.S. government was spying on its own people. *I have a paranoid attorney here.* And then Edward Snowden provided WikiLeaks with a mountain of data purloined from the NSA* that disclosed the government's clandestine surveillance program. Smallman had not only known about it, he had represented Laura Poitras, the documentary filmmaker who had helped break the story and one of only three people to have the NSA files; the other two were journalist Glenn Greenwald and Snowden himself.

So Big Brother was, indeed, watching. But I couldn't pull back. I had started down a path to discover my father's secret life, and each meeting, e-mail, and tracked telephone conversation brought me a step closer to the truth and to him.

"How about we meet at an Iranian restaurant for some Axis of Evil cuisine?" I suggested to David. If our conversations were being monitored I was determined to have a bit of fun, but David was not amused. We would meet at Le Pain Quotidien. Smallman had been busy with his own project—a documentary on spies, drones, and disinformation that was about to debut at a film festival in Norway. All of which set the tone for our meeting nicely. I told him about Callahan. I also told him about a *New York Times* article I'd found listing my father as one of the hostages. The *Times* had not reported on Max's capture but had mistakenly lumped him in with the fifty-two hostages held at the embassy, whose plight was reported every night on the six o'clock news.

"Not so mistakenly," David said, taking a sip of rosé. "They got that list from the State Department—which was likely using your father's name to obfuscate things. In situations like this, the objective is to create confusion and misdirection in Tehran, Moscow, and Washington. It's an information technique. Frankly, it's to no one's benefit that the entire

---

*National Security Agency.

truth be known, except perhaps the revolutionaries. So they have false lists."

The message was clear: If I was hoping to get anything useful from the CIA or the State Department, I was destined for disappointment.

"Listen, Benghazi was an unmitigated intelligence failure. It showed there is a dysfunction between the intelligence and diplomatic communities. And right now, you're not going to find anyone willing to stick his neck out by releasing information on your father. Iran is too sensitive a subject. The only thing you're going to get from them is what will be helpful to them. They'll try to soak you for the information you have, and you'll get nothing. Kevin Callahan was just a preview of that."

He sipped his rosé.

"Unless . . . you gave them an incentive. Can you think of one? Any reason why they should give you the information?"

The dead-father-curious-son angle had worked well. It had also led to some unexpectedly amusing situations. When one Westinghouse executive wanted to know why I was nosing around thirty-five years later, I told him it was because I was now the same age as Max when all this went down—figuring that this bit of personal information would preempt any further inquiry on his part. I was wrong. The executive was not a WASP, he was Jewish, and he did not shy away from intimacy. "So you're having a midlife crisis?" he asked. "No shame in that. Do you want to talk about it?"

Somehow, I could not imagine a State Department bureaucrat wanting to discuss my midlife concerns.

"There is a secret program started by State, using media and cultural programs for psychological purposes," David said. "I can't say any more than that. But think along those lines. You need to create an incentive to encourage a leak."

Increasingly, my conversations with David left me stimulated. He was thoughtful, with good instincts, and I trusted him to root out the truth. In some ways, he reminded me of my father. Smart. Strong moral compass. Capable of parsing complex situations—and holding those complexities without an overly emotional reaction. But could he be any more opaque? How was I supposed to encourage a leak? I was living at the dawn of the twenty-first century, and I was reminded of another man from the 1970s. Chief Martin Brody of the Amity Island Police Department, mechanically dumping chum over the side of the boat trying to entice the shark to the surface.

AS I REPLAYED THE SCENES from 1979 looking for clues, the kaleidoscope began to shift and I started to see Max as something other than a depressed, laconic man caught up in the darkest chapter of his life. In an age where people broadcast their every emotion, spilled their juiciest secrets on TV, and didn't have an unexpressed thought, men like Max were a rarity. My father was a discreet man who took secrets to the grave. But that same quality of discretion was, in some ways, a source of dismay, for it meant we did not know one another well. He wrote me a letter:

> *I know we do not get along as well as I would like, but that does not mean I love you any less. Rather, just the opposite. Why do I always believe I should give you little homilies of wisdom ("Remember the little people!") Do you, my dear son, know why I suggest things like that? If we cannot talk in person, perhaps we can talk with pen. Let's be honest with each other, and open with each other. So often, I think we prefer to avoid matters. It is so easy to do, and so neat and tidy, and non-controversial and neither of us gives or receives anything of importance.*

Our lives would never be neat and tidy and non-controversial, I was beginning to realize. We had lived at the nucleus of a seismic divide between Iran and America, and the fracture between the two countries was written into my parents' relationship and into my bloodlines. I would always be caught between two homelands that maligned and demonized each other. The Axis of Evil and the Great Satan. But maybe what Max wrote in the letter was true. There is virtue in being open and honest with each other. Even though thirty-five years had passed, I could not accept that my father was unknowable, and continued to root through the past looking for answers.

Reading his old letters often brought tears to my eyes—not just for the nostalgic pleasure of seeing my father's handwriting again, but the hand-smack-to-the-forehead obvious realization that he had loved me. I didn't doubt that as a child, but I felt it anew as an adult, and the passage of so many years had only sharpened my regret that I'd not been able to see this more clearly. Some fathers and sons bond over sports. Max knew I liked movies, and so he often wrote about films he'd seen on his trips abroad—paragraphs and paragraphs about performances, plot, costumes. Sometimes it was pure nonsense.

Speaking of movies, I have some (more) questions. What is a gaffer? Is it anything like an old duffer? How would a gaffer describe his job at a party? ("I gaff things." That would end the conversation pretty quickly, wouldn't it?) And, what is a "Best Boy?" By inference, I must assume there must also be a "Worst Boy." Why didn't the Worst Boy get fired if he was so bad? How would the Best Boy describe his job at a party? ("I'm the Best Boy." That is even more of a conversation stopper than the gaffer had.) Finally, can you imagine a chance meeting between the gaffer and the best boy? All of this is obviously leading up to nothing.

My father could be corny, but he could also be a fearsome disciplinarian when the situation warranted. London, 1977: Max had taken Katayoun and me to see the latest Bond flick. We were sitting behind a couple of boys who were cursing up a storm, and my father was growing more and more livid as their behavior worsened. Finally, he got up and planted himself directly in front of them. Backlit by Bond, my dad said, "There are little kids behind you. Have a little respect, or I will throw you out."

I was mortified. But even in a darkened theater my father maintained a protective shield of innocence around us. The film, I note, was *The Spy Who Loved Me*, and after Max silenced the boys, we watched as James Bond donned his skis and zoomed down the ice-encrusted mountain.

Two years later, on the night of December 24, 1979, my father did the same in reverse.

My father hiked to higher elevations to regain a sense of perspective on life. When he found himself confined or upset, or bored by life, he spit-polished his shotgun and took off—as his father had done, and his father before him. Nature rejuvenated Max. Once while he was under house arrest, a couple of weeks before he fashioned his own daring 007 stunt, my mother saw the toll imprisonment had taken on her morose husband and arranged for her brother Mosoul to take him on a hunting expedition. Max pushed his shotgun through the air-conditioning vent, crawled in after it, shimmied twenty feet, then dropped onto an outside ledge adjacent to our house—just clear of the two youths who often stood guard near the front door. He and Mosoul were gone for eight hours. That night, my father returned empty-handed and wind-burned, but flushed with life. It was the happiest I'd seen him in weeks.

But on the night of December 24, 1979, when he hiked into the jagged, ice-ringed Zagros mountains for one last time, this was no hunting expedition. The hunter had become the hunted, and my father knew what all prey know: Stay in one place too long and you're dead. This was his true-life Bond adventure and his mission was a simple one. To save himself.

MAX

I t is a couple of days before Christmas and Max is jubilant.

Before him lies a small pile of necessities: a pocketknife, a coil of rope, a compass, maps, long johns, gloves, matches, a kerosene lantern, a mess kit, a sleeping bag, and his shotgun. In the background, Bing Crosby is crooning "White Christmas." A week from now Max will be a free man.

When the buzzer rings, Shahin comes out of the kitchen. It's one A.M., but she's been busy preparing a few meals for Max to take. Peering down from the second-floor hallway, she watches as a wiry man, attired in a lambskin hat and heavy wool jacket—probably somewhere between forty and sixty, it's difficult to tell with the Kurds—climbs the stairwell. He is trailed by a boy of maybe sixteen.

"Did anyone see you?" Shahin asks.

Outside, the new moon delivered a cloak of darkness, but you couldn't be too careful. Their home was watched. Earlier, Shahin had discreetly smashed the light outside their front door.

Inside the Kurd introduces himself as Ejder. "The border controls are only getting tighter. We wait any longer and the mountain passes will freeze over," he says, then wanders over to inspect Max's pile of necessities. "These will only weigh the horse down. Also your husband is a big man, *mash'allah*. I will need a bigger horse."

"How much?" she says warily.

"Ghabeli nadareh."[*]

"How much?" she insists.

"Five thousand dollars."

"You said three thousand."

"Five thousand dollars, half up front."

That was the problem with meeting at home. Ejder had taken a good look around, factored in Max's nationality, and doubled his price.

"For that price, I assume you will only be transporting my husband? No moochers looking to escape alongside an American."

The trip to Turkey will take three days, through high mountain passes ringed with ice and across rough rivers. This isn't a trip for the weak of heart. Was Doctor in good shape? They'd be passing through high altitudes and treacherous terrain. Last week, a youth had fallen to his death and they'd found his body the following morning—what was left of it, anyway. Wolves, he says offhandedly.

Wolves. Mountain passes. Raging rivers. To Max this sounds like another hunting adventure.

"How many times have you done this?" Shahin inquires.

"We are Kurds," he says derisively. "We have been crossing borders for generations."

In fact, the Kurds had been transporting opium, electronics, wine, whiskey, cognac, and Johnnie Walker (Red and Black) into Iran—more than a million dollars a day—since the revolution began, and other forbidden cargo long before that. But people were a new addition, and it wasn't altogether clear how their vast network would accommodate an American fugitive. Shahin had objected strenuously to Max's plans at first. Everyone knew the Kurds were wild mountain men who would rob, ambush, or kill you without batting an eye. But Max's options were dwindling fast, so Shahin agreed to enlist the help of her brother to locate a reliable smuggler.

---

[*]"Don't mention it."

When Mosoul announced he'd found one, Max knew he was the best of the worst of men.

"Do you know what Ejder's name means in Kurdish?" Mosoul says when he drops by the following night. "*Dragon.* I found a dragon to guard my brother. But you must look out for yourself, Maxy. This isn't like one of our hunting trips. Trust him, but only a little. Hide your passport—no matter what he asks, do not surrender this. The Kurds are not to be trusted. They've lived without laws for centuries, and won't hesitate to advance only their own interests. Lies. Robbery. Smuggling. They are experts in the worst of human traits—for which we must now thank God."

Mosoul takes out a flask and pours a shot. "Can you believe how quickly fifteen years passes? Remember our first trip into the mountains?"

Fifteen years ago, Mosoul and Max had gone hunting in the Tehran foothills, but their expedition was cut short when Max leapt across a stream, landed on a mossy rock, and shattered his shinbone. That morning, Mosoul had hoisted all six-foot-three of Max onto his shoulders, walked across hill and dale to the car, and roused Tehran's finest surgeon from his morning siesta. The operation had lasted ten hours, during which the surgeon inserted a steel rod that held the shattered bone together. Now whenever it rained, Max thought of two things: the ache in his leg and Mosoul's kindness. He also thought: *I will always have a piece of Iran inside me.*

"And now here you are crossing mountains again," Mosoul says wistfully. He pours another shot, then hands Max the flask. "It gets cold up there."

"How did you find Ejder?" Max asks.

Mosoul smiles. "Johnnie Walker didn't walk into the Islamic Republic by himself, did he?"

They drink a final toast to the dragon. Truthfully, it pleases Max that his life will be in the hands of a wily, cantankerous, bootlegging Kurd. Did the revolutionaries think he was a spy? Good. Then he will escape like one. Already Max has grown out his beard to appear less conspicuous.

He hasn't alerted Westinghouse. He hasn't told his parents or the chil-

dren. No use worrying them. The only people who know about his escape
are Mosoul, Shahin, and Ejder. According to plan, Max will travel across
the Zagros mountains into western Turkey. From there a car to the consul-
ate in Ankara. It will be a grueling trip, but he's been practicing—every
afternoon, a hundred flights up and down the stairs like an athlete in training. Maybe it's the exercise or the promise of freedom, but his depression
has lifted, leaving him focused and hopeful for the first time in weeks. He
spends his hours making lists—what to pack, what to wear—and dream-
ing of a new life in America.

AND THEN the hour is upon him. He has kissed the children good night
and now sits in the living room—waiting.

"Call the second you arrive in Ankara," Shahin says.

"You won't forget to call the embassy?" Max replies. "I don't want to get
turned back by some zealous bureaucrat. They should know I'm coming.
And my parents . . ."

They'd been over this a dozen times. While Max was hoofing it over the
mountains, Shahin would orchestrate the family's departure from Tehran.
Already she's sold much of their belongings out of a boutique she'd set up
in Katayoun's bedroom—racks and racks of designer pantsuits, dresses,
and leftover American booty displayed to a steady stream of neighborhood
women. Max had signed a notarized letter giving her the right to leave Iran
of her own volition. These days, all women leaving Iran had to obtain
permission from their husbands—even if he happened to be a convicted
American spy under house arrest.

"What happens if the prosecutor sends someone to check on me?"

"Let's focus on getting you out, shall we?" Shahin says brightly. "In a
week, we'll all be reunited on American soil. I think our luck will hold out
for that long, don't you?"

For now they sit watching the minutes tick by. Midnight. One A.M.
Two A.M.

Max checks his pockets for the tenth time—passport, maps, address and telephone of the American embassy in Turkey, chocolate bars, cheese, money for bribes. Shahin has sewn an additional five thousand dollars into the seams of his jacket.

By 2:30 A.M., Ejder still hasn't arrived and Max is beginning to suspect something dreadful has happened.

The sound of the buzzer jars them both. Seconds later, the same young man who had accompanied Ejder enters the apartment. He looks like he'd be at home in a Dickens novel—ill-fitting clothes, uncombed matted hair, dirty face.

"Ejder couldn't come. He sent me to fetch you," he says.

"Why not?" Shahin says, approaching the boy. "Speak!"

"I don't know," he shrugs. "He couldn't come. He sent me."

"Get out, scamp," Shahin says. "And don't dare come back without Ejder."

But the boy stands there mutely.

"Go. Or I'll call the police," she threatens.

But the boy does not budge. "Call the police, then."

Max turns to Shahin. "I think he's telling the truth. I think I should go with him."

"Absolutely not. My husband isn't leaving with a *child . . .*"

But Max has already begun to gather his things. It's now or never. Taking one final look around, he kisses Shahin and in an instant he is off into the Tehran night.

FOR SEVERAL HOURS, Max lies folded into the backseat of a threadbare truck loaded with fruits, hurtling toward the Caspian. When the truck comes to a sudden stop or swerves, which is often since the roads are lined with hairpin turns, a bushel careens into Max's lap. Pomegranates. Oranges. Persimmons. For hours he watches the dark scenery rush by, assaulted by fruit, but eventually gives in to fatigue, and by the time he wakes it's morning. The driver is different, but the boy is still sitting shotgun. It's colder now and his breath rises in condensed puffs. In his lap, an assortment of fruit rumbles.

He picks a pomegranate from his lap and squeezes it—kneading and kneading until its seeds give way, then bites into the fruit. A spurt of juice flows. Outside, the Caspian glimmers in the distance.

The Caspian. He and Shahin had vacationed here once. One summer, 1974, they'd spent a week watching the kids chase newly hatched chicks, gorging on *chello kebab* and caviar and diving headlong into the world's largest lake. Now he was fleeing along these same shores, cramped and held captive by pomegranates. How strange life is.

The car heads west along the thread of seashore, then into the surrounding foothills. A mist worthy of Merlin has settled across the landscape. Occasionally the driver stops for Max to stretch his legs, relieve his bladder, liberate himself from the fruit. Each time, Max ventures into the roadside trees, anxious to not be seen from the road—but not so far as to lose sight of the truck. The third time he does this, he returns to a cloud of exhaust. The truck is gone.

"Jesus Christ!"

He's in the middle of a long, loud stream of expletives when he sees the boy.

"Hello, *meester*," he calls out jauntily.

The boy leads him through a mossy thicket, toward a house in the foothills, which turns out to be a mud stable, and their accommodations for the day. Inside, the boy lays a pile of blankets for Max on the dirt floor. *Eenja*, the boy says, patting the makeshift bed. Against the far wall, a mangy white packhorse feeds. Max hopes this isn't the beast on which he'll escape; it barely looks strong enough to support the boy.

"*Ejder kojast?*" Max inquires, anxious to know where the absentee Kurd is.

But the boy is gone.

Alone in a stable, Max breathes in the scent of straw and manure. The hut is small, ten feet by ten feet maybe, with a small window against the far wall letting in a fading square of twilight. Soon the boy is back with a cup of tea, bread, and a bowl of rice and cold lamb—the first of Shahin's meals. He lights a kerosene lantern and lays a blanket for himself alongside Max's. Then he draws a cross in the dirt. "Hello, *meester*," he says, pointing to the cross.

Then he gives Max some opium, which Max politely declines.

It is Christmas. Christmas in a stable.

Max had given up Christmas traditions when he married Shahin twenty years ago and converted to Islam. The day he strode into the Washington, D.C., mosque and thrice-repeated, "There is no God but one and Mohammad is his messenger," both Allah and Shahin witnessed the power of his faith in him. Max had converted to Islam out of respect for Shahin's father, a deeply devout man, and also to have a spiritual adventure of his own. He'd never met a Moslem until he left home at eighteen, and as an only child he was intrigued with the ideology—a religion of brotherhood. That day, the presiding imam welcomed Max into the folds of Islam with a handshake, and Max began his new life as a Moslem. But every Christmas, he struggles with the weight of his Christian past. It's not so much the religion, for Max suspects that all paths lead to the same God. But he misses the tradition. The carols and tinsel and eggnog and salty hams. The Christmas Eve dinners. And especially the tree that Dolly sprays with fake snow and festoons with tiny lights. Now as his gaze falls upon the snow-crusted pines outside, Max smiles. The path through these pines will take him home.

In the corner, the boy begins his prayers.

A FEW HOURS LATER the boy shakes Max awake with another cup of tea and slice of bread. It's bone-numbingly cold, but the boy removes Max's shoes and socks and begins rubbing his feet with a wool blanket. While Max eats, the boy continues to rub his feet briskly, gazing at him with piercing curiosity. Later when the boy is feeding the horse, Max checks his belongings to ensure the boy hasn't stolen anything.

Outside the sky is pitch-black, littered with more stars than Max has ever seen. Underfoot, a good half meter of snow has fallen. Before him, the cliffs of Zagros rise in elegant formation—jagged and white, outlined against the darkness. The peaks will be their home for the next two days.

There is an advantage to the snow: Their packhorse is pure white and beautifully camouflaged. But when the boy trots her out, saddled and fed, Max is dismayed to see that she walks with a discernible limp. Something is wrong with her hind leg. Grabbing the lantern, Max circles around and sees she is wounded—a bite mark, it appears.

A boy, a wounded horse, a fugitive. This did not even rise to the level of a fool's errand.

Soon man, boy, and beast are heading up the mountainside. With the boy in front, there is little room to shift or beat his arms for warmth, so Max closes his eyes and tries to call forth a fire within like a Tibetan monk. But it's too cold to focus or meditate, too cold to do anything but be miserable. The wind whips down the mountain and slaps his face. Five thousand feet up, he has never been so cold. When Max's teeth start clattering, the boy wraps a cloth reeking of sweat and opium around Max's jaw.

The trail ahead is a series of switchbacks that zag along the mountain. Where are the opium smugglers? The barrel-chested outlaws with thick beards and fur-lined boots? Max has heard that these trails are traversed by horses so familiar with the route, they are often sent unmanned. But ahead there is only vast whiteness. Soon the incline steepens and the horse begins visibly laboring under their weight. Her breath comes in thick plumes and her body is coated in sweat, soaking the saddle blankets and Max's pants. Wet and cold, Max's joints begin to stiffen. A new round of snow is beginning to fall.

Perched in front, the boy is softly humming a Kurdish song to himself. He seems oddly happy.

Remembering his flask, Max takes a swig of whiskey and finds relief in the spreading fire. Max doesn't share it with the boy—no use hastening his journey out of childhood, he thinks. Then laughs. The boy has probably sampled every liquor and drug known to man. Last night he'd offered Max opium as a Christmas present.

The whiskey's warmth gives way to pleasant thoughts: Back home, Dolly and Pappy are probably sitting around the tree, spiked eggnog in hand, exchanging gifts. He will be home in time for New Year's, hopefully, and they'll laugh about his adventures while firecrackers light up the Texan sky.

But then the whiskey's fire dissipates, and Max is back to his wet, shivering self.

The wind picks up. The air gets thinner. And Max's head begins to hurt.

Ahead, he sees only snow—endless miles of white—and higher peaks.

By MIDAFTERNOON, the light snow has turned into a heavy blizzard and the temperature has dropped. They will have to take shelter. But the boy continues guiding the horse toward higher elevations, singing pleasantly into the snowstorm. When Max tries to get the boy's attention, the boy says, *"Neh, neh,"* and goes on singing. Finally, when it seems like the horse might well drop from exhaustion, they turn a corner and there, cut into the mountain, Max sees a hovel. Dismounting, the boy leads the horse inside and begins rubbing down the spent beast with the saddle blanket. Max takes a second blanket and does the same.

When the horse is dry, the boy fetches a few pieces of wood to light a fire at the hut's entrance, then unties Max's boots and begins rubbing his feet briskly. Everything is methodical, as if the boy's done this a hundred times. Soon Max's toes thaw out and the pain sets in, sharp and unrelenting, but the boy continues to briskly knead his feet until warmth returns to them. Looking at him, Max feels a pang of gratitude. He extracts a couple of chocolate bars, some cheese, and nuts from his satchel and offers some to the boy, who declines them. But when Max places a bar of chocolate a few inches from the boy, it disappears.

The Kurds are a proud people.

SOMETIME IN THE NIGHT, a sharp cry rings out—high and inhuman. The horse is furiously kicking at something. The fire has gone out and in the darkness it is impossible to make out the jumble of shapes, but instantly the boy is up. Grabbing a stick, he begins beating the invader. Max follows suit with his satchel, landing several blows on the invader's rump, but it only appears to invigorate the intruder. This goes on for a good half minute, man and boy beating, horse kicking and crying, shadow lunging and retreating. Eventually the invader backs away, grazing Max's foot on the way out. In its shiny eyes, large head, and sloping back, Max recognizes the features of a wolf. Max relights the fire and what he sees shocks him.

Blood everywhere.

In the corner the horse is audibly gasping—his leg in tatters, bits of flesh hanging, the wound reopened and spurting blood. When the boy sees the extent of the damage, he begins to cry and beat his head with bloody hands. The floor. The boy's clothes. His hands and hair. All inked with the animal's blood.

Max's first instinct is to fetch his shotgun and put the animal out of his misery, but killing the transport is not an option. He goes to work methodically cleaning the wound with handfuls of snow and a bit of whiskey. Then he binds it with a strip of cloth. The wound will certainly get infected, but for now it will have to do.

Outside, it's almost daybreak. The blizzard has dumped another foot of snow. Pulling a map from his satchel, Max mimes: *Where are we?* But the boy only looks at Max absently.

After a breakfast of stale bread and strong tea, they set off again. Another series of switchbacks, white and frozen, lies ahead. At first the horse lumbers along at a slower gait, obviously pained, but able. But as the hours pass, her exertions become more labored. The air gets thinner. The wind picks up. Their faces are warmed by the sun—then burned. In front, the boy is singing another Kurdish song.

Ahead another peak looms, massive and white.

These mountains are the dividing line between East and West. Two thousand years ago, Alexander the Great had crossed these trails en route into Persia—back when the peaks were a throughway for mixed blood, culture, and the high and human ideals of Greco-Persian civilization. At the time of Alexander's invasion in 330 BC, Persia was Greece's sworn enemy, but there was no denying the beauty of her lands or richness of her culture. Alexander adopted their style of dress, took the title of *Shahanshah** for himself, and ordered his officers to take Persian brides so that East and West would meet in the wombs and bloodlines. Two millennia later, confronting the relentlessly white landscape through which Alexander's army had once charged, Max cannot help but feel he is beating a hasty retreat— here where the traffic of high and human ideals has been reduced to fugitives, cigarettes, booze, and opium.

Several times, Max dismounts to check the wound and lighten the horse's load. By midafternoon, he notices that a froth has accumulated on the animal's chest. The boy greets this development with resignation, clicking his tongue and pointing skyward to God, but Max knows what it is. His years on a ranch had taught him one thing: not to overwork a beast. This one was spent.

So WEIGHTED IS HE by these thoughts that he almost misses the cluster of huts in the distance—mere dots on a white canvas. *Look*, he points to the boy. Soon Max is jumping over snowbanks and careening through powder, the hamlet rising and falling according to their elevation. Presently they arrive close enough for Max to take a good look, and what he sees pleases

---

*King of Kings.

him. No industry. No agriculture. Nothing but seven huts. This is likely a smuggler's village, which means they are closer to the border than Max thought.

A half kilometer away, the boy pulls up sharply.

"Petrol," he says, pointing excitedly.

A hundred meters beyond the village, Max sees two jeeps parked alongside a pathway. Did the boy mean to take a jeep across the border? Instead of heading toward the hamlet, though, the boy dismounts and leads them hurriedly into a gully. *Come,* the boy gestures furiously. Fifty feet below, the village is oddly still.

Suddenly it dawns on Max. The village is being raided.

Patrol, the boy meant, not petrol.

Nestled into the gully, Max fishes out another chocolate bar and offers half to the boy. What could they do but wait? Eventually the raid would conclude and they could proceed. As Max chews absently on the bar of chocolate, his mind wanders. Had the wolf not attacked and slowed their progress, Max would be en route to jail right now, he realizes. Then shot. All this time, Max had smiled indulgently when people used the phrase *inshallah,*[*] but now wonders if there's something to it. Was the wolf an angel in camouflage?

The answer probably depended on whom you asked. The horse would surely have other ideas.

By dusk, the horse had taken a turn for the worse and, despite the boy's almost constant ministrations, was in critical condition—from either acute hunger, infection, or exhaustion. *"Bayad beram,"* the boy says, then points to the ground. *"Shoma eenja."*

I must leave. You stay here. As if Max had much choice in the matter.

He cannot blame the boy. The horse is likely the only thing the boy owns in this world. But as he watches the boy and his horse descend the mountainside, Max is beset by a sudden conviction that all this is fated

---

[*] God willing.

anyway. Whatever will happen has already been written. The wolf was an agent of some force he did not quite understand. God, perhaps?

After a few minutes, Max stands up cautiously and takes a look around. Soon the sun will go down and he wants to make sure he has his bearings. Beyond the village, he sees a faint glimmer that catches the fading sunlight and extends for miles in either direction. The light catches and dances reflectively. *Barbed wire.* Which means Turkey is just beyond. Turkey! He is this close to freedom. But the raid almost assuredly meant tighter patrols—and looking across the landscape, Max now notices a half-dozen checkpoints scattered across the mountain. Even if he got across to Turkey, without a guide he would assuredly get lost in the mountains.

His thoughts turn to the boy. A kid in bloodstained clothes was sure to invite questions—maybe it was a mistake to trust him. Below, the hamlet is still deathly quiet.

An hour passes. It grows darker. The air is bitingly cold, and Max is beginning to realize he must move or freeze. Burrowing into a blanket, Max extracts another Hershey bar from the diminishing supply in his satchel. The chocolate of his boyhood might well become the final taste of his adulthood, he realizes. At least he will go out with something sweet on his tongue.

Freedom or death, wasn't that the idea by which Americans lived? Probably this wasn't what Alexander Hamilton had in mind, but when the night winds start up, Max decides to make a break for it. Strapping on the satchel and pulling the blanket tightly around him, Max climbs out of the gully and back up the mountain. Under the slivered moon, it is almost completely dark, but the snow creates a slight contrast by which Max's vision grows sharper bit by bit. The snow seeps into his boots and numbs his feet. An hour later Max descends the mountain again and finds himself a good mile to the left of the hamlet. At least that's what he thinks; it's difficult to tell in the inky blackness.

A hundred or so yards to his left is a guard station not much bigger than a telephone booth. It is lit and Max can just make out the tea-sipping shadow figure of a border guard inside. He will have to ascend again and find another spot to cross.

Just then, a hand slips across Max's mouth and clamps down.

Another hand spins him around.

Max's heart plummets. *This close to freedom only to fail at its doorstep?*

"Doctor," a voice says menacingly.

The musk. The voice. The grip of powerfully corded arms. Wolf or angel? All this time he'd assumed that his life had been strung up between the twin forces of good and evil, fate and happenstance, East and West, but the truth occupied a far murkier and more indeterminate place. Here in this frozen no-man's-land, the white canvas was ruled over by a more mythic beast, neither wolf nor angel.

This was the territory of dragons.

Max was gazing into the grizzled face of Ejder.

PART 4

A Tale of
Two Countries

Shahin

Max has been gone for a few days. There has been no call from Turkey. And Shahin is beginning to worry. But she continues preparing for their departure, selling off their furniture, obtaining school transcripts, and making travel arrangements. Earlier that day, she'd purchased three British Airways tickets to London for herself and the kids— and now as her glance alights on the tickets, it hits her. In a week's time, she will be leaving Iran.

Probably forever.

Shahin had dreamed about London ever since she was a fifteen-year-old girl and spirited a radio to her room, nightly. Under cover of darkness, she spun the dial to the BBC and listened to the pristine diction of its announcers. It was 1946, but it wasn't news of the war Shahin coveted so much as the delicious English accent. "This is the British Broadcasting Corporation, and here is the news," she repeated, having discovered an innate ability to wrap her tongue around strange vowels and consonants. One night, her father caught her listening to the BBC. "I can imitate them perfectly," she boasted. "But I want to learn English properly. Will you send me to Britain?"

"Absolutely not," he replied.

What if she was the number one student in her class?

Again, no. Postwar London was no place for a girl.

If she was the number one student in her city?

Then he should be very pleased—but still no. Why didn't Shahin wish to stay home, get married like her brothers and sisters?

Number one in the entire province, then?

And because Khorassan was Iran's largest province, spanning a hundred thousand square kilometers, and Shahin's chances were thinner than a thread of silk, Abdul Hossein nodded his assent. Two years later when he was called to Ferdowsi Hall to present academic honors, and the red velvet curtains swung aside, there she stood—the number one student in Khorassan. Abdul Hossein looked like he might faint from pride. And because he was a man of his word, the following week a representative of the British embassy delivered Shahin's visa and she flew off to England—at seventeen, the youngest woman to leave Iran unchaperoned.

When Shahin arrived in London in June 1948, she took one look at the landscape and felt her heart sink. The city was in woeful shape, vast swaths strewn with the rubble of bombings. She called her father that night and begged him to allow her to return. Everyone she loved was in Iran. Her siblings. The sounds and scents of her childhood. She entreated him to send her a return ticket, but he refused. "Give destiny a chance to unfold," he advised.

Abdul Hossein had arranged for Shahin to board with the chief of police, whose family kept a town house on Orchard Street in Stratham, and he was confident that given time, she would enjoy her new life. Shahin had a modestly furnished room on the second floor with a bed, armoire, night table, desk, and rocking chair. The chief's boys, Peter and Mark, distracted Shahin from her homesickness by imitating their father. His wife, Kika, clucked about her exotic houseguest and each afternoon presided over tea service. Out came the trolley with a china teapot and tiered silver tray of sandwiches, pastries, and crumpets. "Milk first or last?" she asked, explaining that milk first turns oily when hot tea is added. The finger sandwiches were a lovely delicacy—too lovely, perhaps, with slices of meat as translucent as an onion. Everyone had rations, Kika explained. Bread. Milk. Eggs.

This too was new to Shahin for even during the war, the Malekis had always set a generous table.

Soon, she discovered that London teemed with a strange kinetic life. The postwar fashions captivated Shahin, as did the double-decker buses with their punctilious timetables and cheerfully proper conductors. She rode them everywhere—to the market in Piccadilly Circus, to the outer boroughs and rolling countryside. One day Shahin received an invitation to the Iranian ambassador's house for dinner and, finding herself in need of a gown, went to DH Evans department store. Their flagship store on Oxford Street was known as the primary source of European couture.

"Have you modeled before?" the clerk asked Shahin as she emerged from the dressing room in full regalia—heels, silk gloves, crimson gown. "You're quite pretty. You have maturity and elegance."

"Thank you. About the gown—does it suit me?"

"Small hips. Jet-black hair. Lovely shoulders. You're certainly different from all the other milky girls," she commented, circling Shahin. "Where are you from?"

"Persia."

"Persia! We could use a bit of exotic blood. Would you like to give it a go?"

The clerk wasn't a clerk. She was Mrs. Miller, manager of the DH Evans, and she gave Shahin two bits of advice: Their clothes were quite snug, owing to the fact that Mr. Evans had apprenticed with a draper and enjoyed curves. "Not too many scones at tea, my dear." The second bit of advice Shahin would remember long into old age: "When you walk, one mustn't see daylight through your legs. Heel to toe, heel to toe."

There in the DH Evans salon, surrounded by a colorful array of the latest continental fashions, Mrs. Miller gave Shahin a quick modeling lesson, fanning her skirt out like an accordion to show how a fuller skirt might benefit from a rocking turn. "One must use any accessory at hand," she says, "even something like an umbrella might be used to better show off your clothes." She plucked one from the racks and planted it like a flag, so that it clicked smoothly on the marble floor. Then she opened the umbrella and walked jauntily across the showroom floor.

Shahin laughed. Then, realizing she was quite serious, opened another and copied her walk.

A half hour later, her induction into the world of high fashion concluded with the most important maneuver—the curtsey. DH Evans catered to high society, Mrs. Miller explained, and they expected to be addressed accordingly. One must first lower one's head in respect, while holding one's skirt, placing one foot behind the other and bending one's legs at the knee, and bending one's shoulders forward without sticking the fanny out, all in one fluid motion. Hold for two seconds—three for royalty. Then rise. Could Shahin manage that?

Years later, when it seemed like they'd pluck any refugee off the boat, deny her food, ply her with cigarettes, strip her naked, and do their damnedest to make her look like an opium addict—voilà, a model—Shahin was glad to have come of age when modeling was a respectable profession. But the following week, when a driver picked Shahin up and spirited her to an E. M. Forster–sized mansion on the East End, with a circular driveway and manicured gardens, it hit her: *Modeling?* Her father would be scandalized. She'd come to England to pursue her studies, not model for a duchess.

Two hours later, Shahin had shown a dozen dresses, sold three, and collected a tidy commission, and from that day on, twice a week after classes, a driver whisked her away to cold Tudors outside London, town houses on the Thames, or magnificent rolling estates where young boys played cricket on the lawn. Inside ladies sipped tea and cooed over continental couture. In the gloom of postwar Britain, DH Evans's wardrobes were a bright spot of color. At thirty pounds a visit plus commission, Shahin earned enough for room and board, tuition at London Polytechnic, and a tiny rental on the Cote d'Azur where she escaped Britain's gloomy winters.

Shahin's life grew fuller. Her English improved. The thing she enjoyed most was theater; one weekend she took the bus to Stratford-upon-Avon, where from the rear mezzanine of the Royal Shakespeare Theatre, she saw her first Shakespearean play. How beautifully the language bent under his pen! She loved *Macbeth*, and marveled at the mix of cunning and sorrow that brought Lady Macbeth to commit such a damn ugly crime—then wept at her predicament. Clearly, Shakespeare understood human nature better than anyone. Shahin was shocked to find herself sympathizing with a murderess! In quick succession she saw *Hamlet*, *Romeo and Juliet*, *Othello*, and *A Midsummer Night's Dream*. Afterward, she read each play cover to cover.

Soon, she found herself speaking differently, a bit too literate perhaps, but she could not help it. She blamed Shakespeare. Love. Ambition. Murder. Politics. Sex. Was there nothing that did not seem like a delicious morsel when spoken with the right tone?

One afternoon after a modeling job near Oxford Street, she found herself in front of a building shaped like a top hat and realized she was standing in front of Broadcasting House. This was BBC headquarters, the very building that had drawn her to London on the strength of its radio waves.

"Are you lost?"

"No, no—I used to dream about this place," Shahin said to the gentleman who had inquired. From his accent, Shahin could tell he was Persian. "I came here to study English."

"With a focus on Shakespeare, I see. Is that *Romeo and Juliet*?" he asked, nodding to the copy in Shahin's purse.

"Shall I recite a soliloquy for you?" she laughingly inquired.

There in front of Broadcasting House, Shahin gave a quick performance of "What light through yonder window breaks."

"Mash'allah," he said. "You are rather theatrical, aren't you?"

"If you should call love of language a theatrical thing, yes. What a pity Shakespeare hasn't been translated into Farsi, for our countrymen would enjoy him, don't you think?"

They chatted a bit more. It was growing late, and Shahin sensed that she should be getting back home, but she was having such an enjoyable time talking with her compatriot. Except for the Iranian ambassador and one or two of his colleagues, she'd not met any other Persians in London. When Mr. Golanipour volunteered that he ran BBC Persia, Shahin recounted how she used to spirit her radio under the covers at night, and how the radio waves from this very building had beckoned her across an ocean.

Golanipour looked thoughtful.

"Look," he says, directing her attention to the interlocked rococo statues above the entrance to Broadcasting House. "Prospero and Ariel from *The Tempest*. The Magician and the Air Sprite. It is through the magic of radio waves that the BBC travels through the air. We do a Shakespeare play once a week in English. Perhaps you'd like to translate one into Farsi for BBC Persia?"

Translate Shakespeare? Shahin blushed at the audacity.

"Of course, I will edit the translation," Golanipour continued, "so don't fret too much about getting it just right. Don't worry about making your dialogue too complex. We can always go back and deepen it later. What play shall we choose?"

"*Macbeth*," Shahin said, before she could stop herself.

"*Macbeth*. Perfect. With all its intrigues and double crosses and stories of stolen thrones, it is perfect for Iran."

ACCIDENTS HAVE BEFALLEN the cast. Actual murders committed onstage. Fires and falling scenery. "The Scottish play" was how they referred to it, because even mentioning its title was bad luck. To Shahin, *Macbeth* was the luckiest of all Shakespeare's plays—a bridge to the listening hearts of her countrymen. For three months she labored over a draft, paying particular attention to Lady Macbeth, in whom the forces of ambition and grace, femininity and masculinity collided. Was there ever a greater woman to grace the stage? What a shame Shakespeare dispensed with her in an offstage suicide. If murderous men died glorious deaths in the spotlight, Lady Macbeth deserved the same at least—for wasn't she the real star? Over and over Shahin rewrote her soliloquies, choosing just the right turn of phrase in Farsi, then rewriting it. Women in Iran must understand this woman wasn't a witch or a shrew.

Translating Shakespeare for the radio presented its own challenges. It was difficult enough to lift listeners over the battlefield for Macbeth's soul and show the ruination that ensued, but then Shakespeare's language was so rich with double meanings—wordplay, wit—and how did one translate that? English and Farsi were two wholly unrelated languages, every bit as irreconcilable as their respective cultures. Eventually Shahin realized it wasn't so important that word match word, but rather that each sentence was alive with meaning. She paid particular attention to the soliloquies, knowing that Shakespeare used them to reveal the truth of his characters and build a bridge to the audience.

The winter of 1949 was miserable—copious snowfall that quickly blackened, food shortages—but Shahin had never felt better nourished. Daytimes she attended classes at London Polytechnic. Afternoons, she modeled. Evenings, she translated England's greatest writer into the language of her childhood. If there was a happier woman in all London, Shahin didn't know who that might be. By the time spring rolled around, her *Macbeth* translation was complete.

MR. GOLANIPOUR brought in a half-dozen Persian newscasters to play assigned roles and record *Macbeth* over the course of an afternoon. This worked better than one might have expected, for newscasters had a natural sense of drama. Shahin took the role of Lady Macbeth. Sitting at a bank of microphones with fellow Iranians, recording her translation of Shakespeare, she felt as proud as if she had authored the play herself. It was the most exciting day of her young life.

By then the BBC had become the premier source for news in Iran. Over three million people routinely turned their dial to the BBC. But one day in the spring of 1949, rich and poor, illiterate and educated gathered all across Iran in teahouses and living rooms, bazaars and beauty salons to hear a tale full of sound and fury.

"This is London," Mr. Golanipour announced, "and today we bring you the tragedy of *Macbeth*." With a thunderclap of lightning, the three witches offered their woeful predictions—and for the next hour, Shahin and her fellow announcers held BBC's listeners in sway. It was the first time Shakespeare was heard in Iran.

It was later reported that in a courtroom in Tehran, a judge had postponed a trial until the play concluded.

In cafés in Isfahan, groups of forty to fifty were crammed to the doors, contentedly listening as Macbeth fretted about life's futility.

There were reports that in the farthest villages, school children gathered around the *kadkhoda*'s* radio, enraptured, declaring that this was better than Ferdowsi's poetry, because it was *actually happening*. Wasn't this the BBC? Didn't they report the news? A murder on the radio was a spectacular thing. The only exception was Rasht, where listeners complained that all this high-minded excitement was very nice for cities like Isfahan and Tehran, but they were a practical people with no interest in prophecies and ghosts and sleepwalking ladies. But it was commonly known that Rashtis were Iran's simpletons, the butt of everyone's jokes.

In the Maleki household, the family sat in the *andarun*† and listened to Shahin channeling Lady Macbeth. Abdul Hossein brushed away a tear.

For days afterward the British legation in Tehran was besieged with requests for "more Shakespeare, less news." But Golanipour had other ideas for Shahin. He offered her a position announcing the news. It would be good to have a female announcer, he suggested. Iran was in the process of modernizing and women's rights, and BBC's programs should reflect that.

---

*Village leader.
†Private family quarters of a wealthy household.

JUNE 1, 1951, 3 P.M.,
GREENWICH MEAN TIME

Today marked one year of broadcasts, thousands of stories, fifty-two pay-checks, two-hundred-some odd trips to headquarters, and an equal number of afternoon scones that had thankfully not made their way to her hips. Every afternoon at three, Shahin took the lift to the fourth floor, picked up the white briefings smartly embossed with the BBC logo, entered the studio, and took her place at the microphone. Taking a calming breath, she leaned forward. "Good afternoon, this is Shahin Maleki for BBC Persia," she began, "and these are the headlines."

The briefings were arranged in order of importance. Typically the newscast started with an assassination or election, or a revolt in the provinces, and ended on a less climactic note—a goodwill mission, perhaps. Over the course of a year she had broadcast stories ranging from George Orwell's death to Seoul's fall to the spread of Communism.

As she read the briefs, as the radio waves bearing her voice exited the transmitter and traveled out over London and the continent, across the world, Shahin witnessed her own world unfold and expand in similar fashion. She was shocked to receive a letter from a stranger, complimenting her voice and diction. How was it possible that he could write to her—and for what purpose? It seemed odd. And then small batches of mail began to arrive, two and three letters a month, from destinations as remote as Shiraz, Peking, Lahore, Tangiers—Iranians requesting to meet her, schoolgirls wanting to know how she made it into broadcasting and by the way, could she please send a picture?

As her listeners grew in number, she became part of an industrial engine of media, churning out the world's daily history in sound bites. Burning Buddhist nuns, ritual suicides and mass marriages, the mushrooming disaster of nuclear bombs—she delighted in how the insanity of the world rolled off her tongue into BBC's iconic Marconi microphone. She knew her power in shaping that history, how people sat before their radios, tuning in, absorbing her diction, the sweeping syllables of world events. They sat in their living rooms, in their gardens and libraries and embassies and continental cafés, listening. The magnitude of it thrilled her. Someone once told her that radio waves traveled to outer space. An astronaut thrusting through galaxies light-years into the future would hear those newscasts. She imagined Shakespeare's plays traveling past celestial ears, carrying the bard toward other encounters, mixing with nebulas and colliding with meteors, ricocheting off glinting, weightless pieces of astrogarbage. Measured and steady, her voice would orbit Jupiter's moons.

That year, the BBC would receive more than forty-five hundred letters from Iranian doctors, lawyers, teachers, government employees, farmers, students, and landlords. But the vast majority are not complimentary. Back home, Prime Minister Mossadegh had tried to wrest control of the Anglo-Iranian Oil Company from the British, who have controlled Iran's oil since 1913. A striking figure who frequently appeared in his pajamas and conducted business from his bedroom, "old Mossie" was beloved by Iranians for his insistence on nationalizing the AIOC. But the British refused to budge. And in the wake of this brouhaha, the BBC's reporting wasn't *quite* the objective source its guidelines prescribed. The Foreign Office had instructed the BBC on how to report the issue so as to maximize damage to Mossadegh and the cause of nationalization, on the grounds that it would "ruin Persian economic, political and social structure," "alienate British friendship," and "play straight into the hands of the Russians by whom it may even be inspired," a letter advised. And the BBC obliged. For weeks it ran a series of reports countering Mossadegh. Shahin herself had broadcast several. And the initial trickle of letters to Broadcasting House soon became a torrent.

Shahin read a few. One was from a student whose brother worked at the AIOC's refinery and complained about the slumlike conditions, prompting the student to wonder if his brother wasn't a Communist and avowed traitor. Did the BBC have any advice for him? The letter sent a shiver down Shahin's spine.

"What are we doing?" Shahin asked Mr. Golanipour that day. "Why are we broadcasting so many anti-Mossadegh stories? I thought our only commitment was to broadcast the news."

"Good afternoon to you too," Golanipour said, removing his coat. "I thought you didn't like Mossadegh?"

"I hate anyone who tries to undermine my Shah. That doesn't mean the enemy of my enemy is my friend. My loyalty is to Iran."

"This is the *British* Broadcasting Corporation. You report the news we assign."

We? He was Iranian. He was also twice her age and a friend of the Iranian ambassador, so Shahin checked herself—but found that her voice merely quivered at a lower decibel level. "These letters . . . doesn't it trouble you that the British are using us, under the guise of broadcasting the news, to get to our oil?"

"It troubles me that you've not recorded your segment yet. I don't imagine the studio engineer would be pleased to see you here, bleary-eyed and hoarse, holding correspondence that doesn't pertain to you."

"This morning I received a letter asking if I was a 'mouthpiece for British imperialism.'"

Golanipour closed the door. "You are too young to involve yourself in matters such as this. You mustn't pry. You are an announcer, a valued announcer, but finally an announcer. May I have the letter?"

Shahin handed it to him.

"The Foreign Office will respond on your behalf," he said curtly.

Suddenly it struck her: Had the BBC hired young, pliant broadcasters— mostly students—so that they might not ask questions? Was this why BBC Persia had added a new dawn broadcast, to expand its sphere of influence over Iran when the fate of her oil fields was up in the air?

"You have a good voice for broadcasting, Shahin. Clear. Dramatic.

Detached," Mr. Golanipour said, holding the door ajar. "See that it stays that way."

By September the British had pulled out of Iran's oil fields, announced a blockade in the Persian Gulf, and threatened legal action to anyone purchasing Iranian oil. Production dropped 90 percent. With no oil revenues, Mossadegh's social reforms came to a standstill and massive strikes crippled the economy. At BBC Persia, letters continued pouring in. Caught in the crossfire, the Iranian broadcasters declared to BBC management they would no longer broadcast political commentary, news analysis, or any other program related to oil or Mossadegh's government—a threat they carried out on several occasions.

But something did not make sense. If the BBC was such a biased source, Shahin wondered, why were her countrymen still tuning in? Abolghassem Taheri, a longtime BBC veteran and host of *The Listener's Period*, explained the situation: Iranian media was tightly controlled and not terribly good, lacking brevity, clarity and objectivity. The BBC was only marginally more objective—but mythically powerful. This latest cascade of events contributed to the deep-rooted belief that Britain was behind everything that transpired in Iran. *And what source better than the BBC to find out what was happening in their own country?*

Months passed. Shahin continued working as a broadcaster and model—bending and adapting to British culture as the Persian paisley tree bent under Islamic winds. The thought that her country was a plaything to the West, its oil fields ripe for pillaging, disgusted her. All this over a vast accumulation of animal and vegetable residue that lay rotting beneath Iran's surface, whose pressure had slowly converted it to a black viscous liquid. The West pretended concern for Iranian workers, economic prosperity, and human rights—but it all came down to fossil fuels and pipeline routes. *Not all the perfumes in Arabia could sweeten Western hands.* When would the world let Iran alone? Until then, Shahin learned to do something uniquely Persian: *Besaz-o-besooz*. Burn inwardly and make do. She went to work every morning but kept her opinions to herself. She translated a few more Shakespearean plays: *Twelfth Night*, *Hamlet*, and *Romeo and Juliet*.

In October 1952, Mossadegh declared Britain an enemy and cut all diplomatic ties, tossing all British AIOC workers, engineers, missionaries, and teachers out of Iran. Tensions escalated. And then, when it appeared things couldn't get any worse, they did. That July, a CIA agent named Miles Copeland arrived in Tehran to orchestrate a coup. Eight hundred people died in the ensuing melee. Mossadegh was arrested. And Iran's oil interests were evenly divided between the Americans and the Brits.

The price tag for overthrowing a government? Sixty thousand dollars.

In the ensuing confusion, in the deepest hour, when the distant memory of Iran could no longer defend against the swelling, undeniable battalions of international opposition, a soft soliloquy could be heard, a supplication, coming from the direction of Shahin's bedroom. She spoke aloud at these times, mourning the foreign landscape on which she had built another life, the radio waves that lured her from Iran and now planted seeds of conflict, the indisputable loneliness of speaking a second tongue—even one as gorgeous as Shakespeare's. On such nights, Kika Rodgers stood outside her door with a ready cup of tea, but her assurances that "It's not so bad, luv," did nothing to rouse Shahin from her sadness.

A COUPLE YEARS LATER, an impressionable young man named Sadegh Ghotbzadeh paid a visit to Mossadegh. Broken and humbled, the ex–prime minister had retired to his village home in Ahmad Abad and began selling the beautiful Tabrizi trees he cultivated on his estate. The trees were tall and straight with profuse leafage and fetched a considerable sum. When he called his old friend Hossein Ghotbzadeh for help with the enterprise, Hossein sent his teenage son to apprentice with him. Sadegh spent two weeks with Mossadegh, during which he came to love the charismatic old man with a bald head and beaklike nose. During this time, he absorbed Mossadegh's brand of nationalism—Iran was for Iranians—and his deep mistrust of the West.

Years later, everyone would say 1979 was the year that launched Islamic fundamentalism on an unready world. They were wrong. It was 1953. The seeds of discord had merely taken a few decades to sprout. Soon Iranians would throw their weight behind another idealistic old man, hawkish and charismatic, bent on humiliating the west. Like Mossadegh, Ayatollah Khomeini would be named *Time*'s Man of the Year. Soon the same mix of elements would clash: The intellectuals. The religious fanatics. The nationalists. The Communist *Tudehs*.

And Sadegh would merely transfer his loyalties from one revolutionary leader to another.

A QUARTER CENTURY LATER as she surveys the wreckage of revolution, Shahin couldn't help but wonder if the British and the CIA were up to their old tricks. Did anyone really think Iranians could unseat a twenty-five-hundred-year-old monarchy by themselves? Hadn't the Shah driven the price of oil up and renegotiated Iranian petrol contracts, just like Mossadegh? By then the reputation of the CIA was mythically powerful. Not only had the CIA unseated Mossadegh and formed SAVAK, it was well known that they had a number of tricks in their arsenal: Coups. Assassination plots. Poison pens. Private armies. Biological weapons. What clinched it for Shahin was when Nixon named Richard Helms ambassador to Iran. Helms hadn't even retired from his post as director of the CIA yet—so what was America's number one spy doing in her country in the highest diplomatic office?

Yes, the more Shahin thinks about it, the more she wonders whether the CIA had a hand in the Iranian revolution. Fifty-four thousand Americans were living in Iran at the time; half of them were military affiliates, so it was quite plausible that Iran had a vast network of American spies here.

She just never figured her husband was one of them.

At just this moment, four days after he'd left in the middle of the night, there is a knock at the door. When Shahin answers it, she falls back in surprise. Before her stands a disheveled man in blood-spattered clothes. It takes a second to fully recognize him.

"Max! What in God's name are you doing here? I thought you'd be in America!"

MAX

His feet are numb, his lips blue and chapped, and his supplies almost gone.

His face is burned by the wind and sun.

It is his third day in the Alborz mountains. Standing at the doorstep of freedom, Max looks upon Turkey—frozen and ringed with barbed wire—as an unreachable paradise. Even if he made it past the guards and across the border, then what? How would he make it to Ankara?

When a hand cups his mouth and he is pulled backward, Max thinks for sure he's been caught—and almost loses consciousness, so severe is the shock. Shock turns to relief when he sees it's Ejder. Then elation. *The Kurd has come to transport him to freedom.*

But Ejder is in no festive mood. "Why didn't you stay where the boy said?" he whispers, furious. "I have been looking for you for hours. Bad enough my village is raided, now I have to hunt in icy temperatures for a lost American? You're lucky I found you before the wolves—or the guards," he says, jerking his head toward the lit station a hundred yards away.

"Sorry," Max replies. "I was . . ."

Ejder does not wait for an explanation. Already he is pulling Max back up the mountain.

"But—isn't Turkey that way?"

"You aren't going to Turkey," the Kurd says. "You are going back to Tehran."

Max is certain he's not heard correctly in the high winds. Or maybe his Farsi is too rusty? He is standing a hundred feet from freedom.

"Turkey is that way," he says again.

"My contacts on the border have all been replaced," Ejder says. "Yesterday, the new militia took our belongings and shot our horses. You and I will be next if they catch us."

"But—"

"But what?" Ejder says angrily. "There is no *but*. No horses. No contacts. No Turkey. They invade our village, destroy our business, and shoot our horses. And you still expect to go to Turkey? I can't control the government, can I? Is this my fault?"

At five thousand feet, in subzero temperatures, Max's thinking is increasingly sluggish. But he knows one thing. He's come too far to turn back.

"I paid you twenty-five hundred dollars," Max says. "And I have another twenty-five hundred for you when we cross over the border. The last time I looked, I'm on the wrong side of that."

"If you want to go to Turkey, go," Ejder says, pointing across the snowy field, his voice low and furious. "Go! Be my guest! Blood-covered American on the wanted list—see what reception you get. You think I don't know? Everyone who crosses these mountains is a wanted man. Tell them you were lost. Tell them you were in a hunting accident. Tell them a thousand things, I don't care. I've risked my life to find you, and won't do it again. You're lucky I didn't abandon you to the mountains. Woeful Kurds! We are a hopeless tribe, God's lost people—cursed!"

High in the Alborz mountains buffeted by winds so strong they could barely hear each other, the two men burn with anger and a realization that their fates are driven by forces beyond their control. Freedom and probable death, or retreat—that is the choice.

After a while the Kurd relinquishes his grip on Max. "Maybe we can try again in the spring," Ejder says.

They both know there will be no spring crossing.

That night, Max follows in Ejder's footsteps, back up the mountain and through a series of snowy foothills that eventually leads to a path. They hike parallel to the path for miles. By midmorning they arrive at a clearing. Ejder leads Max into a nearby hut, where a woman serves them tea, bread, and a bowl of hot stew. Shortly afterward, a pickup truck pulls up and Ejder motions for Max to get into the back. As the Kurd draws a tarp over him, the last thing Max sees is the Kurd's eyes. There is a deep and hard-won wisdom in those eyes, coupled with an intent to survive that would have made Darwin proud. In the womb of darkness, the eyes of Ejder loom for a split second more—like a ghost vision. Then blackness, as Max gives in to the sleep he has long coveted. It's been thirty-six sleepless hours since that horrific night in the hovel.

By nightfall, Max finds himself back in Tehran. A "smuggler" smuggled—then returned.

"JESUS, JOSEPH, AND MARY," Shahin says when Max recounts the story.

Sitting at the kitchen table, husband and wife are lingering over tea and the remains of cold kebabs, grilled tomatoes, and rice pudding as the dawn's first light spills across the table and illuminates them. Suddenly it strikes Max that in his blood-spattered clothes he is not exactly a sight for sore eyes. "I don't think the kids should see their dad looking like a hobo, do you? I'm going to take a shower."

"I told them you were on another hunting expedition," Shahin says.

"How about some pancakes for breakfast?" Max replies, padding off to the bathroom. "Maybe with a Tylenol chaser? I don't think my body has ever ached so much."

"Look at it this way," Shahin calls after him, "you can sell your story to Hollywood when it's all over."

"There won't be any story to sell," Max says. "I'm going to die in Iran."

Stepping into the shower, Max luxuriates in the spray of hot water on his spent muscles and watches with satisfaction as the blood and grime of three days in the Alborz mountains washes down the drain. As difficult as the past few days have been, the days ahead will be even more torturous. In a couple of weeks, his family will be leaving for America.

And Max will stay behind in Tehran.

In days to come, he helps the kids pack and as their lives disappear into suitcases, he teases them. *You're taking the Bee Gees? Disco? Haven't I taught you anything?* He asks his children questions, hoping that they will develop probing minds and a sense of curiosity in the lives of others. And he is careful to drop an "I love you" in before bedtime—not so frequently as to belie a sense of desperation. Desperate love is worthless. He wants them to remember him as a man who had faced into the storm. Who made jokes when life was darkest. Max knows a good father would sooner fall on his sword than bare his wounds.

Just as the eyes of Ejder fell upon Max before the tarp came down, a ghost vision that lingered, so do Max's eyes fall upon his children a moment more.

ONE DAY, Shahin returns home with a story. She had been to the airport to see if they might send a few things out prior to their departure, when she bumped into Peter Jennings. Shahin liked the ABC news anchor, if for no other reason than he was the only journalist to pronounce the name of her country properly. Jennings had arrived to cover the hostage crisis, only some of his luggage had gone missing—and he wondered if Shahin might help him locate it. Briefly, Shahin contemplated telling him about Max's plight; maybe he could help?

"Did you?" Max asks when she gets to that part of the story.

"I did not," she says. "I helped him find his luggage, then piled him into a cab. I thought about it. But look at all the TV coverage the hostages have gotten—what good has that done? It's made it worse for them, I think."

Recently, some American clergy had arrived for a Christmas visit, and the footage had been broadcast all over the world. The hostages sat before an array of pastries, fruits, and candies—obviously staged to make the hostage takers look benevolent. Watching the footage on TV, Max felt sick to his stomach. Did they think they'd sway the world to their side with this fake display of Christmas merriment? Afterward, they'd aired more "evidence of U.S. espionage." Some of it made Max laugh, like the Dictaphone they thought was spy equipment. But some of it was quite damaging, like Tom Ahern's multiple passports. Ahern was the CIA station chief, and his fake passports invalidated Ahern's diplomatic immunity and provided grounds to be tried as a spy.

Shahin is right. The eyes of the world are upon the hostages, and the ensuing media coverage has only inflamed public opinion and given the students a spotlit stage on which to air their grievances and bring the world's strongest superpower to its knees.

So Max waits. He keeps an ear to the BBC and an eye cocked toward the hostages, aware that the political temperature—and indirectly, his own fate—is tied to them. And he reads the English-language dailies Shahin brings home. He does not bother calling the State Department, for he knows now that all their resources go into managing the hostage crisis. And that is fine. The hostages have the president, the media, the CIA, and a collection of the finest trained operatives known as Delta Force on their side.

Max has Shahin. He figures it is about equal.

Every day, a few women from the neighborhood drop by and peruse their belongings: Persian rugs. Clothes. Toys. Antique samovars. Kitchen wares. Everything but Max's books, for the volumes are the only things Max will have once his family leaves. The prices of all saleable items are inscribed in a notebook that is always at Shahin's side. How much is this? They negotiate. Shahin doesn't mention that they are desperate to sell— and the neighborhood women don't say they are anxious to have a final bit of Americana before the country closes its doors on the West for good. It's all quite polite.

As the women browse, shop, and linger over their belongings, Max flashes back to the days a year ago when he'd been a one-man pawn shop in an unraveling country. How alive he'd felt! From house to house he went, selling, shutting down, packing up Westinghouse homes and moving on. Now as he watches his wife do the same for their life, he is struck by the strangeness of it all, the circularity of life. But this is *their* life. Still, he does not resent these women or their intrusions. He thinks of them as benefactors who will help his family relaunch their lives in America—even as he stays back in Iran.

He puts on a Frank Sinatra record and gives them music to shop by.

CYRUS

B it by bit, our lives get smaller, lighter.

As my mother prices and sells our belongings, my sister and I scurry through the apartment writing *Cyrus and Katayoun were here* behind bookshelves and under cabinets. I have so many memories of Iran, but what will Iran have of me? The thought of leaving Iran forever turns me sentimental, and I draw a fistful of dirt from the empty lot next to our house and pack it up. Later, I will discover that thousands of other fleeing Iranians all had the same sentimental idea, and Iran's soil was now flung across the world.

"What are your favorite memories of Iran?" my father asks one night.

I remind him of the time he took Katayoun and me to a lush valley outside Shiraz. The landscape was studded with young poplar trees, none higher than six feet and all ringed with a profusion of gold leaves that shook and shimmied in the breeze. The air was crisp, the ground littered with color each time a breeze cut the leaves and sprinkled them liberally at our feet. Through the valley a profusion of small streams flowed, accented with mossy banks and silvery fish. For hours, my father hunted partridge while Katayoun and I explored—the air of the lowlands burning in our lungs and reddening our cheeks, and it was that kind of a cold-warm autumn day that seemed to go on forever. We had found a place known to few, and even as the sun dipped low on the horizon we didn't want to leave. "Look," my father said, picking up a leaf and pointing out the intricate web of chlorophyll that carried leaf blood to its tips. At the angle my father held it, the leaf was shot through with the sun's dying rays. "Isn't that magnificent?"

It was. Eden was thought to be between the Tigris and the Euphrates, but the flood had rearranged the whole of Mesopotamia, and deposited it here—or so I believed.

My cryptic, quiet father. I didn't know what would happen to him—and was only vaguely reassured by my mother's promise that we would re-unite in America one day. He had asked about my favorite memory of Iran, but this was how I wanted to remember *him*. Voyager. Teacher. Explorer. Gatekeeper to the valley.

JANUARY 13, 1980. It is still dark when we arrive at Mehrabad Airport the next morning, but the scene in Departures is predictably chaotic. There are only a few flights out of Iran, and everyone wants on. It's not exactly the fall of Saigon—but close. High above the sea of humanity looms a por-trait of the ayatollah and for the last time, I look at his face and note how angry he appears. How has he duped thirty-six million people? It astounds me that he is loved, adored, worshipped by my countrymen. Just over a year ago, a large picture of the Shah, strikingly handsome in his military threads, had hung in that very place. The difference between his eyes and the ayatollah's is as wide as the Persian Gulf.

Our flight is scheduled to leave at eight A.M.—allowing two hours for bribes, lines, customs, security, and fighting the tearful good-byes of torn-apart families. At customs, an agent pulls my prayer rug out of my suitcase and says it's disallowed. We are each allotted one suitcase, and in mine I have packed my prayer rug on which I'd greeted God, to which I'd brought my confusion, my despair, my inability to be the kind of worshipful Mos-lem I'd seen; the Sears and Roebuck catalog; some clothes; and my ABBA tapes. I placed the Holy Quran on top, hoping the customs agent would see it and leave the rest alone. I did not pack *The Joy of Sex*.

"Disallowed? Isn't this the Islamic Republic?" my mother says indignantly. She presses five hundred *tomans* into his hands and we sail through.

At Passport Control we're stopped again. The *hejabi*˙ woman manning the desk consults her list, frowns, and calls over her supervisor—a portly man with a frightening large pair of glasses through which I can see the veins in his irises.

"Who is Coop-land?" he asks.

"My husband. Why?" my mother asks innocently.

"What is his issue?"

"It's nothing—a technicality."

"The stop list isn't for technicalities," he says, stone-faced. He waves another couple behind us through, motioning for us to stand aside.

"Anyway, we aren't on it. Can we please pass? We're late for our flight," she says, handing him the tickets.

"Women cannot leave without permission."

"It's like a Laurel and Hardy show," she says. "My husband can't leave, but I need his approval?" She lays a notarized letter on his desk—Max's official permission for us to leave, even as he himself cannot.

The *hejabi* woman turns to her supervisor and shrugs sympathetically.

Five minutes pass. Ten. A plethora of people proceed in front of us and by now my mother is getting nervous, beads of perspiration gathering on her brow. Later, I discover this is because she is smuggling diamonds under her hair extension. My sister is also wearing ruby earrings far more suited to a dowager empress than a thirteen-year-old girl; apparently my dad is not the only "smuggler" in the family. Earlier I heard a story about a woman whose leg was wrapped in plaster. Someone called the airport with an anonymous tip: *A broken-legged lady smuggling jewels in her cast.* So the airport officials cut it open, found nothing, and profusely apologized. The following day, she flew out with a cast full of diamonds, pearls, and dollars.

"Will passengers . . . Kat-kat-ayooon, Cyprus, and Shane Copeland re-

---

˙*Hejab*: a veil covering the hair and chest, usually worn by conservative women.

port to Gate Seven," a distinctly British voice says over the loudspeaker. "Your flight is ready to depart."

"I don't care if Mohammad himself, peace be upon him, calls your flight," the passport officer says at my mother's beseeching look. "You don't pass this gate until I say."

Another twenty minutes tick by. More passengers squeeze through— never even glancing at us, lest our bad luck rub off on them. The announcement echoes a couple more times, each time with a rising sense of urgency.

And then the passport officer waves us through—no explanation, he merely stamps our passports and flicks his wrist. But it is too late.

"You've missed your flight," the gate agent tells us. In fact, we are just in time to see our airplane taxi and lift.

I watch as my mother's face slowly gives way and every tiny secret and veiled anxiety about leaving—hidden diamonds, imprisoned husband, and now missed flight—surfaces. Her lips begin to tremble. Her legs give way. She almost collapses onto the gate agent's desk. I'm not sure what it is that distinguishes us from the hundreds of other forlorn people who miss their flights, but the gate agent clucks sympathetically and says, "Let me see what I can do."

An hour later, he hands us three boarding passes and shoos us onto a waiting bus. Across the tarmac we zoom toward a plane whose red and blue tail glimmers promisingly with the British Airways logo. On board, I discover we are its sole cargo to London. The entire 747 is ours.

"There must be some mistake," my mother says when the cabin door closes. "Where is everyone?"

"No mistake, luv," the stewardess replies. "This isn't a scheduled flight. We had an extra aircraft and it's getting returned to Heathrow. Something about avoiding government sanctions on the aircraft and crew, I think. Welcome aboard our phantom flight to London!"

As the plane begins its taxi down the runway and lifts, Iran reduces to a geometric tapestry of oddly shaped tracts and colors. Somewhere down there is my hidden valley. Somewhere down there is Max.

From that phantom flight I remember the salty, barely cooked bacon and eggs for breakfast, followed by a rotation of sodas and pretzels, playing cards, a dizzying visit to the cockpit, and trips to the bathroom stocked with exotic hand creams. I page through the duty-free catalog—which at thirty thousand feet supplants Sears in the impressive array of available purchases. Each of us stretches out over three seats, but we are too wired to sleep. After breakfast, my mother calls over the stewardess and tells her our story, and soon they're both having a good cry.

"Sorry to burden you, my dear," my mom says, "but I had to tell someone."

Afterward she takes our picture. This is us huddled together, *Seh Teflaneh Moslem*, en route to our new life in America.

IN PHILADELPHIA we stay with the Daltons—longtime friends of my parents—where Uncle Jack lets us take turns reclining in his La-Z-Boy and watching a channel called HBO. I am pleasantly shocked at the amount of nudity on television. On our second day, Aunt Mary takes us to Two Guys, where I buy a stereo and the *Grease* soundtrack—my first down payments on my new American life. At Sears, I realize the catalog on which I'd envisioned our new American lives is woefully out of date. They have a new oven called a microwave. Pleated vamp shoes. Car coats and velour tracksuits. My sister proves that the ruby earrings are a bellwether of her expensive tastes. She prefers B. Altman to Sears and repeatedly begs to return there for the pleasure of petting the porcelain animals on the second floor. For a solid week we shop! Marshalls. Macy's. Bamberger's. Our restrictive life in Tehran gives way to a shopping bonanza. And a fast-food fiesta! Back in Iran, Katayoun and I had made lists of all the fast foods we vowed to gorge on—hot fudge sundaes, pickles, burgers, shakes, fries—and now check off every item on the list as we pile the greasy foods into our accommodating bellies.

A week later, my mother deposits us with Aunt Mary's son John Dalton and his wife, Joanne, instructs us to be good, and gives each of us $150 in pocket money. "Three weeks," my mother promises. "Four at the most. Then I'll be back with your father and we'll all be together."

John and Joanne are public schoolteachers and restrict us to two hours of TV each night. But Katayoun and I are starved for pop culture, and in addition to the *Charlie's Angels* pantheon, we soon have every commercial jingle committed to memory—Enjoli to Kibbles 'n Bits.

My mother has enrolled us in different prep schools. The kids at Shipley are welcoming, and in my heart I want desperately to disappear into the foray of joyful, beer-drinking, cussing camaraderie I see around me, but I have no idea how to do that. Everyone is friendly enough. Bruce Hunt is an all-American boy assigned to mentor me. "You need anything, anything at all, lemmeno," he says. With his chiseled face and friendly demeanor, Bruce looks like he stepped out of the Sears catalog. My first day, he treats me to an off-campus lunch at Wendy's and as he pulls his car out of the parking lot, I think, *Uh-oh, student drivers?*

In high school, everyone fits in somewhere. Jock. Rich kid. Brainiac. Cheerleader. Math geek. Valedictorian. Party boy. But I am none of these things. The thing I most identify with is the country I've left behind. Thrilled to discover a couple of Persian expats at school, I talk to them in Farsi, but after a few sentences they always revert to English. I understand why. Here Iran is a four-letter word, and all around me is proof that half of me will always be unwelcome: *Iranian Go Home* signs hurt just as much as the "Yankee Go Home" and "Death to America" cries that punctuated my childhood. The yellow ribbons, the *Bomb Iran* bumper stickers, the poisonous headlines—it is all a reminder that I hail from a hated country.

A curious thing happens. Just as I'd been proudly American in Iran, here I begin to define myself as Iranian. I do not distinguish myself academically or athletically. I look to geography as my wound and anchor. Other Iranians call themselves "Persian"—chiefly, I suspect, because they are embarrassed about the mullahs who'd co-opted their country and because they are (mostly) right to believe that Americans have no idea what the hell Persian is. It is a way of hiding in plain sight and holding on to your glorious past at the same time. It's brilliant—and I want no part of it. I may be half Iranian, but I am no apologist.

My sister is having a better time. She's enrolled in Baldwin School for girls, a stone's throw from Shipley, and already can be found conjugating Latin verbs or playing lacrosse, apple-cheeked, on the rolling school lawns. Disregarding my mother's instruction to wear her tunic at a respectable length, like the Baldwin girls she hikes it *way* above the knees. *She's got it down,* I think. After school, Katayoun volunteers as a Candy Stripe girl at Bryn Mawr Hospital.

At home, she plays ping-pong with John.

"Do you think I'm good-looking?" he teases.

"Don't put me between Iraq and a hard place," she replies.

"You mean *a* rock."

"Whatever," Katayoun says, sealing her status as an American teenager. Like that.

Three weeks becomes a month. Then two. Three. Still no news from Iran. *Where are my parents?*

That spring I rent a white tux like John Travolta's in *Saturday Night Fever*, mousse my hair, and go to the prom—stag.

The only place where I feel comfortable is in the movies. And that's because when the lights go down, I find myself immersed in someone else's life. In the dark and welcoming chill of my local Cineplex, I find there is always a character I can identify with—even inhabit. Dustin Hoffman in *Kramer vs. Kramer*. Robert Redford in *The Electric Horseman*. Peter Sellers in *Being There*. When *Ordinary People* comes out, I see it three times in succession, read every review, write my own for the school newspaper, scour and cut out *People* magazine articles about the actors, and am ecstatic when they are nominated for Oscars. The Jarretts are a family with a closely guarded secret in beautiful Lake Forest, Chicago. When the movie opens to chords of *Canon in D* and the camera moves in on Timothy Hutton's

OFF THE RADAR

raccoon-circled eyes, I see a specter of myself—unhealed, unseen, a phantom harboring a wound I'd carried across the ocean to Philadelphia's Main Line. I don't exactly know what my wound is, and I have no Judd Hirsch to tease it out. Unlike Conrad, I don't go to therapy. I don't go on dates. I have fallen in love with a movie.

There's one scene where Timothy Hutton's character, Conrad, gets together with an old friend from his time at the hospital, but try as he might, he just cannot connect with her. "Conrad? Let's have a great Christmas!" she says. "Okay? Let's have . . . a great year. Let's have the best year of our whole lives."

But Conrad is still tethered to the past, and its pain is the only thing he knows is truthful. He wants to talk about their time in the hospital.

"Would you cheer up?" she finally says, exasperated.

When a childhood friend from Iran visits, I take him to see the movie, hoping he might see how I am having a very difficult time adjusting to my new life. Everyone is telling me to get back to normal, but like Conrad I have no idea what normal is anymore. So I take him to *Ordinary People* to explain things.

But right when we get to that exact scene, he exhales heavily.

"Did you go to your prom?" he inquires.

Fuck you, I think—but like Conrad give no indication that everything is anything but A-OK.

Over and over, I relive this scene. At home. School. Dunkin' Donuts, where I get a part-time job. I want to throw a line back to the painful past, but I have no idea how to do this. The pain is real and truthful and six thousand miles away, but it's also breathing right under the surface of my American life. It is pumping in my bloodlines. It is unspoken and it is undeniably all around me. America surpasses everything I'd envisioned from reading the Sears catalog, but I am still a stranger to this country, and it to me. American in Iran. Iranian in America. I wonder if the two halves of myself will ever be whole.

This is the thing. No one ever personally insults me—not one person.

But beneath the bonhomie and deep in my bloodlines, I can feel it. The hatred between my homelands simmers. And so in my head, I dream up entire conversations and glorious brawls, during which my mind becomes so overheated it is almost comical. I have not figured out how to marry the divergent strands of my dual—and dueling—identity, and so compose imaginary conversations in response to imaginary insults and fight them in the only place I might win. My head. My arguments are angry, meaty, beautiful things! Powered by raw emotion, they are so consumptive that should you glance at me midargument, it is almost plausible that you'd see smoke coming out of my ears. I am cartoonishly angry. And when I am done fake-arguing with my friends, I take on public personas, celebrities, and movie stars. As the years pass, I fight with world leaders, Dutch cartoonists, and overrated English writers with fatwas on their head. I fight with preachers who burn my holy book. And I fight with Gidget.

In the theater, I am watching the trailer for *Not Without My Daughter*, and rejoicing at the happy Iranian-American family I see on-screen—finally! A well-adjusted nuclear family that holds the contradiction of its bloodlines. The bliss lasts all of five seconds. The voice-over turns dark: *Betty Mahmoody's husband took her and her daughter to Iran. He swore they would be safe. He swore they would be happy. He swore they'd be coming home. He lied.* Cut to Sally Field on the run from a population of screaming Iranian women, prayerful masses, deceitful in-laws, gun-toting zealots, exploding bombs, and a husband who smacks her around. Hollywood has stitched together every American fear of Iran and slapped it onto the screen—fronted by Gidget. How do you fight with Gidget?

Be the change you want to see in the world, Gandhi said. But I am too angry. My interior landscape is aflame, fueled by the media and dabblers and dilettantes who make a name for themselves by demonizing my homeland and religion. I am not by nature a fighter. But I want to be.

I'm a fool, of course. What kind of person looks to Hollywood for an example of how his life might end up? I do. And there, lurking in the shadows, is my answer. Some vaguely Middle Eastern–looking, Alfred Molina–

like guy with a pronounced accent and ominously arched eyebrows. His eyes burn with conviction. *Please don't be that guy,* I think. But he is always that guy. In Act II he will take his wife hostage, highjack a plane, detonate a device, destroy the White House or die trying. He is either Iranian or Moslem, and there is invariably an American who will foil his attempts. I am both the villain and the hero in this movie. Do you know how exhausting it is to play both roles?

And in my head, the monologue loops and catches fire, and I charge into battle all over again.

Would you cheer up, Conrad?

Lord knows I want to. I flash back to the end of *Ordinary People.* The camera lifts across the frozen landscape of the Jarretts' backyard. The sun is out. Conrad and his father are locked in a hug. But something is off. His father is apologizing to him, saying he just wasn't listening and attentive to Conrad's troubles. And Conrad says, no, he wasn't putting out many signals, and there was nothing his father could have done.

I'm the one who's sorry. I wasn't listening. And Max wasn't putting out signals.

I will never have a moment like this with my father. Frosted landscape. Locked in a hug. Sun warming our tear-stained cheeks. Where the hell is my father, anyway? I am beginning to realize that no matter how hard we try, we Copelands will never be *Ordinary People.*

Cyrus

Thirty-three years later, another movie about Iran came out.

The story of *Argo* was a remarkable tale—six diplomats escaped the American embassy the morning of November 4, 1979, and made their way to the Canadian embassy, where they were given refuge by Ambassador Ken Taylor. Months later the CIA devised an audacious scheme to pull them out of Iran, disguising the diplomats as Hollywood filmmakers who'd landed in Tehran to make a sci-fi movie. Never mind that revolutionary Iran wasn't atop the list of scouting locations or that the presence of Hollywood and its objectionable values would raise a major red flag for any Islamic militant, or that a cardinal rule of covers is that they be as unremarkable and close to real life as possible. On January 25, CIA agent Tony Mendez flew into Tehran with fake passports, gave them each a cover legend, and, seventy-two hours later, flew them out on a Swissair flight for Zurich.

It was a plan so incredible, it could only happen in the movies.

And three decades later, it did. In the winter of 2013, I saw *Argo* and was both riveted and disgusted. The movie retells the caper from the CIA's perspective—taking more than a few liberties with the truth at the expense of the Canadians, the Kiwis, the Brits, and most predictably the Iranians who are shown to be a nation of goons, zealots, and cretins. (Astonishingly,

Mendez is inspired to stage his exfiltration by watching *Planet of the Apes*.) It was *Not Without My Daughter* all over again—sub in six diplomats for the daughter, the CIA guy for Gidget, and thirty-six million angry Iranians. A timeless tale.

"*Argo* was designed to embarrass the Iranians and make them look stupid," David Smallman said. "Think about the message of that film. Think of how it was perceived internationally. Both *Argo* and *Zero Dark Thirty* were made with the CIA's cooperation. Two Best Picture nominees in the same year? Lately, there's been a lot of saber-rattling to go to war with Iran, and movies like *Argo* set the stage handily." It was true. And it made me wonder if Hollywood wasn't an instrument of foreign policy. The drumbeat was growing louder. Thirty-five years after the hostage crisis, the movie had gotten the public all riled up again. "I'm not taking military options off the table," Obama said.

In Iran, the movie offended just about everyone. "The Iranophobic American movie attempts to describe Iranians as overemotional, irrational, insane, and diabolical while at the same time, the CIA agents are represented as heroically patriotic," the Iranian state press said.

The Iranians weren't the only ones upset by *Argo*. All across the world, a chorus of displeasure rang out. Canada was peeved to find their role relegated to an afterthought. Hadn't their ambassador hidden and fed the diplomats for months, while Mendez had spent less than seventy-two hours with them? New Zealand and England were offended too. The culprit? A single line, tight and crystalline as a country music lyric.

"Brits turned them away, Kiwis turned them away, Canadians took them in."

It was a status update on the escaped diplomats—a throwaway line meant to heighten the drama—but it was a lie. And it rankled the Brits, who'd assisted the American fugitives, and especially the Kiwis, who had not only *not* turned them away, but sheltered them, rented them a safe house with CIA funds, wined and dined them, and then driven them to the airport the morning of their escape. Offended, the New Zealand

Foreign Ministry made a fuss over the slight, and the fuss ricocheted in newsrooms all over the world.

All of which mattered little to the moviegoing public. On February 24, 2013, Ben Affleck ascended the steps of the Dolby Theater and collected the Oscar for Best Picture—presented by Michelle Obama via a live video link from the White House. Was there ever a better image cementing Hollywood and Washington's bond?

But it mattered to me. But for that silly throwaway line and the flurry of press it provoked, I'd never have found out the truth of what happened to Max.

In movie terms, when the hero is at a dead end, something happens that delivers him from impending doom and spins the action around in a surprising new direction. This is called a plot point. It's what separates the different acts of a movie. But *Argo* was no mere plot point. It was a true-to-life instance of Hollywood movie magic. A moment when reel life converged with real life. For thirty-five years, I had believed that the movies could show me a fundamental truth about who I was in the world. Instead, Hollywood had shone the light of truth into the dark corners of my father's life. And it all went back to that silly line and the furor it caused.

It had been a year and still I'd heard nothing back from the CIA, and nothing from State. What had happened that was so secretive that it took an entire year to sift through the information for my FOIA request and release it to me? According to guidelines, they're supposed to reply in four weeks. So when President Carter's national security advisor, Zbigniew Brzezinski, advised me to pay a visit to the Carter Library, the official archive for his presidency, I thought: Why not? When Zbig gives you a heads-up on locating sensitive information, it's best to listen. My friend Erica lived thirty minutes from the Atlanta institution and volunteered to go.

She called back the following day. "Sorry, Cope-meister. I went through twenty-five boxes of memos, meeting minutes, notes, and telexes of pretty much everyone in Carter's cabinet. Brzezinski. Vance. Jordan. A search of the White House Papers turned up nothing. Most of the important papers have been 'sanitized'—the librarian's word, not mine—or are just missing. Although I found a couple of memos about Sadegh and the ongoing back-channel negotiations about the hostages. Pretty fascinating. Shall I send them?"

"Sure," I said, dispiritedly. "So there was nothing on Max?"

"Well—there was one thing—a memo from this guy Hal Saunders. Don't get too excited, it's just one sentence."

Hal Saunders had been head of the Iran Working Group at the State Department and reported to Cyrus Vance. His memo was a daily update on the group's outstanding initiatives in Iran, everything from a bio on Khomeini's American heart doctor to Ghotbzadeh's bid for the presidency. But it was the final line that got my attention.

> *We have asked the New Zealand embassy to assist an American,*
> *Max Copeland, who was prevented from leaving the country*
> *because of some unknown difficulty with the Ministry of Justice.*

It was just one sentence—and the last one, which indicated he wasn't high on their list of priorities. I reread it. "Some unknown difficulty" sounded very vague, in a way which made me think Saunders knew exactly what the difficulty was. The memo had been marked SECRET but was recently—and I suspected, mistakenly—declassified. A glance at the distribution list showed that everyone in the Iran Working Group had discussed Max that morning. But it was the date of the memo that lifted that one sentence, gave it context and clarity: January 25, 1980.

I flashed back to *Argo* and the New Zealand fuss and did a little arithmetic. Exactly two days before the Kiwis had driven the American diplomats to safety, the State Department had asked them to "assist" my father. The wording on the memo was vague, but there was no mistaking what they'd asked for.

Another extraction.

The realizations cascaded. *So the U.S. government had tried to get my father out.* They had waited until we left Iran on January 13, 1980, to green-light the extraction—knowing it would be easier to communicate with Max solo and make the necessary arrangements without his wife and kids. No one wants to believe his father had been forgotten by the government entrusted to protect him, but for thirty-five long years, this is exactly what I'd assumed. The silence from State and the Agency had only solidified that. But now, here was proof that they'd tried to rescue Max, that he'd been a valued citizen right up there with their diplomats—the subject of a side-by-side operation!

Even better, armed with this bit of evidence, I could finally pressure them to release Max's files. Surely Uncle Sam and the CIA couldn't cooperate on the production of a Hollywood blockbuster, then claim events of the past were too sensitive?

Except that they could. When I tracked down Saunders at the Kettering Institute in Washington, he denied any knowledge of the operation. And when I professed incredulity—I had the smoking-gun memo!—he gave me a brief lecture on office protocol. "Do you know how a bureaucracy works, son? When you have a position like mine, other people are authorized to act on my behalf. The memo was probably written by my deputy Peter Constable. And he's deceased."

I remembered how Saunders's group had released a list of hostages that "mistakenly" included my father. Before joining the State Department, Saunders had been with the CIA and the National Security Council. He had a boot in several camps—the White House, the State Department, and the intelligence community. Later, he would write that there was great stress on the State Department because of the attention on the number of hostages, forcing them to adapt a misinformation strategy. So was I now being misinformed?

Chuck Cogan was Saunders's CIA counterpart on Argo and professed no knowledge of a follow-up rescue for Max. All across Washington, the same chorus rang out.

"I don't recall."

"Sorry, son, it's been more than thirty years."

"I'm a bit embarrassed not to know a thing about this."

"Can't do much about a faulty memory, can I?"

And having let the Argo cat out of the bag, the New Zealand Foreign Ministry now worked furiously to stuff it back in. "Give me a couple weeks," ex–Deputy Head Commissioner Brian Lynch offered. Then–Kiwi ambassador to Iran Chris Beeby had extensively debriefed Lynch in London in January 1980. "Let me see what I can dig up. I think we might be able to fill in some of the holes in your father's situation," Lynch said. Weeks later, I received a terse e-mail from him.

> I regret to advise you that the relevant files are still under wraps for some time yet. My former foreign service colleagues have explained the sensitivities involved and I have to respect their judgment.

Sensitivities meant this: The Kiwis have a thriving trade relationship with Iran.

Sensitivities also meant nukes. As one of the most conspicuous nonnuclear states in the world, New Zealand has a long history of involvement with nonproliferation and disarmament issues—and yet it remained relatively silent on the issue of the Iranian nuclear program.

And sensitivities meant intelligence. New Zealand is one of five countries with an ongoing intelligence-sharing relationship with the United States. The Five Eyes program includes Australia, Canada, New Zealand, Britain, and the United States—all of whom are bound to cooperate in intelligence matters. Edward Snowden described the Five Eyes as a "supranational intelligence organization that doesn't answer to the laws of its own countries." Documents released by Snowden revealed that the Five Eyes have been spying on each other's citizens—then sharing the data with each other to circumvent restrictive domestic regulations on spying. It is the most powerful espionage alliance in world history.

Standing in the eye of the storm was Tony Mendez—the CIA agent who'd pulled off the Argo operation. But he wouldn't talk to me either. That was particularly frustrating; Mendez's specialty was disguising and smuggling CIA assets who needed to be brought in from the cold. He had arrived in Tehran on the exact same day that Saunders circulated his memo. While in Tehran, Mendez had leaned heavily on New Zealand's number two diplomat, Richard Sewell. ("I am not sure how it came about that he was the driver and advisor to Tony Mendez regarding how best to navigate Tehran during those dangerous times," one of the Argo houseguests wrote me, "but that was in fact his role. Prior to Tony's arrival, Richard arranged to rent a safe house . . . which I understand was paid for by the CIA, so he was already working with them.") It was all starting to add up. But Mendez would not talk and denied any knowledge of the operation through the Argo houseguest. I took that with a grain of salt. He was a former intelligence officer with a half century's practice in obfuscation, and basking in the glow of his newly burnished Oscar reputation. Why tarnish it? Truth was, Tony Mendez had been in Tehran at the same time, strategizing with Sewell, doctoring passports, and hanging out in the Canadian embassy, which was seven kilometers—ten minutes—from our house.

Stonewalled by Washington and Wellington, I recalled something I'd learned from the Westinghouse executives: Retired folks like to chat. And so I threw my final piece of bait overboard.

It was ten A.M. in Wellington when Merwyn Norrish's phone rang. Ambassador Norrish had been New Zealand's man in Washington at the time, and I hoped that the Foreign Ministry hadn't yet silenced him on the issue.

"I just saw *Argo*," I said, "and it reminded me of your kind offer to help my dad escape Iran as a Kiwi. Max Copeland. He was stranded in Tehran at the same time. Do you recall?"

The overseas line crackled with silence.

"Yes," Mr. Norrish finally said. "It was my responsibility to tell the prime minister what Chris Beeby and Richard Sewell wanted to do. We got the word: 'Well, okay, but we didn't tell you so . . .' It was one of those occasions where a couple of our people ran considerable risks. Those people who say diplomacy is just cocktail parties don't really understand the things that can happen—and your father's operation was one of them."

We spoke for fifteen minutes. He told me about the dynamic duo who'd worked undercover to pull my dad out. "Chris Beeby was one of the most intelligent folks we've ever had—a Renaissance man and an international lawyer of great repute," he said, adding that he was also a first-rate fencer and an excellent cabinetmaker in his spare time. His sidekick, Richard Sewell, was considerably younger but was "thought of very highly by his colleagues, and was an excellent consular officer in terms of looking after people in distress.

"We basically left it to them to do what they reasonably could without running undue risks or without involving the New Zealand embassy," Norrish continued. "Our relationship with Iran was an important one in trade terms. Chris kept us informed to the extent that he could, when he could."

Would there be any files or records about Max, I asked.

"I don't recall. Certainly they wouldn't want to release them."

It didn't matter. I had finally found the leak that David Smallman had suggested so many months ago. For weeks I sat assembling the pieces. How had Max's exfiltration been planned? Chris Beeby and Richard Sewell were both dead, but I spoke with some of the other gentlemen of Argo, including rescued diplomat Mark Lijek, who knew State Department protocols and talked freely about his own extraction. I also talked at length with Roger Lucy—first secretary at the Canadian embassy—who became my sounding board on exfiltration logistics. His knowledge was based on real experience of having helped orchestrate the Argo operation. I combed through the Canadian ambassador's situation reports from Tehran, looking for any mention of Max. And I chatted with the friends and family of Beeby and

Sewell—all of whom painted an honorable picture of the men who had tried to save my father.

In retrospect I can understand Washington's and Wellington's desire to forget all about the whole affair—and but for that single sentence, it would have been relegated to history's dustbin. I still had a slew of questions. Why hadn't they combined the operations and flown them out in one scoop? President Carter had green-lit Argo—so did he know about Max's operation too? Didn't anyone think the revolutionaries would figure out the relationship between Canada and New Zealand? But what mattered was this: They'd tried to save my dad. The operation was a carbon copy of one of the most audacious rescues in history—minus the idiotic Hollywood option.

Too bad it all went down in flames.

PART 5

ONE LAST TRY

MAX

TEHRAN, 1980

It is a particularly brutal January, even by Tehran standards. Gray skies. Mounds of snow that quickly turn sooty. Oil shortages that drive everyone under the *korsi*. Even the roaring crowds at the embassy gates begin to thin out a bit—though whenever the cameras show up, the demonstrators crank up their anger and passion.

With Shahin and the kids stateside, Max is alone. Twice a week his brother-in-law and wife, Taghi and Aghdas, bring groceries, play backgammon, and together they watch dubbed American movies. Max has always loved Shahin's family, six siblings that provide a warm counterpoint to his solitary childhood. "You are like our brother," they say when he protests their many kindnesses. *"Natars. Een ham meegzareh."* Don't worry. This too shall pass.

Daytimes he dives into books—his tastes range from Melville to Michener, Dickens and Churchill to modern authors like Sidney Sheldon and Ian Fleming. He is a voracious reader who devours books in a single sitting. If he particularly enjoys one, Max parcels it out in multiple readings, parsimoniously, like a box of fine chocolates. In the tundra of Tehran, in the winter of his discontent, a book becomes something rare and precious—a lifeline that pulls him from the rubble and lifts him into another narrative, far away. That winter he goes through fifty-plus books.

Occasionally, he composes a falsely cheerful letter to his parents in which he never mentions his house arrest, his loneliness, or his doubts. Lately Max misses America, but wonders if America misses him. He is beginning to suspect his government has forgotten him. And now with the Soviets in Afghanistan he's even less hopeful about getting the White House's attention. On the radio, Max flips back and forth between the BBC and Voice of America: The U.S. embassy in Libya is ransacked. Saudi Arabia beheads sixty-three people for the Grand Mosque raid. The Shah is in a military hospital in San Antonio. Paul McCartney is arrested in Tokyo for marijuana possession.

And of course, nonstop dispatches about the hostages.

Ear to radio. Pen to page. Book to book. In this way a week passes.

THE NIGHT OF JANUARY 20, Max wakes to the sound of an insistent doorbell. Peering downstairs, he sees a shock of light brown hair in the entrance light.

"Hello, mate! Name's Richard Sewell—but you can call me Moses," the man says when Max opens the door. The visitor is fairly tall, maybe six feet, with an angular face and the friendly, twinkly-eyed demeanor of a fraternity boy. Midthirties. Ruddy complexion—made ruddier by the cold. "Mind if I come in? Doesn't look good for us to be chatting in the stairwell like this . . . Didn't they tell you I was coming? Probably not, the lines out aren't the safest. How about a cup of tea? It's awfully cold."

"Sorry—who are you?"

"Sewell. New Zealand embassy," he says, stepping around Max. "The State Department briefed us on your, uh, difficulties."

The State Department had been in contact with New Zealand? That made no sense. Switzerland was representing American interests in Iran these days.

"It's all being handled—can't say *exactly* how, it's *quite* clandestine—but you've got the attention of some interesting people, Mr. Copeland. In fact, if all goes well, in two weeks' time you'll be on a plane out of Mehrabad. Oh, sorry, did you envision a midnight border crossing by helicopter, or stuffed into the trunk of a car? No. It'll be through the airport on a commercial liner. Coach."

Sewell thrusts a telex at him from the State Department, confirming their request for "assistance."

So he is still on their radar.

"Thank you," Max says, "I'm much obliged, but there's no way I'm flying out of Mehrabad. One, my name is on the stop list. Two, I'm on a first-name basis with most of the customs agents—many of whom I've bribed. And three, they're all familiar with my, let's say, situation. They think I'm CIA. So there's no way I'm flying out of Mehrabad."

"Which is why you'll be in disguise," Sewell replies.

"Like—hike up my collar, look left and right?"

"No, a proper disguise. Beard. New glasses. The works. You, sir, are going to be an honorary Kiwi—and I am going to be your agent of transformation. We've got ourselves a properly clandestine operation here. Have you anything to eat?"

Sewell had a comforting, take-charge way about him. The two men retreated into the kitchen, where over leftover kebabs, grilled tomatoes, and rice Sewell lays out the bones of his plan.

"As I was saying—you've got the attention of some interesting people, Mr. Copeland. Max. Mind if I call you Max? I should begin by saying this is a covert operation handled at the highest levels of both your government and mine. There's twenty million dollars on the line here."

Max is stunned. "The U.S. government paid that much to save my ass?"

"No, mate—this is about mutton," Sewell replies, laughing. "Probably this kebab was fattened on the hills of New Zealand. Iran is our number one buyer of lamb, see? In fact, recently there was a muddle when the ayatollah declared it *haram* to eat frozen meat, so Ambassador Beeby—my boss—dropped everything and flew to Qum, and convinced the old man that New Zealand's slaughter and storage was in line with Islamic dictates. That move saved us quite a bit of money."

Max is not sure where the conversation is headed.

"So," Sewell asks, "how do you feel about being a meat inspector?"

"You want to give me a job?" Max asks. And then the realization hits him. "Oh, you mean for a cover?"

As it happened, Max had toured Tehran's largest cold-storage facility only months before. The facility was owned by Shahin's sister Mahin, and the day she'd taken Max on a tour was frozen into memory. Huge carcasses of beef and lamb swung from hooks, while Mahin teetered around on heels, dodging slabs of meat and clutching her shivering poodle Joo Joo to her chest. A meat inspector. It was perfect in its simplicity. More importantly, it was unremarkable and would not invite questions.

"To mutton!" Max says, raising a glass of tea.

"Just one small problem," Sewell says. "At the airport, arriving passengers fill out an embarkation form—a copy of which is kept and retrieved upon departure. It's to prevent enterprising Iranians from doctoring their visas, and to catch foreigners who've overstayed their welcome. The original can be forged. But because you, good man, will be traveling on a fake passport, there won't be any duplicate copy. If the passport officer goes looking for it, we are sunk."

Sewell takes another bite of kebab.

"Luckily, a few Canadian diplomats have been leaving the country and taking note of airport regulations, which shifts are lax in security, et cetera, et cetera. They feed this information to us at the New Zealand embassy. We know early mornings are the best time to leave—before Mehrabad becomes a zoo and the Revolutionary Guards are looking over everyone's shoulders."

What Sewell does not tell Max is that two months ago, he himself had been stopped by a Revolutionary Guard who insisted on searching his diplomatic pouch. This was a flagrant breach of international protocol, and only a last-minute call to the chief of protocol had prevented the breach.

But news of the incident circulated. Canadian ambassador Ken Taylor telexed Ottawa:

INCIDENT MAY HAVE BEEN PROVOKED BY ARREST YESTERDAY
OF ALLEGED CIA AGENT MAX COPELAND WHO WAS HELD
FOR ATTEMPTING TO SEND EIGHT BOXES OF RADAR EQPT
OUT OF COUNTRY.

Soon the entire diplomatic community in Tehran—seventy-five embassies—was on guard because of Max.

"Max, listen to me, I've done my fair share of airport runs and gotten out of some fairly tricky situations. Early mornings, no one is paying attention. It's winter. We'll put you in a hat . . . maybe arrange for a diversion in the customs line. You're in our hands, so let me worry about this, okay? Do you trust me?"

Had he given it further thought, Max might have wondered why Sewell was so familiar with forged documents, disguises, and airport intelligence—or why Canadian diplomats were reporting to the New Zealand embassy about airport security. But for now he sweeps any instinctual curiosities aside. He will be leaving Iran. That is what matters.

"I do," Max says.

"Good. Familiarize yourself with these," Sewell says, handing him some brochures on New Zealand lamb. "Remember, twenty million dollars is on the line."

Not to mention my life, Max thinks.

THE NEXT DAY, Sewell drops off a handful of "pocket litter"—luncheon receipts, Maori pins, anything a meat inspector might carry, as well as a biographical dossier with instructions to memorize it. John Moffett is Max's new name. For his passport, Sewell says there are two options: Either Sewell can issue him a real one via Wellington, which will take a while, or an emergency passport can be obtained from the Foreign Ministry, which is likely to raise suspicions at the airport. If they issue an emergency passport, Sewell will accompany Max to the airport and use his airport pass to squire him through.

"I'll take the real passport," Max says. Comforting as the thought of Sewell's airport companionship was, the thought of marching into the Foreign Ministry, Sadegh's territory, is even more unsettling. "But how are you going to get the forged visa and embarkation forms?"

"There are ways," Sewell says mysteriously.

That afternoon, the two men begin the process of transforming Max from jailbird to meat inspector. Sewell takes out a bag of beards and mustaches, and Max spends an hour trying on facial hair with ridiculous names like the Che Guevara, the French Fork, and the Van Dyke. Most look like comic book beards, but when Max tries on the Professor, a moderately clipped beard inflected with gray, it suits him nicely. He looks like an inspector. Sewell adjusts the beard and paints a few wrinkles on Max's brow with a greasy pencil. At the airport, Max will wear a hat—perfectly acceptable given Tehran's subzero temperatures.

When Sewell is finished, Max takes a look in the mirror. He looks different—but different enough? Draping a white sheet across the wall, Sewell snaps a passport picture of John Moffett, meat inspector.

"The secret to a successful cover is, you have to believe the lie. It's not just being a good liar. It's that you believe in the lie so much that it becomes the truth. You really *are* a meat inspector. Let's give it a go, shall we?"

Upon which, Sewell himself dons a fake mustache and conducts a mock immigration. When did John arrive in Iran? What is the purpose of his visit? Which facilities has he visited? How much meat did Iran buy last year? Why is he going to London instead of back to New Zealand? A couple of minutes into the interview, Sewell stops. "You seem to think you're British. Kiwi is more of an Aussie accent—but clipped."

He writes *Pass the pasta, pastor* on a napkin and asks Max to pronounce it.

"Poss the posta, pastoh," Max says.

"Shorten the vowels and lop off the *r*'s—the result is a modulated murmur. Try again. Pess the pestah, pasta."

"Pass the pastah, pestah."

"Pess the pestah, pasta. It's in the mixed-up vowels. Think of it as 'irritable vowel syndrome.' Again."

"My wife's the linguist," Max says. "I'm an academic. I can't do accents. Besides, you think some *komiteh* thug is going to recognize a Kiwi accent?"

Sewell furrows his brow. "I thought this might be a problem. Here," he says, diving into his satchel and pulling out a record: *Radio New Zealand's Greatest Interviews.*

"Play this. I want you to pay particular attention to the intonation. You'll notice how every sentence sounds like a question? That's because when a Kiwi talks, the inflection always rises at the end. But mostly I want you to listen to the vowels—that's where the truth of this accent lies. You're going to play this record again and again until you sound like a Christchurch tour guide."

He gets up to leave. "I'll be back tomorrow with a few more goodies."

When he reaches the door, he turns around again. "And yes—if you're detained, I can guarantee that they'll bring in some *komiteh* thug who knows the difference."

Suddenly it strikes Max the extraordinary lengths to which Sewell was going to in helping a Yank. Language training. Disguises. Forged documents. Aiding and abetting an alleged spy for the Great Satan, to say nothing of putting New Zealand's relations with the revolutionary government—and $20 million of lamb sales—at risk. Why had the State Department chosen New Zealand anyway? Why not Britain? Or Canada, which was closer, with an easier accent?

THE ARGO ESCAPE had been in planning for several weeks when State contacted the Kiwis and asked if they might add one more to the list.

Ambassador Beeby agreed on one condition: The two operations would be run separately. The diplomats wouldn't know about Max and vice versa. Even the Canadians would be in the dark. That way, should anything go wrong with either operation, the other might still be salvaged.

Meanwhile, Richard Sewell was a very busy man. In addition to his regular consular duties and Max's extraction, he was spending quite a bit of time with the American diplomats. He had rented a safe house for the diplomats with CIA funds and stocked it with provisions, picked up blank embarkation forms from a British Airways friend at the airport, brought the diplomats beer and broke bread with them, and grew so close that after their escape one of them wrote a book dedicated to Sewell. And when CIA agent Tony Mendez blew into town, Sewell squired him about Tehran and observed as the CIA operative practiced his tradecraft. His familiarity with disguises, forged documents, and escape protocols was unusual for a diplomat—but not for someone engaged in one of the most audacious rescues in CIA history.

Back in Washington, Hal Saunders's Iran Working Group called the families of the Argo diplomats once a week to update them, but Max's rescue was a new development and the Working Group failed to include Dolly and Pappy in the loop. Distraught that they had not heard from their son in over a month, they sent a letter to their senator, Lloyd Bentsen, who ran their letter up the flagpole. The State Department's response did nothing to allay their fears. Their son Max "was charged with being a CIA 'agent' and with attempting to smuggle electronic equipment out of the country," the letter advised. The word *agent* was in quotes, as though the *particular* CIA designation was of some dispute. It went on to say that they have "requested assistance from another friendly government through its embassy in Tehran."

Back in Tehran, Max is blithely unaware that his destiny is tied to the six American diplomats a few kilometers away.

A FEW DAYS LATER, Shahin returns from America with two suitcases full of candy, clothes, and books. She has been gone less than two weeks, but

Max is delighted to see her. And in such a good mood! She has all the vim and vigor of the old days. No wonder: Half of Saks Fifth Avenue now spills onto the floor. "Look," she says, running her hands over the merchandise. "These will fetch a good price!"

"I thought we were supposed to be selling off our inventory—not restocking with the new spring line," Max teases.

"Don't be a spoilsport. I also have a couple of presents for you," she says and hands him thrillers by Robert Ludlum and James Michener.

For hours Shahin regales him with tales of America—riding top down in a red convertible, dropping by a bank where machines spit out money electronically, wandering the wide-open aisles of an American supermarket. She was particularly enchanted by the checkout scanners that, *ding*, registered the prices automatically. Her enthusiasm is infectious, and Max soon finds himself daydreaming about hunting in the highlands, going to movies, and signing his name and savings away to a mortgaged house on which acorns will rain down. America! After so many months, it appears he will finally be going home.

Home. What a delicious syllable. But somehow it does not seem like the right time to break the news to Shahin: *Guess what? While you've been gallivanting, I've become the subject of a major covert international operation.* Even when she tells him how she had contacted Max's parents and told them she'd have their son out "come hell or high water," he says nothing. That would have been a good time. The date of the exfiltration has been set: Early next month, Max is booked on two successive flights out of Tehran, in case there are any problems. In the meantime, his passport has arrived and is being held in the New Zealand embassy safe.

On January 27, Max is enjoying a morning coffee when a news bulletin crackles through the radio: Six American diplomats have escaped Iran. He bolts up. According to the BBC, the six had been in hiding with the Canadian ambassador and had flown out of Iran as Canadians. They are currently en route to Dover Air Force Base, where they will be reunited with their families.

By now, the hostage angle is showing signs of fatigue and the media is anxious to latch on to any other storyline coming out of Iran. The "Canadian Caper" does not disappoint—a feel-good story featuring a covert rescue and international cooperation (the CIA angle will not surface for decades), it gives way to a flash flood of hope and renewed patriotism. CBS, the *New York Times*, and the *Philadelphia Inquirer* have all been sitting on the story, and once it breaks they rush to press and to the airwaves. Soon newsrooms around the world are rolling out the story. At a press conference in Paris, Canadian ambassador Ken Taylor finds himself flanked by over a hundred journalists and their camera crews. He talks about the exfiltration—barely. "I got the passports and the rest is what you call a trade secret," he tells the crowd. One reporter chalks up Taylor's caginess to "persistent rumors that there are more Americans hiding in Tehran whose safety might be jeopardized by full disclosure of the story."

Others press him about a rumored "seventh man." But Ambassador Taylor won't say more. He thanks everyone for coming, then retreats into the chancery building.

In Iran the backlash is immediate. Within hours, Ayatollah Khalkhali issues a statement declaring that American spies have taken refuge in other embassies and must be eliminated. Accusations fly through the various branches of government as the inevitable search for a scapegoat begins. The daily *Bamdad* reports (correctly, as it happens) that the CIA had jointly planned the operation with the Canadian government. At the embassy, one of the hostage takers—apparently unaware of the concept of irony—announces, "That's illegal!" Even Sadegh jumps into the fray. Canada will pay for its actions, he promises, and if the escape of the six Americans makes life more difficult for the hostages, this will not be the fault of the Iranians.

It is toxic and electrifying, and it feeds the suspicion that CIA agents are everywhere.

Holed up in the apartment, Max spends the day with his ear glued to the BBC. *What the hell was the State Department thinking? Did they really think they might execute two rescues with the exact same subterfuge? Now the entire country will be on the lookout, and airport security will be a nightmare. Why didn't they piggyback him, save all seven at once?*

Angriest of all is Shahin. "They used my idea to fly their diplomats home! When I called them, they told me, quote-unquote, *We aren't in the passport-doctoring business.* And now the diplomats will get a hero's welcome, while we're here sweating it out under the mullahs' thumbs!"

Sewell calls at midnight. His words are circumspect but the message is clear. The operation is being postponed.

IT IS NEVER ANNOUNCED how they connected the dots, but eventually the militants realized that the Argo caper was not a purely Canadian enterprise. One clue came from the Canadians themselves when they transferred their unclassified materials to the New Zealand embassy and asked the Kiwis to assume Canadian interests. Four days later, on the night of February 4, a band of militants erected roadblocks on either side of the street, broke into the New Zealand embassy, and ransacked it. They spent the night rifling through unsecured documents, upending desks, looting visa plates, and drilling into the safe. When Ambassador Beeby and Deputy Sewell arrived the next morning, they found their embassy in shambles.

When the story breaks, Max flies into a rage.

"It's just the New Zealand embassy," Shahin says, perplexed. "Who cares?"

"Proof I was born under an unlucky star!" Max counters, retreating under a cloud of black anger.

They won't even bother with a trial this time. Just as Tom Ahern's multiple passports at the U.S. embassy proved that he was CIA, the discovery of Max's Kiwi passport—hidden in the safe—will likely cast him as a double agent, spying for both the U.S. and New Zealand. It will be enough to get him executed. Max cannot suppress the instinct to run.

But where? Soon there will be a knock and a band of revolutionaries will cart him away again.

"Stop wandering around like a wounded animal," Shahin says, unable to fathom why Max is so restless.

Soon a curious stillness descends. He fixes himself a sandwich and waits. The minutes tick by. Morning turns to afternoon. On television, the crowds outside the American embassy are louder than ever—but inside the stillness grows deeper and more profound. They're getting close, he can feel it.

It is dusk when the phone rings.

So tightly coiled is Max that he thinks it's the doorbell, and nearly jumps out of his skin. But it is Sewell ringing from London. He and Ambassador Beeby have caught the first flight out of the country.

"What the hell happened?" Max asks, pulling the phone into the living room so as not to wake his jetlagged wife. "Didn't you think the revolutionaries would discover the link to Canada? You should have run me out *before* the diplomats."

"I can't say too much. Between you and me, it didn't help that Canada assigned us to look after their interests. I thought we had more time, but a journalist threatened to break the story—so we had to send them out first. There is one stroke of luck, though. Apparently the militants tried to break into our safe but ran out of gas cylinders. I have your passport and materials with me. Lucky stroke, eh?"

Max isn't quite ready to concede luck.

"Sorry it didn't work out, mate. I'm sure the State Department will be in touch. Cheers."

Back in America, the Argo diplomats had been reunited with their families and are being feted by President Carter at the White House. Soon the morning talk shows will come calling. "State Department briefers will impress upon them the inadvisability of going into detail or saying anything which might conceivably jeopardize the lives of the fifty remaining hostages," an internal memo articulated.

Fifty hostages. All at the embassy. And Max once again off the radar.

Back at Langley, Tony Mendez is already making plans to use elements of his Argo operation to pull the hostages out. Six Americans had escaped. But a seventh was still behind enemy lines—an alleged CIA operative himself. And he grew increasingly more fretful.

In retrospect, Max thought it a terrible sign that the State Department had chosen a Kiwi to rescue him. The bird was notorious for not being able to fly.

SHAHIN

Months pass.

Winter gives way to spring. The flower shops in Tehran are hawking tulips and hyacinths and goldfish—hoping the mullahs won't cancel the Persian New Year. A couple weeks ago, they had threatened to do away with No Rooz, a celebration of fertility, good luck, and hopefulness, because it predated Islam. Just last year, Ayatollah Khalkhali had suggested bulldozing Persia's greatest historical treasure, the twenty-five-hundred-year-old Persepolis, because it reminded Iranians of their monarchical history. Did they really think they might rewrite history by razing it?

Back at the embassy, the militants are busy reconstructing American history—the documents that had been shredded the morning of November 4, 1979. They have brought in traditional rug weavers who carefully patch thousands of strips a sixth of an inch wide, matching edges and rows of each strip, certain, finally, they have proof that the American hostages are nothing more than CIA agents. The list of agents will be released to the public, and the agents tried and executed. The carefully reconstituted documents span everything from cryptograms and routing instructions of the various U.S. agencies to details of CIA spying on Israel. There is a document from Cyrus Vance about the need for CIA agents in Iran. Another from Thomas Ahern with a cover propping him up as a Belgian businessman. Several dozen classified Military Assistance Advisory Group documents. All these and many more will eventually be released in a sixty-volume archive titled *Documents from the U.S. Espionage Den*. Predictably, the CIA would "neither confirm nor deny the validity of the material," but the disclosure constituted the biggest loss of classified information sustained by the Agency since World War II.

For now, though, all that floats around are wispy rumors of the CIA list.

"Are you on that list?" Shahin asks Max.

"Don't think so," he says obliquely.

When the first documents come to light, they show that over five thousand Iranians had been on the CIA's payroll. And three of the diplomats are indeed revealed to be CIA agents. But there's no mention of Max. Perhaps Max really is just a quiet academic who has fallen into all this without motive or means.

How do you prove someone isn't a spy? Again Shahin finds herself thinking about the warehouse. It was the hub of all Westinghouse operations in Iran—the epicenter through which all their military equipment passed. When she'd threatened to go to the warehouse and dig around before the trial, Max had refused her a key. "Everything has been confiscated by now," he'd said. But again and again the thought returns to her. Somewhere in that cavernous warehouse, Shahin suspects, is a clue—one that will deliver or damn her husband. Exonerate him or prove his guilt conclusively. The following day, she slips off to visit the facility at daybreak but finds it ringed with barbed wire, padlocked, and fronted by two implacable armed guards. *Closed on order of the Revolutionary Guards* says a handprinted sign.

"*Salaam aghayan,*" Shahin greets the guards. "Can I talk with the manager of this warehouse?"

"No manager here, just the two miserable guards you see before you."

"How about the shipping agent? Any idea where I might find him?" she says, peeling off five thousand *tomans.*

An hour later, Shahin is standing in the living room of a Mr. Nargesi in northern Tehran. Judging from the gold-plated chairs lined up against the wall, plush carpets done in ornate Tabrizi colors, and a vase filled with peacock feathers, international shipping is a good business in a country on the verge of collapse. Off to one side, a parrot is squawking in a gilded cage.

"A shame what happened to your husband, *khanoum*. I always thought he was always a gentleman."

"Thank you."

"I never thought Dr. Copeland was a smuggler, but what else could I do? After he was arrested, I went back to the warehouse; they wouldn't let me back in. And then I read about what happened to Doctor in the paper. Is he okay, *khanoum*?"

"You knew of his troubles?"

"*Khanoum*, I wrote a letter to Dr. Copeland—didn't he get it?"

"A letter?"

"Perhaps these things are best forgotten. Tea?"

"What did the letter say?"

"Let us move on from unpleasant discussions," he says.

Shahin laughs. "Mr. Nargesi, when your spouse is tried, convicted, and sentenced to prison, then let us pass over unpleasant discussions. What did the letter say?" she asks for the third time.

Nargesi sighs. "In March of last year, five boxes belonging to Mr. X—I don't recall his name, only that he was an employee of Westinghouse— were delivered to Dolphin Shippers. Four boxes were packed by our workers; the fifth was PBO. Packed by Owner. At the time I wondered how and why he had packed and bound such a large carton himself but gave it little thought. Mr. X was very methodical. Back then our warehouse was busier than the noonday bazaar; this was the beginning of the revolution, and Americans were fleeing by the planeload. Westinghouse employees would dump their belongings at our warehouse, often without waiting for a receipt. But he was different—he was quiet. Very calm. He waited while I wrote out a receipt for all his belongings."

"That month, more than five hundred boxes were delivered to Lufthansa—including the five belonging to Mr. X. But there was a mix up, and there wasn't adequate space in Lufthansa's cargo, so the bill was canceled. Many boxes sat in our warehouse for several more months. In September, we got a telex from Westinghouse saying a specific carton hadn't arrived, and to please ship it immediately. Can you guess which carton it was?"

"Packed by Owner?" Shahin says.

"Yes, Mr. X's shipment. A thorough search turned up the carton, and that afternoon it was sent to the airport along with a few other packages. But the customs agents had become very suspicious lately, and the shipment was inspected. And that is when everything fell apart. The next day I received a visit from the Revolutionary Guards, accusing me of exporting espionage equipment. Espionage! They wanted to know if I ran a smuggling ring. How much I was paid by the CIA to do this. Who my contacts were. *Ay dod-e-be-dod!*" They turned my life upside down, *khanoum*! Because as you know, the carton contained radar equipment belonging to the air force. I admit I was angry with Dr. Copeland. Apparently the radar had been packed inside the personal effects of Mr. X—as if to disguise its contents. That afternoon they took Dr. Copeland away. At the time, I was very surprised to realize Dr. Copeland was a smuggler. It wasn't until later that I realized it was the very same carton that sat in our warehouse for months, long before Doctor arrived. So you see, Doctor couldn't have been responsible! It was packed before he arrived in Tehran."

A cascade of joy floods Shahin. She's found a man who would attest to Max's innocence—perhaps even ignorance of the whole operation! A slew of questions arise in her mind. Does Max know this? Has Westinghouse set him up? Why hasn't Mr. Nargesi come forward before? And above all:

"Who is Mr. X?"

Nargesi hangs his head. "I've tried to remember his name—but you know American names, so confusing. I remember he had a very peculiar mustache. Afterward I went back through the files to find them, but the day after they took Dr. Copeland, the Revolutionary Guards sent over a

---

*"What a catastrophe!"

team and they ransacked the place," he says, covering his eyes. "I cannot imagine why Doctor didn't get my letter."

"It was probably intercepted by the guards outside our house. Never mind. You will write another letter saying what you just told me . . ."

"My apologies, *khanoum*. Such misfortune doesn't look good for anyone. Not the air force, not the Revolutionary Guard, not the Ministry of Justice. And not me. Perhaps you can find another way to prove his innocence."

"Perhaps I haven't been clear? My husband has been falsely convicted of a crime. His life has been stripped from him. And you have the only proof of his innocence. Sir! You have a moral responsibility! In Islam it is the greatest of sins to shirk this."

But Nargesi is resolute and immune to her reasoning. He is sorry for what had happened to Dr. Copeland, truly he is, but his life has been ruined and nothing *khanoum* can say will persuade him otherwise.

Almost nothing.

"Ruined? You seem to live rather well, Mr. Nargesi. International shipping is a rather interesting business, isn't it? I wonder if the Revolutionary Guards have been thorough enough. Old money is suspect, but new money is worse. Isn't it? Is that a genuine Louis the Fifteenth chair? I thought I recognized its beautiful gilt. Tell me, was this lovely furniture adorning your tastefully appointed living room purchased with your hard-earned money—or is it forgotten merchandise that never found its way out of the country?"

"I am an upstanding businessman, *khanoum*. I live by the principles of the Islamic Republic."

"You live better than ninety-nine percent of its citizens. But of course I've been too hasty; forgive me. I'm certain that no other packages have gone missing, and that a review by the Revolutionary Guards will prove correct."

"No packages! Ever."

"Then why are you shaking like a motherless baby sparrow?"

Silence.

"That letter. Just write everything you told me, and I'm certain we can put this whole affair behind us.

"Let's see. Perhaps I will write the letter this evening and you can pick it up tomorrow."

"You will write the letter now," she says, handing him a pen. For the next half hour Shahin sips tea, shells pistachios, and admires Mr. Nargesi's library while he puts to paper and details a small piece of history that has not come to light.

WHEN SHAHIN FINDS SADEGH in his office later that afternoon, he looks a good decade older. His eyes are swollon and bloodshot, framed by knotted eyebrows. But beneath the rapid advancements of age, Sadegh is still Sadegh—obstreperous and witty. "Shahin *khanoum*, what a pleasant surprise. Have you come to witness the slow death of an old friend?"

The ensuing months had brought nothing but difficulty for her old friend. Two months before, Sadegh lost the presidential race to his onetime friend and now bitter enemy, Banisadr. It was humiliating enough to get less than one percent of the vote. But then two days later, the six American diplomats had escaped under his nose and Sadegh was hung out to dry. Banisadr had kept him on as foreign minister, hoping Sadegh might solve the hostage crisis while he kept his own presidential hands clean.

"I'm sure you'll survive. The Sadegh I know has bounced back from worse."

Sadegh chuckles. "Life hasn't turned out the way either of us antici-pated. How is Dr. Copeland?"

"As well as can be expected for an innocent man held against his will."

"Still you cling to the belief he's innocent? Why am I not surprised."

"Have you seen the documents released by the students?" Shahin asks. "There are fifty-two hostages—and only three have documents linking them to the CIA. Three. All over Iran this hysteria about American spies is being used to distract people from the real problems at hand. The economy. Unemployment. Inflation."

Sadegh raises an eyebrow.

"You knew about the six diplomats, didn't you?" Shahin continues. "But you said nothing because you knew they weren't spies. And beneath all this bloviating and posturing, you know my husband isn't a spy either."

"Do I?"

"Five thousand Iranians, two Americans, but no mention of Dr. Copeland? Wouldn't his name have appeared *somewhere* on those shredded documents so artfully reconstructed by the rug weavers? Here," she says, setting Nargesi's letter on his desk. "Perhaps this will convince you of my husband's innocence."

Sadegh peruses it.

"You want me to overturn a case on the flimsy letter of a fired manager? No records, no documents or shipping ledger? Only a letter implicating a Mr. X. This isn't an algebra equation."

"Sadegh, I don't have the time to go looking through a warehouse for a few pieces of paper that have likely been confiscated. Even if I found them, can you imagine overturning an espionage conviction? The political fallout would be monumental: The Revolutionary Guards, the air force, and the Ministry of Justice would be hugely embarrassed, and it would prove that these revolutionary tribunals have made a mockery of Islamic justice. No. Even I know an innocent American is a dangerous thing. But you have to do something!"

"Political fallout? Do not cheapen this by talking like an American defense attorney, Shahin. Do me the favor of that at least."

Above them, a thumping reverberates heavily.

"I see the chargé d'affaires is keeping his exercise regimen," Shahin says.

Sadegh groans and buries his head in his hands. "Goddamn hostages have become the bane of my existence. The only thing worse is those students at the embassy. I fought a lifetime for this moment, only to find it undone by a bunch of damned students!"

"Twenty-five years ago that was you," Shahin says. "At Georgetown, re-member? Your demonstrations and your sit-ins, your occupation of the Ira-nian embassy?"

Sadegh laughs. "I never took hostages. I had a *reasonable* list of de-mands."

"To overthrow a twenty-five-hundred-year-old lineage of kings, as I recall."

"And no one said congratulations," Sadegh adds bitterly. "The world is riveted by the fate of fifty-two men who've done nothing but be at the wrong place at the wrong time."

"Fifty-three," Shahin says. "I think we might consider my husband a civilian hostage, don't you? The forgotten hostage."

"If *hostage* is the new word for spy."

"But you won't free him because there's no political payoff."

"Is that how little you think of me, Shahin? Even after all these years?"

"Why won't you help him, then? I'll tell you. He won't get you the Shah's head or a place in Iran's history books. But consider one thing: It might buy you peace of mind—and the conviction that you've done the right thing by God and your old friend Shahin."

For a moment, they rest in the silence of their conflicted friendship.

"What is one more American?" Shahin says. "Release him—one less headache. I will never darken your doorstep again!"

"*Akhhh* . . ." Sadegh groans and buries his head again. "I have never worked so hard in my life for so little. Do you remember at Georgetown, all those times I demonstrated against the Shah and put a paper bag on my head so SAVAK wouldn't recognize me? Now the Shah is dying, I have fifty-two hostages, and your husband is under house arrest. No one got what they wanted! I thought we might fix the world; now I just want to hide from it. Where is that paper bag?"

Upstairs, the thump of Bruce Laingen's physical fitness regimen con-tinues.

"I'm sorry things didn't work out for you. But they still might for me and my family. Will you not help an old friend and release my husband?"

"You seem to think I am American president on his last day in office," Sadegh scoffs. "Perhaps these *are* my final days, but despite what you think of me I am a principled man."

"Yes, I always wondered what happened after you left Georgetown. Twenty years later, suddenly there you are in Paris as Khomeini's right-hand man—risen like a phoenix. How did that happen? How did you finance yourself? How did you get so close to Khomeini?"

"Is this how you appeal to people? It's very effective."

"Max thinks he's going to die in Iran," Shahin says. "Forgive me for not whitewashing my words."

"Did you vote for me?" Sadegh asks.

"Excuse me?"

"Just answer: Did you vote for me?"

Such a tacit admission of vulnerability and personal disappointment is unlike Sadegh—but then, all of this is. It seems like he is unraveling quickly, in all directions. Suddenly Shahin notices that Sadegh's windows have been entirely painted over.

"Sadegh, what is going on? Your windows . . . the whole ministry seems in a state of disarray." On her way in she'd noticed an array of cots in the hallways, banks of rice in tin containers, and huge jugs of water. "Are you"—she lowers her voice—"are you being targeted for assassination? Are you *living* here?"

"It's not that."

All at once Shahin understands. There have been whispers about this. She is looking at the ruins of his latest—last—attempt to solve the crisis. The blacked-out windows, the cots, the covered platters of food and small piles of soap and personal effects. Sadegh had meant to have the remaining hostages transferred to the Foreign Ministry!

History would show just how close he had come to solving the crisis and freeing the remaining Americans. Only days ago Sadegh had secretly met with Hamilton Jordan and Harold Saunders in Paris to hammer out an agreement for a UN delegation of Islamic nations to visit, hear Iran's grievances against the United States, meet with the hostages, then pronounce the whole situation "un-Islamic"—compelling the students to release them. When Khomeini announced that the hostages would be handed over to the Foreign Ministry, it was an astonishing victory. Immediately, Sadegh brought in cots and armchairs, had the windows painted over for protection, and ordered five helicopters to transport the hostages, as well as a few decoy cars. The following day, a young ruffian showed up at the Foreign Ministry—the sort who had become the bane of Sadegh's existence.

"Everything is ready," the student had said, "but we must have a letter from President Banisadr confirming Khomeini's order."

"You will transfer the hostages regardless of any damn letter!" Sadegh exploded. He detested the students.

The student grew rigid. They required a letter.

Sadegh called President Banisadr, who agreed to the request. But an hour later the promised letter still hadn't arrived. In a white rage—the hostages were *this* close to being freed—Sadegh threatened to go to Khomeini with details of his insubordination. The letter arrived instantly.

But it was too late. The student had left. Sadegh turned on the television to see thousands marching against him and the hostage transfer. Any attempt to transfer the hostages would get them killed—and when Khomeini saw the demonstrations, he'd reverse himself anyway. Devastated, Sadegh watched as from the walls of the embassy Ayatollah Khalkhali and the students announced that Khomeini had never approved the transfer and Sadegh was a liar and a cheat.

Politically, Sadegh was an emasculated man.

The following day the UN delegation left minus the hostages, and as their plane taxied down the runway Sadegh and the students stood on the tarmac hurling insults at each other.

What Shahin sees now is the shell of a man who had come close to solving an international crisis, redefining the revolution, and boosting

Iran's standing in the world—only to fail at the eleventh hour. Instantly Shahin switches tactics.

"I'm sorry that your plan didn't work out for the hostages. But there is a fifty-third American. No one need know about this except you, me, and the God presiding over us both. Imagine the considerable embarrassment to the State Department if you did what Max's own government couldn't—wouldn't—do."

Sadegh shakes his head. "My God, the political science professors at Georgetown would be proud of you, Shahin *khanoum*."

"Of us both, I should think—for doing the right thing."

"Who knows what is right? I thought I knew once."

Suddenly, the thump of Bruce Laingen's fitness regime becomes too much. "Shut up!" Sadegh yells at the ceiling. "Goddammit!"

"Sadegh—look at you. Here you sit in the Foreign Ministry babysitting three hostages, giving press conferences even you don't believe anymore. Forgive me for saying, but it seems like the hostages have taken you hostage. Get out of the spotlight, my friend. You were meant to be the power behind the throne—or turban. Not dancing in the spotlight of fame!"

"You think I'm doing all this for personal glory?"

"Aren't you? The moment Khomeini appointed you foreign minister and handed you this mess, you thought, 'I can solve the revolution's biggest international crisis.' Do you deny it?"

"Remarkable," Sadegh scoffs. "You appeal to my vanity even as you deride it."

"But forget all that. Forget the thirty-six million people who didn't vote for you. Forget about the fifty-two hostages. For the time being it's just you and me, old friends. Will you not free my husband? No one need know, and nothing will come of this but the gratitude of an innocent man and a worn-out friend. Come, are you that hardened?"

"What a shame *you* didn't run for office," Sadegh says. "But the benefits to me are considerably less clear."

Later President Carter called Sadegh "really gutsy" and applauded him for taking "a lot of personal risks in seeking a resolution to the hostage crisis." By the time those risks came to light, the world had long forgotten the name Sadegh Ghotbzadeh. The hostages would remain in captivity for 444 days, but by then Sadegh had antagonized almost everyone—the students, Banisadr, Iranians who saw him as the hostages' protector, the West who saw him as Iran's face, and Khomeini who marginalized him. But that day Sadegh took yet another risk. Perhaps it was a final act of forbearance or resignation or friendship, or grace. Perhaps it was a final retaliation against the students who'd emasculated him. Or perhaps it was an act of kindness between improbable friends. Sadegh was an inscrutable man.

But on that day, Shahin got what she came for.

"Go to the Ministry of Justice and introduce yourself to Fereydoon Eshaghi," Sadegh instructs. "He will give you a letter. Do it soon. I don't know how much longer I will be here. Do it now."

"Thank you," Shahin says, turning to go. "Perhaps after all this is over we might enjoy a quiet tea? No politics."

"What else is there?" Sadegh replies.

When Shahin holds out her hand, Sadegh merely bows and touches his heart.

It is the last time she will see Sadegh.

En route to the Ministry of Justice, it strikes Shahin how depressed her friend seemed. He'd lost an election. Lost face. Showed up by a bunch of students and embarrassed on the international stage. Then denied by the spiritual father he'd brought home. Was she walking into a trap at the Ministry of Justice? What if Sadegh is using Max to reassert his power and prove he isn't aligned with the Americans once and for all? Prove that he is a loyal revolutionary? Sadegh is a desperate man. And desperate men cannot be trusted. Pulling up to the ministry, she remembers something else: She has left the letter from the shipping agent—the sole proof of Max's innocence—with Sadegh. For a split second, Shahin finds herself faced with a torturous decision. Should she go into the Ministry of Justice or retrieve the letter? *Do it soon. Do it now.*

Soon the government offices will close for the New Year. But Max has been under house arrest for almost four months now—and it is killing both of them. It's now or never. Sadegh is her last and best, and worst, hope.

Sadegh wouldn't do that. Would he? Shahin makes a split-second decision.

She strides into the Ministry of Justice.

Cyrus

A lfred Hitchcock once spoke about how movies often began with a "MacGuffin"—the mechanism that launches the storyline. Rosebud in *Citizen Kane*. The titular Maltese Falcon. "In crook stories, it is almost always the necklace," Hitchcock explained in a lecture at Columbia University. "And in spy stories, it is most always the papers."

I had stumbled upon Max's Radar Affair over a year ago, and that MacGuffin had led nowhere. It had taken some interesting twists, all right. I still couldn't fathom that the U.S. government had staged an extraction for him—and that it was almost a carbon copy of Argo. A covert operation staged at the exact same time, blocks apart, then buried—only to emerge at roughly the same time as Argo? It was remarkable, really. And when Michelle Obama bestowed the Oscar on *Argo*, it was as if Max's own life had been reassembled, whipped into a cinematic froth, then given Oscar's imprimatur.

But in the end Argo told me nothing about Max's Radar Affair—and I still had no idea if my father was CIA.

In spy stories, it is most always the papers.

There was one set of papers I hadn't looked through yet. Last seen on Sadegh's desk, the letter from Nargesi would almost certainly have been destroyed by now—by either Sadegh himself or his successor.

I found the president of Dolphin Shippers in the Los Angeles White Pages—like 95 percent of Iranian expats—but when I spoke with him he knew nothing of my father's trials. The company's files from the revolution had been destroyed. But, he added, he was in touch with Mr. Nargesi, who'd since begun his own shipping company. Would I like his number?

It was midafternoon when I reached Nargesi in Tehran, and he remembered the whole story. "Back then, our warehouse was filled with the belongings of American companies," he recalled. "Westinghouse. Bell Helicopter. Xerox. There were thousands of boxes, but in my forty years of shipping, never has one box caused so much difficulty!" He then recounted the tale of the radar consoles, with one difference.

Mr. X had a name.

"Lewis. Mr. Lewis," he repeated. "After your mother left that day, I tried hard to recall his name—but it was just beyond my grasp. That night a Jerry Lewis movie came on TV. The minute I saw it, I remembered. Lewis! But I had no idea how to reach your mother. And I didn't want to write another letter. I prayed your mother would return so I could unburden myself of this name, but she never came."

Lewis. It was a frustratingly common name, but it was a start.

A quick survey of Westinghouse retirees yielded a couple of tidbits. Turns out there was a John E. Lewis working in Iran who had been an engineer with the company's Integrated Logistics Support Division. Apparently he liked hang-gliding. "Used to hang-glide all over Iran," an executive recalled. Oh, and Mr. Lewis had worked on the ADS-4 radar installation.

After months of searching, had I finally found the Holy Grail? The one person who had shipped the radar back to the United States, who had inadvertently left Max holding the bag, who could finally solve the riddle of Max Copeland?

"John Lewis? Of course I remember him," George Demougeot's daughter said when I reached her by phone. "He was a friend of my father's. He moved to Maryland with the rest of the Westinghouse gang—then left. I haven't heard from him in years. Maybe they played golf together?"

Max's boss was friends with the man who'd packed the radar consoles? Interesting.

Demougeot's ex-wife sent me a couple pictures of Lewis. With his handlebar mustache, glasses, and a thick head of hair, he looked more like a carnival barker than an engineer. An oddly nerdy and sweet one. The photos were taken a month apart in 1972. His dyed, meticulously groomed mustache suggested a degree of vanity. A closer look revealed sallow skin and an early double chin. He was probably a smoker and drinker, sun damaged, midforties, not well preserved. Which meant he was in his eighties now—if he was still alive.

I imagined Mr. Lewis on the eve of the revolution, knee-deep in personal belongings and open suitcases, receiving the phone call from Demougeot. Would he mind helping out with a corporate issue?

By the time the radar consoles were discovered, camouflaged by Lewis's personal effects, Lewis was long gone. And Max was hauled off to prison. For the umpteenth time, I found myself wondering if he'd known the cartons contained the radar consoles.

When Westinghouse sued the Iranian government for compensatory damages in the World Court eighteen years later, Demougeot was called as a witness, but the consoles were never mentioned, and neither was John E. Lewis. But Lewis had continued his employment with Westinghouse upon returning to the States in their Baltimore office. The wife of a retired Westinghouse executive sent along an old company phone book from 1991— and there was Lewis's number and his classification in the Integrated Logistics Support Division, which provided support for the company's defense projects. A full decade after the smuggled radar, he was still working for the company in a sensitive division. Which meant that Westinghouse had known about the smuggled consoles—and sanctioned it.

Was that why Westinghouse had not lifted a finger to help Max? Forget about violating the Foreign Corrupt Practices Act with their illegal bribes, the revelation that Westinghouse had sold its clients' merchandise and then smuggled it back would not sit well with their international clients.

Or did I have this all wrong? The only person who could speak to these issues was John E. Lewis himself. So I began my search. I cast my net wide, hoping for any bit of information. Engineering organizations. Hang-gliding organizations. I sent out a query to six hundred Westinghouse retirees, but not one person responded. I called Westinghouse too, of course. These days Westinghouse is a fairly closed company by dint of its work in the nuclear industry. The old iteration of the company no longer exists—the name had been sold, and resold, until it finally landed in the hands of Toshiba and a few licensees who turn out lightbulbs, TVs, and kitchen appliances. Legally, the old Westinghouse is defunct. A kindly archivist offered to help see what she could dig up, but nothing ever came of it.

There are over three thousand John E. Lewises in America. I began calling and got to number fifteen before I remembered three salient facts:

1. Westinghouse had housed CIA operatives. Non-official covers, they were called, and they operated in a quiet but often sensitive capacity.

2. If Lewis was CIA, that would explain why Max's Radar Affair never became public.

3. A couple of Westinghouse execs struggled to remember him—but no one recalled much more than vague wisps. Other Westinghouse executives kept in touch. Iran had been a bonding experience for them, and decades later they told and retold stories about it. Not John E. Lewis. He left the lightest of imprints.

And now, after a decades-long career with the company, he'd effectively gone off the radar again. Thirty-five years after hiding the radar consoles in his household goods, John E. Lewis had disappeared—aided in his quest for an anonymous life by his perfect name. He was back to being Mr. X.

I feared that all chances of solving this mystery, once and for all, were lost to history.

MAX

I t's the Wednesday before No Rooz.

In a few days spring will officially arrive—and with it the profusion of hyacinths, goldfish, sweets, and other things symbolizing the Iranian New Year. No Rooz is an elemental holiday, tied to time and the mysterious workings of the universe itself. It is the moment the sun crosses the celestial equator and equalizes night and day. A time of balance. Of renewal and rebirth. Sweet air and soft earth. Typically Shahin brings presents for the children, cooks dill rice and salmon and faithfully sets the *haft seen.** The Persian New Year is considered a major turning point in good fortune, and the children below whose voices rings with the chants of purification remind Max of this.

Take my sickly pallor, give me your fiery red color.

Tonight, children all across Iran are leaping over small fires. A prelude to No Rooz, the bonfires are a national pastime dating back three thousand years to the Zoroastrians, who believed that the fires would keep the

---

*A table set with seven things that begin with the letter *s* in Farsi: *sabzi* (sprouts), symbolizing rebirth; *samanou* (sweet pudding) for affluence; *senjed* (dried orleaster) for love; *seer* (garlic) for medicine; *seeb* (apple) for beauty; *somagh* (sumac) for the sunrise; and *serkeh* (vinegar) for old age. The table is also typically adorned with a Quran, a mirror, goldfish, sweets, and hyacinth.

sun alive until morning, and that jumping over them gives the jumper good fortune and dynamism in the year ahead.

To Max, good fortune seemed like such a distant prospect. And after four months of house arrest, he *was* a little pale.

But tonight Shahin comes home looking quite pleased with herself. "Guess what I've got?" she says, holding her hands behind her back.

"My No Rooz gift?"

She opens her palm, revealing a British Airways ticket.

"Happy No Rooz!" she says. "Your flight is scheduled to leave tomorrow morning."

"My flight," Max repeats.

"Just think, tomorrow you'll be en route to London. Twenty-four hours from now you'll be a free man, wandering Piccadilly Circus, having fish and chips!"

"Um—you know my name is on the stop list, right? That if I'm caught leaving they'll haul me back to jail? No questions, no mercy. Those were the judge's words."

"Never mind. Please pack, we don't have much time."

"I'm not leaving, Shahin. Whatever this is, it won't work."

Why Shahin thought he could escape undisguised through the very place he'd been caught for smuggling radar was beyond him.

"Don't believe me all the way to the airport, then. Just pack, okay? It's cold in London and I won't have you dying of pneumonia—not after all we've been through."

"I won't pack because I'm not leaving."

"Max," she says wearily.

But thirteen months in revolutionary Iran has cured Max of the belief in miraculous escapes. He retreats to the bedroom with a book. It is his fourth month under house arrest and he has been through all the books in his library at least twice. This week was his third go at *The Collected Works of Sir Winston Churchill*. The bombast and high philosophy of Churchill, once a tonic for the mind, was now reliably good at sending him into the arms of Morpheus. He spends as much time as possible sleeping—fewer hours in the day to fill.

Outside, the neighborhood children continue their purification ritual.

The following morning the argument continues. "Just wait, you'll get to England and realize, 'I should have listened to my wife.' Just pack a few things. Is that too much? It takes two minutes!"

"Fine," Max says.

He retreats to the bathroom and reappears a moment later. "I'm packed."

In one hand he holds up his toothbrush, in the other his American Express card. "I'm traveling light. The one thing I've learned from Persian nomads."

Deep in his bones, Max knows he isn't going anywhere and resents Shahin's insistence that he is.

It is dark when they set out for Mehrabad Airport, and between bouts of silence and last-minute questions—*Did he have his passport? Would he remember to call on arrival? Perhaps he might stay at the Sheraton on Hyde Park?*—Max gazes at the landscape. It's the first time he has been outdoors in months. Outside the acrid coal smoke and ever-present propaganda banners and anti-American graffiti bears down—accentuating the menace he feels in his heart. When they pull up to a stoplight, Max sees a sanitation worker jump off his truck, empty a trash can, then do a round of jumping jacks. The world grows stranger by the minute.

He knows what will happen at the airport with cool precision: They will check his name, note that a spy has casually waltzed into their trap, and throw him right back in prison. Probably Evin. Why is Shahin forcing him to do this?

"I have a bad feeling about this," he says as she pulls around the circular drive, then parks in front of the glass-and-concrete terminal. "We shouldn't do this."

Shahin playfully grabs his sleeve.

"I'm serious. This won't end well. I know it."

"Know it?"

"Know it," Max says definitively.

This appears to give Shahin pause, but she forges ahead. "You have a bad feeling because you've not had breakfast. Let's get you something to eat."

Inside there is no sign of the Revolutionary Guards. They usually show up after nine, when the airport transforms into a bustling transportation hub. Out of the corner of his eye Max sees a customs agent he knows. Siamak Ziai had always been mildly resentful of Max, his petulant demeanor unaided by the countless gratuities Max had forked over. The other agents had been solicitous, even jovial, but Siamak had turned from ornery to openly resentful. Just then Siamak locks eyes with Max.

"I'm not hungry," Max says. "Maybe we should check in?"

Has Siamak recognized him? Max is tempted to bolt through the airport, O. J. Simpson–style, but Shahin keeps a steadying hand on his sleeve. At the British Airways desk, the agent checks Max's passport and issues him a boarding pass.

"Might I accompany my husband to the departure lounge?" Shahin asks. "Sorry to impose, it's just that in his state, I'd rather not subject him to these hoodlums. He has a touch of food poisoning."

Max does look rather pale. *Clever,* Max thinks appreciatively.

"Bad kebab, eh?" the agent says. "Come on, then."

The agent leads them toward customs, flashing her badge at successive gates. To his relief, there's no sign of Siamak—only three long lines of passengers in varying stages of desperation. At the head of each line, *komiteh* members are meticulously searching every suitcase and tossing out forbidden items: rugs, antiques, gold, jewelry. Just ahead of Max, a businessman is caught trying to smuggle out ten thousand francs.

With only a toothbrush and his American Express, Max sails through. "The benefits of traveling light," he says to Shahin.

At the next checkpoint, a *pasdar** searches him while Shahin is searched

---

*Informal term for Revolutionary Guard.

by a female. All the while, she maintains a breezy chat over the partition. *Sorry she's thrown out his T-shirts with holes, but it was really time for him to get new ones. Was he looking forward to seeing his parents? The kids?*

Two months ago when they were planning his escape, Richard Sewell had prepped Max with a variety of advice, but the only thing Max recalls now is: "Be confident. If they suspect anything they'll give you a cavity search—it's not that uncommon."

"You okay?" the guard says, patting him down. "Are you upset to leave Iran?"

A small pool of sweat courses down his back. Another into his palms. Upset to leave?

"Better not get too close to him," Shahin cautions the guard from the adjoining kiosk. "He has the flu."

The guard waves Max on.

Food poisoning. The flu. Was Ebola next? That should clear out the airport nicely.

By now the British Airways agent has left them, and they proceed to Passport Control. Of all the places where Shahin's plan might go awry, this is the last. Passport Control is home to the infamous stop list, and a casually dropped sickness wouldn't solve that problem.

The line snakes through a long hallway and around a corner. Minutes pass with excruciating slowness. Any moment Max expects a deftly placed hand on his shoulder. *Dr. Copeland?* At last he was next.

The desk is manned by a young woman in a tightly wrapped *hejab*, backed by a couple of *pasdars*. Max hates these men on sight—their guns, their arrogance, their insistence that God resides in the facial hair.

"Passport?"

Max lays it on the table. Seeing the *NOT VALID FOR DEPARTURE* stamp on Max's passport, she peruses her list—and there, halfway down, is his name. She locates it precisely with her index finger. "Your name is Coop-land?"

Shahin pulls a letter out of her purse. "Excuse me, I was told to give you this."

One of the *pasdars* steps forward and reads the letter, then frowns. He instructs Shahin and Max to step aside, then disappears behind a smoked-glass door with the letter and passport. For several minutes, Shahin and Max wait while a stream of others pass them, cleared, en route to Departures.

What is in the letter? Max wonders. Just behind the door, he can make out the figure of the *pasdar* talking on the phone. Momentarily he's gripped by the conviction that the letter is his arrest warrant, that it contains details of his activities, his conviction and jail terms—everything. Then he remembers Shahin had given him the letter.

Still, he has an urge to run.

Precious seconds tick away. Should he?

"What does the letter say?" he asks Shahin, but her face is implacable.

"Not now," she says almost inaudibly. Occasionally, the *hejabi* girl glances at him with a sad smile.

The *pasdar* returns and unceremoniously hands Max his passport.

"*Befarma,*" he says. Glancing down, Max sees a red stamp over *NOT VALID FOR DEPARTURE* saying *CANCELLED.*

Cancelled. What does that mean?

"*Doostan khoobi dari,*" the pasdar says. *You have good friends.*

Immediately, Shahin thanks the *pasdar* and pulls Max toward Departures, but it's not ten seconds before the young *hejabi* woman comes running after Max. There has been a mistake. Again Max's heart leaps and plunges. But the only error is that they neglected to match the white emigration form to the yellow original. Ten minutes later, they have found the original and once again Max is dispatched to the Departures lounge.

Where he waits.

Here Revolutionary Guards wander around in fatigues checking identification, but their attention is mostly confined to Iranian nationals. Max keeps his head down for the entire time. When his flight is called a half hour later, they board a bus to the idling plane. Again, Shahin talks her way past another checkpoint.

On board the 747, she takes a seat next to Max, chattering about London, this and that, whiling away the time. Eventually someone claims her seat, but even then Shahin refuses to leave, wandering the aisles and pretending to look for something until the departing announcement comes.

"We did it," Shahin says with a triumphant, exhausted smile.

"You did it," Max says, astonished that he is on a London-bound plane. "How did you do it?"

"A story for another time," she says. "Call me when you get to London?"

For the first time, Max notes how Shahin—who has been chattering on mindlessly all this time—is really, truly nervous. The realization floods him with gratitude. That was her. Always pretending problems were smaller than they really were.

"I guess I'll see you in America, then," he says, kissing her on the cheek.

As Shahin turns to go, he is gripped by the need to say something—anything—that reverses everything. The trial. Prison. House arrest. But just like that she's gone, the cabin door locked, and the engines begin to rumble.

The plane taxies, lifts, and Tehran becomes a dollhouse village.

Even then, Max can't quite believe it. Eventually they will discover their mistake and turn the plane around. Or send fighter jets to shoot it down.

The plane banks and climbs. Below Max spots Mount Damavand, from whence he'd witnessed his first sunrise across the Iranian plateau. Fifteen years ago, on a hunting trip with Mosoul, Max had watched slack-jawed as the light spread across the plateau, thinking: *There will be days and days like this.* His arrival in Iran had signaled the beginning of a grand experiment to bring East and West closer through the bond of education. And now Max is leaving Iran a vastly different man—himself educated in ways he does not fully understand yet.

He still cannot believe he's going home. It's only when the pilot announces they've cleared Iranian airspace that he believes he is actually en route to Britain. The knowledge floods him with relief. He orders breakfast and relishes the barely cooked bacon, buttery eggs, and burned coffee. A movie comes on, but Max cannot focus. The projector in his mind continues to spin out imagery, memories, shards of a life.

Katayoun on a fishing trip.

Shahin in a wading pool, her eyes hidden by sunglasses. She is holding Cyrus in an inner tube, afraid he will float away into a current of refracted light.

Max sitting astride a pile of carpets in the bazaar, sipping tea, steam rising.

Slowly elements of the past sift into the present.

He orders another breakfast.

Five hours later when the plane lands at Heathrow, Max realizes: *I only have a toothbrush and my American Express.* And laughs.

SHAHIN

At the airport, Shahin stays in the terminal until the very last minute, eyes glued to the plane that holds her husband, watching for any sign of trouble. When the plane finally takes off, a great cry rises from the depths of Shahin's being. The deed is done. Now there is nothing to do but wait for news her husband has safely arrived.

For a few hours, Shahin wanders Tehran aimlessly. She stops in a pastry shop and buys a handful of almond cookies, nursing the sweets with a cup of tea. Outside a parade of children cavorts in the streets, smiles plastered on their faces, hands wagging with plastic baggies of goldfish. The signs of No Rooz are everywhere, but these symbols of good fortune only exacerbate the hollowness in Shahin's heart. On the day of her most improbable accomplishment, she feels only a sense of loss and emptiness. It eats away at her, hovering just beyond consciousness.

"Can I have some cookies?" a little girl asks.

"Go to the counter and pick out anything you like," Shahin says. The girl points to a cream puff, and Shahin orders a dozen to be boxed. A huge smile crosses the girl's face. But a moment later the girl is gone, and Shahin is once again alone with the feeling that all is not right. That afternoon, Shahin cycles through all available distractions, unable to locate the source of her despair.

Five hours later, she turns the key at 25 Kooyeh Pehleh, their home for the past year. By her calculation, Max will be landing at Heathrow soon, and she wants to be here when he calls. When the phone rings a moment later, Shahin's heart jumps—but it's her brother Mosoul with No Rooz tidings. She tells Mosoul that Max has finally left Iran, then hurries him off the line. A plethora of similar calls follows. Hours tick by. By midnight, Max still has not called.

Exactly a minute after midnight the phone jingles—and because it is well past Max's arrival time, and Shahin is angrily preparing to give him a talking-to. How dare he keep her on edge! But it is Mahin, the last of her siblings.

"Bad news. Max has been re-arrested and returned to Mehrabad."

Max? Rearrested? Returned? Reaching for the kitchen counter, Shahin tries to steady herself but misses and lands on the floor, pulling a tea set down with her. *Max is back in Iran.*

"I'm kidding, Shahin *jan*. You do realize the elder isn't supposed to call the younger sister?"

"I don't understand. Is Max okay?"

"Of course. I have no idea where Max is; I'm sure he's fine. Next time don't make me wait until midnight to remind you to call me."

She places the receiver in the cradle and cries anew. Her sister always did have a curious sense of humor.

When Max finally calls at three A.M., it is to jubilantly inform her he is in London, and his luck has turned. He's won seventy pounds at blackjack. Seen a musical. Taken a luxurious suite overlooking Hyde Park. For several minutes he goes on, concluding with a detailed description of his stroll through the thick London fog.

But the call has the reverse effect. Instead of allaying Shahin's fears, it exacerbates them. She cannot quite place it. The sense of looming darkness that has followed her through the day, cut into her heart, drained like a sieve into her soul—that is still there. Soon, Shahin has such an overwhelming sense of foreboding that she dives under the blanket.

Outside, the gaiety of No Rooz has given way to perfect stillness. The city is finally quiet.

The following day, Shahin begins the inevitable process of shutting down her life in Iran. Paying off debts. Closing bank accounts. Packing up clothes. Saying her good-byes.

Of all these, Mosoul is the toughest. She is close to her other siblings, but she loves Mosoul the best—recalling how as children, he'd taken her to the cinema and bought her rosewater ice cream. Shahin has always been fiercely devoted to her older brother. He is the salt of Iran's earth, a mullah-baiting, whiskey-drinking bon vivant who knows how to make his own fun. Even now, when everything looks bleak and Shahin is closing out her life here, Mosoul makes her laugh with a cache of fake accents. French. Russian. German. Italian. There isn't a language he doesn't fake-speak, vaulting from Nazi officer to Italian paramour to French baker in service of a farewell laugh.

"You drove Max to his trial. You spirited him away on hunting expeditions. You showed him his first sunrise from atop a mountain. You even procured a Kurdish smuggler to take him to Turkey. Is there anything you won't do?"

"You want me to kill someone for you?" he valiantly and only half-jokingly offers.

A MONTH LATER she is alone in an empty apartment. Husband and children have been rescued. But on the eve of her departure, it somehow seems she is leaving the most crucial part of herself behind. Shahin had left Iran for the first time as a girl of seventeen. When she returned, it was with an education, husband, family, and the conviction that she would eventually die in her beloved Iran. How do you bid good-bye to a country that formed your very soul?

Shahin does a final sweep of the apartment. She has distilled her life to two suitcases. The sole remnant of their once-vibrant life is a TV, which Mosoul will collect tomorrow. To pass the time Shahin turns it on and sees yet another mullah spouting nonsense. There has been an uprising in the provinces and the mullah is counseling restraint, beseeching viewers to remember that Iranians are one family, made of one fabric. *One fabric?* Shahin thinks. *One fabric in the color of black. The color of mourning, sadness, and death.*

Instantly, Shahin understands the darkness that had been trailing her like a looming storm from behind. It is not depression. It is a vision of her homeland's demise—how twenty-five hundred years of glorious history will be reduced to dust scattered across the Iranian plateau, its oil wealth siphoned and stashed in Swiss bank accounts. Its people massacred by sadists who hijack her religion for profit and power. They will take this country back a century, close it off to the world, suck the Iranian psyche dry—and then justify it by the tenets of Islam, itself sullied and abused. *One fabric? Mullah, we aren't one of your cloaks!* We are a Persian carpet—one fabric, but made of cotton, wool, and silken threads woven with all the colors under the sun: reds and whites, salmon, pistachio, blues and ardent greens, even gold and silver. You can wrap us up in chadors, but our colors grow only richer, our knots tighter. These unique knots make Persian carpets the most desirable in the world. *This* is Iran.

The following morning she wakes as if from a feverish dream and begins hunting for a pen—lest the words escape her.

I am soaked with the love of my country
And rightly so—the name of Iran ennobles me
For all the historical achievements of Iran, I am proud
And ever so delighted to contemplate her artistic, historical, and
*   scientific victories*
If science and art are the measure of man
Iran is the winner, as usual
There is nothing in this world stronger than the love of one's country
Nor will there cross one's mind a dirtier thought than her foe
A nation will never lose the love of her countrymen
Nor release anyone from the bonds of allegiance
I am a daughter of Iran

And ready to shed with love and sincerity every drop of my blood in her
  name
My life will never be complete
Until once more I kneel to touch the fertile earth of home.

She channels this on the back of an envelope. There isn't a single crossed-out line, as though it had arrived fully formed in her heart.

Later that day, Mosoul comes to drive her to the airport. The streets that had echoed with wicked slogans, with hope and with angry demonstrators, now only pulse with silence. Shahin will always be a daughter of Iran. When her plane lifts and banks, and the great Alborz mountain range comes into view, Shahin turns away.

In her heart, she has already said a thousand good-byes.

MAX

It's spring 1980. After the longest and darkest chapter of his life, Max is home.

Home. He turns the word over in his mind. A week ago, he was convinced he would die in Iran. Now he is enjoying a Frosty at Wendy's. The magnolia trees are in full and vibrant bloom. And there is a fresh slate of movies to see.

On his second day back, Max walks into a used-car dealership, plunks down $1,000, and drives out in a white Chrysler LeBaron. Long confined to smaller Iranian cars, Max stretches his limbs, rolls down the window, rests his left arm on the driver's-side door, and cruises up and down that verdant stretch of suburban Philadelphia known as the Main Line. Max loves the area for its greenery, placidity, and rich educational heritage. Acorns rain down from pin oak trees. Prosperous ladies spend hours at lunch. Men talk golf and finance. On spring nights, Max enjoys driving to the local Dairy Queen, ordering a Freeze, and luxuriating in the fading sun. On the car radio, John Lennon's "Starting Over" is playing almost nonstop.

Before Max can start over, there is something he must do. On his third day back, he drives to Washington and participates in a number of debriefings with government officials. What is said in those meetings remains classified, but Max likely shares his knowledge of the ADS-4 consoles, the air bases he visited for Westinghouse, airport security, his own escape, and Iran's security protocols. Some of the matters discussed pertain to the hostages still at the embassy. And Max comes away with the distinct impression that plans for a rescue operation are being prepared.

A month later, the details of that operation would hit the front page of every major newspaper. On April 24, 1980, eight helicopters fly into Iran as part of a Delta Force operation. Before they even get to Tehran though, their mission is beset by an array of unforeseen problems. A sandstorm. Hydraulic problems. Cracked blades. So they decide to abort. But en route out of the country, one of the helicopters crashes into a transport vehicle, sending a huge fireball into the desert sky and killing eight American servicemen—the final stroke in a long line of misfortune related to the hostages. It was a humiliating and very public debacle.

As Max watches the coverage on TV the following morning, he says a renewed prayer of gratitude for Shahin. Larger and stronger organizations, and a handful of very brave men, had not managed to extract a single hostage. Shahin had used a different approach. No military. No media. Hers was more like a backroom game of chess, dependent only on wits, strategy, and patience. The game had originated in Iran two thousand years ago, and it was central to understanding the Iranian mind-set. Cunning was needed. Pieces would fall. Kings would be vanquished. But Shahin kept playing the game until Max was the only piece left on her side of the board and—through a brilliant series of attacks, counterattacks, and sacrifices— she saved him. Then deftly took him off the board, folded it up, and exited. She had played her most exquisite game when she needed to most. In chess, it was called a brilliancy, and it happened maybe once or twice in a chess player's life.

IT IS MID-MAY and Max is waiting in the Arrivals lounge with an armful of red gladiolas. When he glimpses Shahin through the crowd he nearly drops them. It has only been six weeks since they parted in Mehrabad Airport, but the sight of her trailing luggage like a weary traveler melts Max's heart. She does not look like a bravura chess champion. In her overstuffed suitcases, Max sees her intention to bring her homeland, her past, her ambitions across the ocean as she'd once done so many years ago.

En route from the airport, Shahin briefly recounts the trials of her final weeks in Tehran. Max counters with the joys of his new life in America. He says nothing about his meetings in Washington. From now on, there will be no discussion of politics, no discussion of America and Iran. For now, the Copelands will focus on rebuilding their lives.

But everywhere they look is a reminder of the life they left behind. "What are all these yellow ribbons?" Shahin says after they pass the tenth oak tree wrapped like a present.

Max laughs—then pulls the car aside, unties the yellow ribbon from the tree, and presents it to Shahin. "For you," he says, handing it to her.

Shahin fingers the silky, weather-beaten strip.

"This yellow ribbon means coming home," Max says, "You brought me home, Shahin. I thought I'd die in Iran, and now here we are, and I have you to thank. You are the most courageous person I know, mouse. You pulled me out when I had no hope of ever seeing my children or parents or country again. And I don't know how I can ever repay you. Suddenly it strikes me as the height of presumption, but I have one more favor to ask. We've spent our entire lives crossing borders, you and I. Do you think America could be your home once again? Because I'd like that."

"Max . . ."

"No, just—all I'm asking is that we start fresh. A lot has happened. I've made some mistakes. But can we just let the past go? Someday? I'd like for this dilapidated ribbon to symbolize a fresh start."

"I'm here, aren't I?"

"Do you think you could consider America home?"

She looks at him wistfully. "I've watched a revolution destroy my home, sold everything, and said good-bye to my siblings and my beloved country—the only thing that has ever anchored me. I've seen twenty-five hundred years of monarchy felled by a mullah, and watched helplessly as my king has wandered from port to port like a Flying Dutchman, unable to secure a home from so-called friends. I've defended a husband from accusations I don't understand—on faith. Our savings are gone. Our friends are scattered. The life I knew is gone. It's gone. And I don't know what to do about it except keep moving forward. So here I am. But I will always be a daughter of Iran, Max. Always. A proud and distraught and exhausted daughter of Iran. So please, right now don't ask me to accept that this is suddenly my new home."

For a while, they both sit by the side of the road, silent, a puddle of yellow ribbon in Shahin's lap. Finally, she speaks again.

"You bought a car, I see."

"I did. You like it?"

"It's comfortable," she says, gingerly touching the bleached leather seat. "White's a bit impractical, isn't it?"

FOR A FEW WEEKS, the Copelands live in the Divine Tracy Hotel in Philadelphia. The establishment is run by a stringent Christian sect that forbids commingling of the sexes, and houses the family on different floors. Founded by Father Divine, the hotel prides itself on offering decent accommodations at affordable prices, provided guests adhere to a strict code of conduct enumerated on a lobby sign: *No smoking, drinking, obscenity, vulgarity, undue mixing of the sexes, eating in your room, visitors, miniskirts, receiving gifts, presents, tips or bribes.*

"It's worse than revolutionary Iran," Katayoun says. "How about the Sheraton across the street?"

"It's twenty dollars a night," Max replies. "You'll stay here and like it, shrimper."

At least the family is back together. Separately.

Father Divine's picture gazes down from walls on every floor, reminding guests to conduct themselves as dignified Christians. A charismatic man who rose from obscurity, Divine had been a pot-stirrer and a bit of a loon. And the Copelands aren't the only Copelands to have followed in his path. Back in the day, Divine had ruffled a few feathers, and a handful of local preachers had him arrested for lunacy. But a lawyer named J. B. Copeland defended him pro bono, and he was found sane—in spite of having given his name as "John Doe, alias God" when arrested.

"You aren't a direct descendant of J. B., are you?" the elevator attendant asks Max. "Because we need a bit of help carrying on Father Divine's legacy."

That does it. Within days Max has found alternate accommodations, a comfortable ranch-style house on an idyllic, shaded street in the heart of Haverford. The first week he brings a brown lab puppy for the kids. Mornings he makes pancakes. Weekends he gardens. From the fertile soil, Max pulls forth a variety of vegetation that is the envy of neighbors, to whom he totes bushels of tomatoes, squash, and freshly cut gardenia blossoms. He sees movies. Takes long drives. Grills burgers. Reads voraciously. All of which brings him renewed pleasure. But in the wee hours, questions about his life still loom large—and they will not be silenced by the beauty of small things. What does he have to show for his years? "I've made enough to pay for Cyrus's education—four years at the finest university," he writes his mother. "Next up, Katayoun's college fund!" But their savings are going fast, dwindling by the week, drained by private school tuition, rent on the Main Line, and the expenses of beginning life anew. Max and Shahin decide to exchange the LeBaron for a Volkswagen with better mileage.

The promised job with Westinghouse has not materialized. Max had called Demougeot several times, but the man was unreachable. Last Max heard, Demougeot had divorced his wife, married his secretary, and moved to Arlington.

A book. He will pen an eyewitness account of the Iranian revolution. Was he not an expert on Iran? Fueled by visions of a runaway best seller, Max takes out a legal pad and begins scribbling. An outline quickly emerges. The early chapters are promising—a lighthearted but detailed lens on the first days of the revolution, and the oddity of being a one-man cleanup crew in a rapidly devolving country. He writes so fast he can barely keep up with the flood of memories. What's an Okie doing in the middle of an Islamic revolution anyway, selling off appliances? He even has a name for it: *The Forgotten Hostage*. A couple weeks later, the writing grinds to a halt. There are things Max has no desire to relive. Max has a reportorial eye, but he will not cast it upon the darker chapters of his own life. And so after three nights of pencil chewing, fitful trips to the fridge, and waiting for words that won't come, he puts his legal pad aside, and with it his literary ambitions. *The Forgotten Hostage* is soon forgotten.

He places another call to Westinghouse. Then decides, the hell with it, he won't work for a company that left him to rot in jail.

Academe is an option. That is one of the reasons Max loves the Main Line: Within ten miles you'll find a cluster of the finest liberal arts colleges. Max would make a fine dean—or perhaps a political science or history professor? He writes the colleges about the Pahlavi-Penn exchange program, figuring its multicultural appeal will hook them, but the hidebound colleges send back kindly rejection letters. Up and down the eastern seaboard, a flurry of letters goes out to academic institutions, corporations, and nonprofits. But the envelopes that pile up in the mailbox each afternoon are always disappointingly thin.

"Maybe send a letter to President Carter," Shahin suggests. "If anyone can help with your job search . . ."

Max is too proud to write the president, so Shahin pens one to President Carter's wife—woman to woman. The letter is an emotional pitch that lays out the family's trials. "Now that my own stamina and capacity to cope has dwindled, does it not fall within the human and legal scope of the government to lend a hand and help rebuild our lives? My husband is a self-made, honest and hardworking American with an exceptional dedication to his country . . ."

Weeks later, Max is pleasantly surprised to see an envelope embossed with the White House logo in their mailbox. And even more surprised to see that Mrs. Carter has written back with a proposed solution to the family's troubles: Counseling.

Counseling. No wonder the American economy is in the toilet. The president's wife believes the solution to joblessness is a visit to the therapist.

ONE AFTERNOON, as he is busily scanning the supermarket circular for coupons and sale items, Max hears a familiarly shrill voice ring out across the aisles. "Max Copeland? I heard you were back. Lemme get a good look at you . . ."

Mollie Harnwell is the wife of the ex-president of the University of Pennsylvania. Her husband, Gaylord, had brought Max on to oversee the exchange program with Pahlavi University he'd pioneered. Fifteen years later, Mollie and Max stand in the aisles of the Acme supermarket and renew their friendship. "What are you doing next Thursday?" Mollie inquires. "We have a ladies' club every month and our speaker just canceled. Would you like to come talk to us?"

"About?"

"What else? Iran! It pays five hundred dollars and a good lunch. What do you say? Don't bother answering, you must come. I'll have my driver pick you up next Thursday at eleven."

Main Liners can be so wonderfully bossy, and Mollie is quintessentially Main Line—a blue-blooded, idiosyncratic woman who wears dressing gowns while clipping roses, gives expensive gifts then tucks the ribbon back into her purse, and is generally used to getting her way. Max finds her delightful. That night, Max fans out the notes he'd made for his book and weaves them into a narrative of the Iranian revolution. He touches on American foreign policy, oil, the mullahs, the hostages, and the Shah. By midnight he has the bones down. The following night, he retreats to the attic and works on the speech—reading it aloud until he owns the words, inflections, and carefully timed pauses. From reading Churchill, Max knows that a good speech is both detailed and high-flying, equal parts bombast and pathos and rolling drama. Max will never be an orator like Churchill, but he has one advantage—he is an eyewitness to one of the most discussed, misunderstood events of the twentieth century. And his version of it eventually clocks in at a perfect forty-five minutes.

When Thursday rolls around, Max is suited—and more prepared than he has been for any interview. And nervous. Suddenly he is a historian for the Iranian revolution? Entering the hall Mollie's group has procured, he sees a couple hundred women—all staring at Max expectantly. Mollie Harnwell has evidently called every society matron in the state.

He takes a sip of water and begins.

"Two thousand five hundred years ago, in a great empire located at the fault lines between East and West, Cyrus the Great was crowned Light of the Aryans and laid the foundation for what would be the longest-running monarchy in the history of the world. The empire he built was the birthplace of human rights. Domestic post service. Algebra. Chess. Standardized weights and monies. Sanskrit, which is the mother of all languages. And the first legal code. As the years passed, the empire expanded and contracted, and birthed dazzling contributions to world culture. But the monarchy stayed. It was the one constant coefficient to Persia. Until just last year when Reza Shah Pahlavi, Iran's last king and stalwart friend to America, packed up his family and flew to Egypt. The light of the Aryans went out. The monarchy, which had withstood invasions by the Mongols, by Islam and the Arabs, by Alexander the Great, had been felled by a cleric with a tape recorder. And Iran, America's greatest friend in the Middle East, instantly became its number one enemy . . ."

Half an hour later, Max looks up to the sound of steady applause.

It is not thunderous—they are decorous women—but neither is it simply polite. And Mollie is smiling exultantly. A slew of hands shoot up. Why do Iranians hate us? Why do the women cover themselves? What is it like for women? Is it true the Shah tortured people? What will happen with the hostages? What does Max think of U.S. foreign policy?

"So what the hell happened to you over there?" Mollie says afterward, plucking a shrimp from a passing tray of delicacies. "I figure, as your booking agent I should know. You go over there as an academic advisor and return a spy? It's me, Max—and I'll have nothing less than the full story."

"Alleged spy. I wasn't aware that you'd heard."

"I hear things. I'm disappointed you didn't spill the beans—I guess five hundred dollars doesn't buy much these days."

But Max can tell Mollie is pleased. He had not spoken about his personal difficulties, focusing instead on the history that had brought Iran and America to fisticuffs, and it had galvanized the women. Mollie, the dowager empress of the Main Line, had introduced him as "our resident expert on Iran," and he'd delivered. "You must come over and see Gaylord," she declares. "He will be delighted to see you. You can relive your glory days at the university!"

Secretly Max entertains a glimmer of hope that someone at the University of Pennsylvania will hear about his speech and offer him a job. Instead, the following week he gets a call to address an insurance consortium. Then a student group. Other requests roll in, leading Max to wonder if Mollie has called everyone in her Rolodex. In a matter of weeks, Max finds himself addressing college students, international organizations, Rotary Clubs, anywhere there is an interest in Iranian affairs—which is apparently everywhere. The audiences are small. But soon Max is averaging an engagement or two a week which, at $500 to $2,000 a pop, is enough to refill the Copeland coffers, send the family on vacation to the Bahamas, and pay for a tailored Italian suit.

"If you're going to be an expert on Iran, you should look like one," Shahin says, pulling suit after suit into the Bloomingdale's fitting room. "This isn't some academic conference, you know. You're speaking about Iran."

They still have not spoken about what happened. For now, Shahin pats his lapel and gingerly discusses his version of Persian history—especially as it pertains to her beloved Shah, who had died the previous summer. She felt awful that her king had died in loneliness, felled by a lymphoma he'd kept from the world. His death was a dark spot on America's soul, she felt, for after courting him and cozying up to him, America had turned away in his hour of need. Now the king was dead and the monarchy would never be restored.

But there was the matter of his legacy. "What did you say about him?" she'd asked him after his first talk, "when they asked about torture?"

"That I never saw anything."

"Good," she reflected. "But maybe point out how the CIA trained SAVAK?"

His audiences are modest, but each time Max steps behind a microphone, he grows more confident with the weight of history, and his speeches shape-shift from professorial talks to something imaginative, theatrical, and playful, ripe with dramatic pauses—as if penned by Mary Renault. That summer and into the fall, Max finds himself addressing an improbable assortment of curious minds. Housewives. Students. Economists. Managers. Professors. Iranians and Americans. Afterward they all ask about the same things—hostages, torture, international friendships gone sour, women's rights. To Max's great surprise, several professors come out of the woodwork—Persians he'd sent to Iran decades ago under the Pahlavi-Penn contract. These men hear no bitterness or recrimination in Max's voice, only the vast arc of history, and afterward they drop by to thank him for sending them home—all too briefly.

Occasionally he gets a "how did it feel" question. *How did it feel hearing "Death to America" echo all around you? How did you feel when you first heard about the hostages?* But he deftly sidesteps these questions. For now, he is comfortable channeling history and burying his own under the weight of it, even as he wonders: Will his future always be tied to his wife's conflicted homeland?

And if Max is not quite through with the past, the past is not through with him either. On November 3, 1980, while perusing the headlines over his morning coffee, Max receives a shock. There on page eighteen of the *New York Times* is a list of the hostages—and it includes a name he never expects to see: Max Copeland.

The paper of record has identified him as a hostage.

The misprint—if it is that—prompts a series of calls. First from Max's mother, who is beside herself. Then a call from an international banking consortium that he is supposed to address next week, and now wonders if he is still available? Mollie also calls. "I suppose you will be upping your speaker's fee? Nice move. The only official hostage who is a free man. Congratulations, Max, you never cease to amaze me."

When Max calls the editor and asks why he was identified as a hostage, he is informed that the State Department provided the list of names. And once again Max wonders if he is a pawn in a high-stakes game between nations that he will never understand. In Iran, Max had lived alone and always in the shadow of those held at the embassy. And as he sits and reads the morning paper, he realizes that shadow has somehow extended across the ocean.

PART 6

An Experiment
in Understanding

CYRUS

It has been a year since our return to America and the speaking engagements have dried up. One night, my father appears at the dinner table with an announcement. He has found a job—in Saudi Arabia.

"I've interviewed for every job I'm qualified for, and many I'm not," he says. "Companies say I'm too academic. Universities say I'm too corporate. And no one seems too impressed with my experience in Iran. Except Aramco. They offered me a position as director of training in Riyadh. And I am going to take it."

Curiously, it is the same position that had taken him to Iran with Hughes Aircraft. But if he is troubled by the apparent trajectory of his life into mercurial Middle Eastern territories, he says nothing. And if we Copelands are troubled by all the trouble it's taken to get here after long and painful months of separation, only to watch him leave again, what's to be done? A job's a job. Within a week, he is packed and off to Saudi Arabia, with promises that he will return twice a year, or perhaps meet us in Europe.

And like that, we are back to being *Seh Teflaneh Moslem*.

My mother goes back to work, too. Over the past two years, a great Iranian diaspora has spilled across the world, and in Philadelphia's lush suburbs, she perceives an opportunity. She opens a Farsi school for Iranian expats. Every Saturday at eight A.M. our dining room hums with the voices of young children singing the (unofficial) Iranian national anthem and learning the complexities of their mother tongue.

And, because education isn't exactly a gold mine, she also takes a couple of courses in real estate on the side. Within a year, she is one of Coldwell Banker's rising stars—selling posh homes to financiers, company presidents, stylists, Philadelphia lawyers, even Hollywood auteurs. When a young man claiming to be a director for the Walt Disney company says he wants a quiet home on the outskirts of Philadelphia, she shows him an assortment of houses, thinking: *Disney director? Right. He's barely thirty.* But a week later, she has found a lovely Tudor for M. Night Shyamalan.

Our dining room table is the best barometer of my mother's success. On Saturdays, it is buried under school supplies and Farsi books, and the rest of the week, under client files and glossy flyers trumpeting my mother's growing real estate distinctions. The President's Council. The Multi-Million-Dollar Club. The Circle of Excellence. In her second year she lists a $16 million home in the Poconos—a mansion so over-the-top, it has its own helipad. Should the Carringtons ever relocate from Denver, they would feel right at home here. Accordingly, she dubs the mansion "Belle Reve."

And indeed, life does seem like a beautiful dream. With astonishing fluidity, my mother has traded the Iranian dream for the American one— even adapting her name along the way. Her new professional name is Shane, which is easier for Americans to remember.

"Like the Western?" a client inquires.

"No, Middle Eastern," she replies, unaware she is following in Alan Ladd's gunslinging footsteps.

IN SAUDI ARABIA, my father is decidedly not having a *belle rêve.* He writes home a couple times a month. At first I get the impression he's doing okay, since most of his letters to me are about me—and those that aren't contain suggestions he believes will benefit me. He is being fatherly from six thousand miles away. And since it's no skin off my back, I don't object. But I do not register for the draft, open an IRA, take ROTC courses (really?

ROTC?), or anything else he suggests. Frankly, I cannot believe that he wants me to take courses in military science. Does he know me at all? And then, on the eve of my high school graduation, I get a letter that clears everything up.

> *Whether you like it or not, you have been temporarily blessed with intelligence and ability. I say "temporarily" because if you do not constantly and consistently use and expand your possessions, they will wither. If this happens, you will have lost the ability to control your own career. You will have to accept any job that is offered to you, because you will not be in charge of your own life. Last night, I was so utterly exhausted that I didn't even feel like going to have dinner. I left the office around 8:30 P.M. (having started at 6 A.M.) and went home. I turned on the TV, got some crackers and a soda, and started to eat. Fifteen minutes later, I woke up with the crackers still in my mouth, turned off the TV, and fell asleep on the floor. Life is not fun and games for those who cannot control their career. I strive hard because I have to, because times are difficult, and because I am afraid they are going to become even more difficult.*
>
> *Before I came to Saudi Arabia, we were almost out of money. There would have been no one to turn to, no loan, no help from the government, and no private school for you or your sister. With this four-page letter, this tired old man has one request. Wad the paper up and consign it to the waste basket, but keep the thoughts contained in these pages in your able mind.*

I read it once, then fold it up and file it away. I don't want to contemplate his version of the world—a catch-as-catch-can place where you've only got yourself to trust. Eventually I will realize that this is his worldview because *this has been his life.* No wonder his letters are packed with advice for an uncertain future. If a man of his sizable talents and outsized smarts couldn't find a job in the States, well, something was wrong. Near as I can make out, something had irreparably broken in Iran—between Iran and America, and maybe within my father's heart.

But I am too young to see all of this. When I get that letter, I find myself resenting his foreboding fatherly advice—and cannot help comparing his spent and difficult life to the effervescent one that my mother has created for herself. On one side of the Atlantic, my mother wheels and deals, hobnobbing with movie directors and Main Line cognoscenti. And on the other, there is Dad—alone, exhausted, and worried about a safety net. It is the eve of my graduation. I am on the brink of adulthood. And if six thousand miles isn't enough distance between us, my father's letter drives me even deeper into my mother's orbit.

YEARS LATER, Max returns from Saudi Arabia. But his physical absence has exacted a steep toll on our already tentative relationship. We have grown even more distant. He sends me cards and presents and letters, asking about my new life in Manhattan. By then I have moved to take a job on Madison Avenue, so maybe I am the distant one? I cannot quite figure it out.

One night, on returning to Philly, I find myself sitting on the side of his bed before he falls asleep. It is a rare moment of communion. Both of us are feeling a bit wistful.

"Hey, could you draw me a map to the valley—you know, the one you took us to in Iran?"

"Why?" he says, suddenly alert.

Fifteen years have passed since that magical day—but tonight for reasons unknown to me, I need to draw a line back to boyhood. I recount the day to him, hanging on each detail. The gold-coin leaves. The peanut butter that clung to the roofs of our mouths. I remind him how Katayoun and I had taken along a whistle to scare away the partridge he hunted. I tell him it was the best day of my young life.

"In that case, might I offer a word of advice? Don't go back. Let it live in memory."

Gingerly, I insist. I do not want advice. I want a map. Briefly we argue about it; he is disappointed I will not take his fatherly counsel about this— or anything. Eventually he draws me a map on the back of an envelope.

A month later, he is gone—permanently.

Dead of a heart attack at age fifty-seven.

AND I AM PULLED UNDER by a tidal wave of grief, regret, and guilt. Of these, guilt is the strongest. It wasn't supposed to happen this way. I always assumed my mom would be the first to go and that I'd have Max's old age to make things okay with him. By then, I imagined he'd be living in a shack on the edge of the woods, finally and always a hunter, maybe living with all the animals he'd made lists of on the backs of envelopes during the revolution so many years ago. He would have a fireplace and a rocking chair, like his grandmother once had. I would bring him soup. And we would sit back and talk.

But my version of his future wasn't to be—proof, perhaps, that my father's life would never be a predictable, comprehensible thing. I'm certain it didn't work out quite the way he thought it would either. Dead of a heart attack at fifty-seven? The death certificate says his immediate cause of death was "acute subendocardia myocardial infarction" and that the interval between onset and death was four days. The language is medical but the meaning perfectly clear: My father died of a slow-breaking heart.

The morning after he dies, I show up at my mother's doorstep, bleary-eyed, exhausted, and dirty from having spent the night sitting on the floor of Pennsylvania Station, weeping while I waited for the first train out. The house is immaculate. For the first time in years, the dining room table is cleared of files and flyers. Shahin and Katayoun have stayed up the entire night cleaning. Around midmorning, we head to the hospital, where a nurse walks us through the basement corridor, opens a door, and there is my father's body laid on a gurney. Instantly, my mother is kissing his forehead, his hands, whispering prayers—but I can't bring myself to do anything so nakedly expressive. In death as in life, there seems to be an invisible barrier between us. Instead I touch his forehead, which is shockingly cool. Of all the things about death, this is the one I recall the most—the chill.

"Kiss your father," my mother instructs.

So I do. And I say prayers for his soul.

Later that day, I take a crack at writing his eulogy. Here are the facts about my father: Max Copeland had traveled the world. Married exotically and above his station. Bettered his mind through continual exposure to books. He'd loved books as much as anything—more. And he'd left behind a hard-drinking life on a ranch and moved across the world in the service of love and education.

But when I try to compose his eulogy, none of these things come to mind. Instead, I keep remembering the day he took us to that valley outside Shiraz—and so I write about that.

It is, frankly, an unexceptional eulogy for it says little about Max.

TWENTY PEOPLE SHOW UP for his memorial service. The Sowers. The DeRoses. The Kings. John and Joanne. The Coffeys. As I look around the room, I realize how few people know my father, really know him, and the knowledge that he has died unknown to the world plunges me into an even deeper despair.

I take a deep breath, compose myself, and tell the gathered about our day in the valley—how from the time Katayoun and I were young, my father had taught us how to be explorers in life and search out hidden vistas. When people talk about valleys at funerals, it is usually the valley of the shadow of death, and those people are priests. But my father had showed us its earthly opposite—alive and hidden and magical. That low-lying valley was the high point of my childhood, and as I spoke the words, haltingly, a vision of the valley arose before me yet again. The breeze. My sister's whistle. Her red cheeks. The silvery fish and mossy banks and gold leaves. And of course, Max. He is over yonder, keeping an eye on us. It is the valley of the shadow of the best day of my life—and maybe Max was right after all to insist that it live in memory.

ONE OF THE CHIEF EFFECTS of his death is to reinvigorate my life. After seeing how young he died, how few people attended his funeral, I swear to myself I will live with greater abandon, and return to Manhattan full of death's sad vigor. I will travel. Make a dozen new friends a year. And write! After composing his eulogy, an idea occurs to me. What about doing a book of eulogies of famous people? Movie stars, scientists, politicians who have all left an imprint on our world.

I do what we all do with our flashes of brilliance—nothing. Instead, I return to my job in advertising, my expense account, and my busy New York life. I am not a writer, I am an ad man with blue-chip clients like HBO and Chase, and they are waiting on strategy memos. Within a week, I am living the exact same life I lived before he died—the promise I made in his memory all but forgotten.

Occasionally I dream of Max. One night I find myself in a stately white house. My mother, my sister, and I are waiting for Max in a room lined with white foods and frosted cakes on silver platters. In an adjacent room a wedding is taking place. The house is a ceremonial house for important life events, and the knowledge that my father will soon be joining us gladdens me. I did not have a chance to say good-bye to him. When he finally appears, white and spectral as the foods, I know we will not have him for long. Behind him, a robed priestess waits to escort him back through the door again. He says nothing. Instead, he lies down on the floor and I lay my hands upon him. At the hospital, I was reluctant to touch him, but now I rush forward and put my hands on my father. A current of energy passes between us. Then he is gone—again.

———

FIRST IT COMES AS A WHISPER. Then a rumble. And finally an all-out explosion you cannot ignore. It is life's invitation to change. Ten years later, on a cloudless Tuesday, as the southern tip of Manhattan burns, I awake to the reality that our world has changed—undone by men with box cutters. My beloved city is awash with pictures of the dead. By now I have spent a decade shilling products and pitching clients and am deeply ambivalent about my life and career. I dread going to work in the morning. What is my place in this post-9/11 world? I sincerely, achingly, want to know. From almost every wall the eyes of missing people stare back at me, and from every church remembrances of the dead echo. It is a time of deep and exquisite grief—nothing is crystalline, nothing, but in the haze I remember the idea I had a decade ago.

It is life calling me back to it. And this time I listen.

When the book of eulogies comes out, I become for a brief time death's spokesperson. Suddenly I am giving interviews to the *New York Times*, guesting on NPR, and traveling the country as a speaker on the funeral director circuit. A newspaper editor dubs me "the Goodbye Guy" and it sticks. At parties all over Manhattan, I regale people with death-related trivia and can hold a dinner party spellbound on the topic of celebrity good-byes. Shortest eulogy ever delivered? Lee Harvey Oswald's—one sentence. ("Mrs. Oswald tells me her son Lee Harvey was a good boy, and today, dear Lord, we commit him to your care.") Strangest place for a eulogy? Timothy Leary's in an airport hangar, just before his ashes were blasted off into space. Best close? James Woods on Bette Davis: "Fasten your seat belts, it's going to be a bumpy eternity."

Joseph Campbell observed, "it is by going down into the abyss that we discover the treasures of life." This is true. As I read through the eulogies, I find the veil between worlds lifts. Scientists, actors, writers, visionaries, politicians, musicians—a stream of ethereal guests come to visit. Like Max, they often appear in my dreams. Now whenever a celebrity dies, I get calls from the press. The *Washington Post*, the *Boston Globe*, the *L.A. Times*, suddenly my name is everywhere—linked to death. One morning, I awake in the Minnesota Marriott and, glancing at my freshly pressed black suit, think: *I am now an educational speaker on the funeral director circuit. How the hell did that happen?*

Funny thing about death—it gives new life to those left behind. There I stand before hundreds, miked and spotlit, waxing eloquently about the art of good-bye. But privately I still grieve for the man I wish I'd known better. The man whose unexceptional eulogy started all this.

CYRUS

On the twenty-first anniversary of Max's death, I took a candle to the beach and sat for a good hour, digging my toes into the sand and watching the moon as it rose above Long Island Sound. I said a prayer for him and bade my mother and sister light candles in their homes, too. We were living apart and alone, but united that night in remembrance of Max. I took a picture of the hurricane lamp enclosing my candle and sent it to Katayoun, who pointed out how the moon had refracted the candle into three separate reflections under the moon.

"It's like he's watching over us," she declared.

The last dream I had about Max was a year ago. "Follow me," he had said. I had tried to do that. I had sent out inquiries about Max around the world. I wrote to President Carter, to Westinghouse employees, to archivists, to government agencies, all the while believing the answer to my father's identity somehow lay in the files my mother had labeled "Max's Radar Affair." But no single source could explain a man—much less one as complex as Max.

That night over dinner, I recounted Max's upbringing to a friend. I explained how Max had launched himself out into the world from the sleepy town of Grove, Oklahoma. When I got to the part of the story where Max converted to Islam to marry my mother, my friend asked what religion Max had been.

"He was a Christian," I replied.

"What kind of Christian? Catholic? Presbyterian? Baptist?"

I dug into my pasta.

"You don't know what sect your father was?"

"Ummm . . ."

"I think you have to go to Grove," my friend said.

"What!" I cried, seeing no correlation between my ignorance and such strident punishment.

"Your father had a life before you—aren't you curious what that was? You have to go to Grove," he repeated.

Faced with the choice of claiming my heritage from a princely Persian tradition or from an Oklahoman cattleman, I had gravitated to the former. I had a vague idea that Max had lived on a ranch somewhere and palled around with someone named Owen Butler. He had an adored grandmother he called Mammy. I knew he had been fond of a college professor named Percy. Max hunted. He rode horses. In college, he joined a fraternity and was a damn good journalist for the school paper.

That is pretty much the sum total of my knowledge of my father's childhood.

My friend was right. I booked a flight to Oklahoma that night.

As I sat on the plane weeks later, it occurred to me why Max had looked so youthful in my dream—so much so that I hardly recognized him until he whispered, "Follow me." I put a lot of stock in the mystical quality of dreams. And I now realized, Max had not wanted to take me into the darkest chapter of his life, rather his youthful one. He was trying to communicate with me, to convince me that to understand the adult Max who was my father, I had to understand the youthful Max who became that man.

———

GREEN HILLS. Pastures. Cattle. Clear streams and pine trees. Oklahoma was just like I never imagined it. If you listened you could almost hear the wind whistling down the plain—fresh from the Ozark Mountains that loomed in the distance. My father had grown up in the shadow of those mountains, south of Route 66, which still delivered dreamers to their destinations out west. The hills were barren but stunning in their naked, curvy architecture. I found myself mesmerized by Oklahoma's stark beauty.

Grove itself was a good decade behind Tulsa in "coming along," but the town sported a bustling Main Street, several strip malls, and a DQ with $1 Oreo mint freezes I soon became excessively fond of. My father's best friend, Owen Butler, insisted that I stay with him, and, thinking it might be a good way to honor Max's memory, I did not object. This turned out to be a very good decision for several reasons—not the least of which was the opportunity to meet Owen's wife, Claudia, a real sweetheart and an exceptional cook. Night after night we revisited the past over grilled tuna steaks, shrimp cocktails, spiced couscous, and brownies.

"They used to call us Mutt and Jeff," Owen recalled over dinner the first night. "I was the short one."

"What religion was Max?" I inquired.

"Methodist. Everyone here was either Baptist or Methodist. Back then, Grove was a town with one movie theater, one stoplight, and one Jew . . ."

That was cool. I loved the nonjudgmental nature of Methodists.

"Did he go to church?"

Owen laughed. "Max? I suspect not. He was busy causing some kind of mischief or 'nother."

My father, a naughty boy? Owen also retained somewhat of a fun-loving gleam in his eye, and confessed he had been a "spitballer par excellence" back in the day.

"But Max? You'd never believe Max was mischievous—which was why he got away with an awful lot. Your father used to plant tacks on the chairs of fat teachers. And he loved listening in on the party line. Why, he'd get on the phone and pretend to be the town pharmacist, doling out advice and telling people their prescriptions were ready for pickup and whatnot . . ."

For hours a vision of Max's bucolic boyhood unfolded before me—and with it, the ghost of my father rose before my eyes. So he had been a rascally boy. A smart boy, perhaps the smartest in the class, whose taste for history was well known.

And as an only child on a sprawling ranch, probably a lonely boy.

I had brought along my father's yearbooks, and for hours I thumbed through them with Owen, who was my guide into the Sooner past. It was lovely seeing Max's youthful face staring back from the pages. I learned Max was editor of the high school newspaper and wore number 31 on the football team. That last fact surprised me. I knew Max had an agile mind, but I had no idea he had been an athlete. In college, he pledged Sigma Nu. One picture showed him at a meeting of the International Club sandwiched between two Asian students. At six-foot-three, he towered over everyone else in the photo. He was remembered as a quiet, shy, funny young man. People called him Tex. Grovey. Soupy. Poncho. Maxy.

The cumulative effect of which was to amaze and shame me, for I knew none of this.

"Greatness comes not from the common herd," Henry Beechhold wrote in Max's yearbook, "but from those rare people—I include you here—who have the courage to think and act on their principles in the fact of seemingly insurmountable odds."

Having come to Grove, I understood why my father loved it—and why, in 1956, he left. Apparently, he really did want to leave the herd, and not just the herd on the Copeland ranch. "I often think of the times we spent on the porch, talking about running away from people," he once wrote his grandmother.

His yearbook provided a few insights into my father's life. But it wasn't until I cracked open his journal, a spiral notebook filled with pages of his loopy handwriting, that I saw what my father had run toward. After he died, Katayoun and I found his journal in a trunk full of memorabilia. I sat on the floor and began reading, fascinated by the prospect of a final story from Dad. "Hello World," it began. The diary was about a trip he took to Asia after graduation. I got to page six before I realized there were a dozen things to do. Death leaves a lot of work for the survivors. Items to pack. Papers to get signed. I told myself I would read the journal later.

Later was today. After Owen and Claudia went to bed, I opened it again.

I did not expect it to yield anything particularly revelatory, but as with most things pertaining to my father, I was mistaken. Interestingly, there were two copies of Max's diary: one handwritten, one typed. I assumed it was because of his illegible scrawl, but soon noticed disparities between the two, things he crossed out or purposefully omitted. I wasn't surprised my father had things he wished to conceal from the world—but these were not crushes on girls or drunken collegiate nights. They were references to clandestine jobs. Geopolitical observations. Characters he'd met. A heart attack suffered by his professor. In the reading and comparison of the two versions of my father's past, it became clear to me that these missing details pointed to something much larger.

And so it was that with Owen's help, a yearbook, a diary, and a few newspaper clippings, I began to carefully put together the pieces of my father's life, and answer the question that had set me on this path.

MAX

M ax is ten when the Copelands move to Grove, Oklahoma, a small
town on the southwestern edge of Cowskin Prairie at the foothills
of the Ozark Mountains. Once settled by Indians, the area was thinly populated until the 1880s. Back then, a spring at the base of the hill provided
a welcome campsite for travelers on the trail between Southwest City and
Vinita. When the Copelands move here in 1944, Sam Copeland buys a
ranch off Lake Road 6 with wooded views in all directions—two thousand
acres where cattle and sheep roam. The ranch house has two fireplaces and
beamed wood walls that run diagonally instead of parallel to the floor—a
distinguishing feature. Out back, a spring gives birth to a stream in whose
gentle currents watercress grow.

Because Max is one-sixteenth Cherokee, he inherits a deep affinity for the
land. The other fifteen-sixteenths wants to get the hell out of Grove. At
night, he can almost hear the echo of a stagecoach and horse hooves, for outside his window a sycamore tree marks the spot of the old stagecoach depot,
and a light depression indicates the tracks in which the coaches had once run.

His first year in Grove, Max attends a one-room country schoolhouse
with a mix of Indians and hillbillies. His teacher is a wiry woman with
steel-rim glasses and hair pulled into a bun. Each day after the Pledge
of Allegiance, she leads the class in a rousing rendition of "The Volga
Boatmen," a Russian folk anthem about the joys of unremitting toil that
sets the tone perfectly. The schoolhouse has no indoor plumbing, two out-
houses, a hand pump from which students drink, and in the winter months

a potbellied stove over which they warm their limbs. The following year when authorities begin busing students into Grove, Max is delighted. The new school in town has a library where he gets acquainted with Russian masters such as Chekhov, Dostoyevsky, Tolstoy, and history tomes in whose pages Max takes comfort and flight.

Life in Grove is not quite as idyllic as a Rockwell painting, but it is close. When Max is not milking the cows, feeding guineas, herding sheep, or studying, he is pranking the good citizens of Grove with his best friend, Owen Butler, three grades behind. Summers the boys hunt, cut brush, gig for fish in the lake, or go to the movies, where they are advised about the dangers of marijuana by a strung-out, scantily clad girl in a preview clip.

Max learns to drive at fourteen, and smoke and drink shortly thereafter. Back then, if you are big enough to do it, you do it.

At eighteen, Max enrolls at the University of Oklahoma and pledges Sigma Nu, earning a BMOC designation and the admiration of his house mother. "In his quiet way and without forcing anything, he quickly made a place for himself in the fraternity, and has become a general favorite with us all," she writes to Dolly. But beneath his affable and quiet exterior, a feeling of terrible anxiety begins to gnaw at Max. "I have a virtual fear of being a failure," Max confesses to his mother. On the exterior, Max seems easygoing, but he burns with the need to do something consequential with his life.

Journalism holds some allure. He is good at telling stories and lining up facts, and reporting gives him a sense of contributing to the world's well-being. He writes for the *Oklahoma Daily* and works nights at another paper as the sports editor.

Yet his anxiety continues unabated.

FROM THE MOMENT Percy Buchanan sets foot on campus, he is the object of almost continuous controversy and speculation. By age forty-seven,

Percy has been ordered out of Mongolia, imprisoned in China, bombed by the Japanese in Shanghai, headed up the army's intelligence language school in Washington during World War II, visited Korea on special assignment, and directed counterintelligence training in Japan. His knowledge of Asia does not come from armchair studies—it comes from life.

On campus, girls swoon over his chiseled looks. A charismatic speaker, Percy is a frequent guest on TV and radio for a segment called *The Orient in the News*. At the university, Percy establishes the Institute of Asiatic Affairs and organizes regional meetings. He writes and mails—largely at his own expense—a bimonthly report on the Orient to around five hundred interested parties. And he is faculty sponsor of the university's International Club. These are not traditional career-making moves for a professor, but then Percy is hardly typical. His classes are routinely packed due to not only his mastery of the subject but also his propensity to enliven things: Occasionally he catapults himself into the classroom through the transom, then smooths back his thick hair and delivers a riveting lecture on the Far East.

"Hello, I'm president of the university," he says to pretty coeds. "Anything I can do for you?"

Percy approaches the hallowed halls of academe with a gleam in his eye—which earns him the mistrust of colleagues, and tenure by a hair.

THE YEAR Percy is voted "Oklahoman of the Year," Max is a junior. Curious to see what the fuss is about, he enrolls in Percy's class on the Far East and is instantly hooked by the charismatic professor. Soon the terrible anxiety that afflicts Max and drives him to despair about the future begins to abate—replaced by an acute interest in Asia. He becomes Percy's protégé.

Upon graduation, Percy floats an idea. He calls it an Experiment in Understanding: Twelve students. Three months. Seven countries. "It is *not* a pleasure trip," he specifies. "You will travel third class, stay with middle- and lower-class families along the way, and conform to local customs. There will be no porters, so take only what you can carry." In each country, the students will live with locals, eating, sleeping, and working as their hosts do. On the itinerary: Japan, Singapore, Indonesia, Thailand, Malaysia, the Philippines, and Hong Kong.

Interestingly, almost all these countries are newly vulnerable to Communism.

To Max, it is a long-awaited passport out of Oklahoma.

ON JUNE 15, 1956, Max and eleven other students board the SS *President Cleveland* out of San Francisco. The group includes Owen Butler and a part-time student in her forties, Alberta Pennington. On board, Max and his classmates are known as "the group from Oklahoma" and solidify their reputation by singing the title song to *Oklahoma!* at the passenger talent show. At night, Max sleeps on deck—a relief from the feverish steerage cabins, until the crew hoses down the decks just before dawn. A luxury liner the SS *Cleveland* is not. "One crew member has a delightful game he likes to play," he writes in his diary. "It's called 'Wake Up Max.' No matter where I sleep on deck, he finds me promptly at 7 A.M. The first morning he ensnared me with ropes."

Other European and American lines refused to carry Americans in steerage, claiming it lowers the prestige of Westerners in Asia, but Percy has somehow booked the Sooners in "Asiatic Third Class"—along with three hundred Japanese, Chinese, Indians, Filipinos, Malays, and Indonesians, all jammed into the poorly lit, labyrinthine cabins and recreation areas at the back end of the ship. It is like a floating Asian dorm. In the dining room Max attacks Japanese salads with chopsticks—and finds it impossible to get the ingredients into his mouth without sending bits of peas, celery, onions, and boiled beef flying.

Daytimes in the passenger lounge, Percy teaches class. Nights the group sees first-run movies like *The Egyptian* or *Johnny Concho*. There are dances. Concerts. The air-cooled lounges have tables for cards, checkers, or chatting. Max particularly enjoys talking up returning Asians and finds their impressions of America endlessly fascinating. He writes up his first story, "Grove Student Meets Homeward Bound Chinese," and sends it to the *Miami News Record*. A couple of the students have signed on to write articles about their trip—at twenty-five dollars per, it will easily pay for their souvenirs and a few dinners.

But halfway across the Pacific, misfortune strikes. Percy suffers a massive heart attack—then a second. He summons Max to his cabin. "The pains were still hitting him when I got there," Max writes in his diary. "There was no doctor aboard the ship and there was nothing we could do for him. Although I agree with Percy in most of his philosophy, he made the following statement to me. 'If something should happen to me, have my body cremated and scattered in the Pacific. Don't send it home. All the reservations are already made, so you can finish the trip if you want to. Everything is taken care of. Alberta and I have a joint checking account.'"

A joint bank account with a student? Max is touched that Percy trusts him and Alberta, and tells the others Percy has a bad cold. Over the following forty-eight hours, Max and Alberta, and later a fellow student, Martha Watson, take turns mopping Percy's forehead with a cool cloth, bringing food, and, when Percy is not looking, washing his clothes. When Alberta tells Percy about this, Max writes, "he wiped a tear off his face. That was more than enough thanks." For several days, the threesome hover over their ailing professor.

By the time Port Yokohama looms on the horizon, Percy has recovered and Max has begun calling him "Old Walrus" and teasing him with songs like "Too Old to Cut the Mustard." The incident has bonded the men— but it sets Martha wondering: Exactly what was the nature of Percy's relationship with Alberta?

In Bali, the group tours the island on the back of a pickup truck, and when it runs out of gas, they sing "Oklahoma!" to the locals.

In Singapore, Max visits Singlop Lane—an enclave where the Chinese take their elderly to die, twenty-five to a room. Max and Owen serenade them with "Enjoy Yourself, It's Later Than You Think."

In Kuala Lumpur, they stay at a Chinese whorehouse.

In Manila, they dine on *balut*—developing duck embryos. Glancing into the swirl of bilious purple, green, and gray in his bowl, Max thinks he sees a bluish eyelid and tiny pinfeathers and nearly loses consciousness.

In Batangas, a cockfight.

Endless hours are spent comparing the price of cigarettes, shoes, and shirts with locals or answering questions about democracy and segregation in the United States. Everywhere they go, the students are treated like dignitaries or movie stars—posing with politicians and followed by a pack of fascinated children who scamper when Max takes a step toward them. "I can't understand why," he writes. "I'm only 6-foot-3." But by the time they land in Manila, the group has noticed an odd pattern: After disembarking, Alberta and Percy always leave the group. "Quite mysterious," Martha Watson later recalls. "In most ports, they'd go off and we'd never see them until it was time to leave."

Although Owen thinks they are an item, Martha's intuition tells her otherwise. Back home, there had been a flurry of stories in the university press about the Experiment in Understanding—including a prominent cover photo of Alberta, Percy, Owen, and Max. Martha knew that people went out of the way to hide affairs, not publicize them on page one. Percy was married. He was also an ordained minister and admired professor hoping for tenure.

There are other things. Percy had promised they would stay with the locals—but after crossing the Pacific in steerage, several students find themselves housed by prime ministers, generals, mayors, diplomats, university professors, and business titans. Martha has a fleeting thought: "I began to wonder if Percy and Alberta were with the CIA. Think about it, we were a bunch of students abroad in Asia—it was a perfect cover. This was 1956. The shadow of Communism was everywhere we turned."

IN THAILAND, Max finds the Orient he dreamed about—deer who nuzzle your palm, the *clang* of temple bells, Chinese hawkers, the overcrowded buses loaded up with people, pigs, chickens, and ducks. Up north, women up to their knees in mud and water plant terraced rice fields while the dying rays of sunlight glaze the slopes. The sight of these things brings him to a state of near worship—life, it is so fragile and dirty and beautiful. People say Bangkok is filthy, and they are right. It is also the holiest place Max has ever seen. Up and down the Chao Phraya river, Max sees the diseased, the miserable, the homeless and the ill. Men with goiters. Three-month-old babies with adult-sized heads. Lepers. "When I see all the injustice and misery, I don't feel sorry for the people but just mad enough to want to do something about it. I'm like a philanthropist without money," he writes to Dolly. "This is the hardest letter I've had to write. I won't be returning to America. I've decided to stay in Thailand. I plan to use my time here canvassing in the fields of education and health care."

The OU students throw him a party. "Several of the girls cried. Percy couldn't say anything," Max writes. "He's been like a father to me on this trip . . . he even gave me $10 for my birthday."

His final gift to Max is a job and a place to stay. Percy has secured a position for Max at the American University Language Association, and accommodations with General Sudasna, the head of the Army Staff and Command College. "If I do not experience a good cross-section of the country, then it won't be the General's fault. Every other sentence is aimed at this objective. He keeps apologizing because his family isn't middle class. He is really a card—he cusses like a sailor and we get along perfectly."

OVER THE NEXT FEW MONTHS, a volley of letters flies over the Pacific detailing Max's life in Thailand, his impressions, his experiences teaching English. He touches on spicy Thai food and marvels at the fruit that grows roadside—a variety of coconuts, mangos, mangosteens, and a type of grape that puts the Concord to shame. He gains fifteen pounds. "I sincerely enjoy this teaching racket," he writes. "It takes a great deal of patience and a smattering of knowledge." The racket must have been particularly good because soon Max takes another position teaching English at the YWCA. Then the general asks him to teach a course in geography at the Army College. At twenty-two, Max holds down a full courseload all over Bangkok.

He particularly enjoys his courses at the Y. After class, his students ply him with icy Cokes, candy, and fruit piled so high Carmen Miranda would have bowed down in humility. Then Max plays "Chopsticks" on the piano and reads the girls' palms—first dusting each with a handker-chief, which sends the girls into high peals of laughter. "Other Americans are proud and snobbish," one tells him, "but everyone likes you." The Thai are not too fond of two nationalities—the Japanese for their war atrocities and the Chinese for their stronghold on business, but lately everyone is cussing American imperialism too. "I was sorry and humble at this re-mark," he writes in his diary that night. "I hope to be a different kind of American."

And he is. In Chiangmai, Max hitches a plow to a carabao and volun-teers to till the fields. When children shout *"Farang!"* ("Foreigner!") as Max goes by, he yells right back: *"Mai chai. Pen khon Thai!"* ("That's not right, I'm a Thai!") And when the skies open, Max continues working in mud up to his knees, plowing ten perfectly straight rows—sealing his accomplish-ment with a glass of palm wine and the applause of a small crowd of locals, who survey his accomplishment from under a shed. "I'm happier than I've been in a long time," he writes Dolly. "I'm busy nearly all the time now, but

I don't have that terrible feeling of ambition constantly. It's sort of like living in a dream—although I'm not on opium yet."

He attends a Benny Goodman concert in Lumpini Park.

Goes deep sea fishing and catches nothing but a sunburn.

Plays chess under the rising moon.

Travels to Burma.

In dimly lit back-alley restaurants he sits in rickety chairs and samples fiery cuisines served up by saucy waitresses.

But his favorite hours are spent on the Chao Phraya river. Boarding a ramshackle boat, Max floats past temples and houses, opium dens and late-night dance clubs from which the cha-cha blares, past teahouses in which he has slurped bowls of spicy noodles and bathers who use the river as their personal bathtub. One night he sees locals launching their own boats from the shorelines—tiny vessels fashioned from banana leaves, cradling flowers and small candles—and quickly finds himself surrounded by a slow-moving maelstrom of light and incense, gold coin and flower petal. It is the loveliest thing he's ever seen.

MAX HAS BEEN IN THAILAND three months when the general summons him to a special social function. At 1900 hours on the dot, Max appears downstairs doused with a bit too much lemon verbena cologne and finds the general in full military regalia. Shortly thereafter two Rolls-Royces pull up. A door opens.

And there sits the king of Thailand.

"Get into the second car," the general commands. For a half hour Max rolls through Bangkok, running his hand along the Rolls's plush interior—wood accents, meal trays, baby blue leather seats. *I'm riding in the king's Silver Cloud*, Max thinks. He lights a cigarette and blows plumes out the window. Three months ago he'd arrived in Bangkok knowing no one—now he is in the king's entourage. A half hour later the Rolls pulls up outside Bangkok's oldest movie house, the Sala Chalermkrung, and Max is escorted to balcony seats by two statuesque women in traditional Thai dress. The theater routinely plays American fare to packed houses, but to-night the theater is empty. Inside, Max sees the general and the king sitting below. Spicy papaya and fruit juice are brought. The lights go down. And for the next two hours, Max finds himself watching *The King and I* with the king of Thailand.

Unfortunately, the Hollywood version of Thailand is one of Siamese twins, white elephants, and giggly, deferential women, and the king is a despot with multiple wives and slaves. Essentially, he is Rousseau's noble savage updated. In the balcony, Max's head swings like a pendulum be-tween Yul Brynner and the smaller, quieter monarch below, silhouetted by Hollywood's shadow. *What is he thinking?* Two hours later, King Bhumi-bol's picture flashes across the screen, and Max stands at attention while the national anthem plays. If King Bhumibol has been insulted, he does not let on. With a serene face, he climbs back into his Rolls.

Back at the house, the general explains that the king had heard about the movie and, wanting to see what the fuss was about, hired the general to be his bodyguard for the evening. The following day, *The King and I* is banned, and anyone caught showing the movie will be subject to a strict fine and jail term.

Max had attended the first—and last—showing of that film.

Again and again, Max thinks about the movie. It is a silly movie, but on some deeper level it is a reflection of something he struggles with. Like its heroine, Anna, he had come to Thailand and stayed to educate the people, which he believes is the key to lifting the country out of pov-erty. "Buddhism is changing in Thailand," he writes. "The religion, as you know, places emphasis on spiritual, and not material, well-being. In my esteemed opinion, this has held the country back. Because the people see TV sets, cars, radios, etc., they naturally want them. The religion is then forced to adhere—but still retaining something of the old. These days priests give sermons on TV. This is beginning to snowball and in a country where 80% of the people are farmers, and about the same % of illiterates, it could be tough. Education is the answer, but it's a question of time."

Max has devoted himself to education, with questionable results. "The rose-colored glasses have slipped off my nose," he writes Dolly. "I thought I knew quite a bit about Asia and the people here. I now see how really ignorant I was. I had the mistaken idea my presence here would magically raise the standard of living, help the people, etc. I was a real missionary. On this score I was entirely wrong. I now see that my training in Far Eastern affairs has not helped them. It has been of immeasurable help to me, it is true, but none whatsoever to them. But this isn't the worst part. I find that I am now indifferent to pain and suffering. This is terrible to admit but true nonetheless. And I'm not that old yet!"

His letters home turn snippy and dark. "If it doesn't start a downpour soon, no one will be able to plant rice, which means that taxes will go up in the States, due to the fact that half the nation will be on public welfare, which means that the Thai politicians will get richer, because they'll be taking a large scrape off the great big bundle of dough we'll give Thailand." A season abroad has toughened Max, turned him into—if not a cynic, then a realist about American assistance.

GIVEN THE POVERTY AND ILLITERACY, it is no surprise Thailand is the latest battleground for Communism. Recently American weapons sales to Thailand have skyrocketed to $56 million, strange for a Buddhist nation, but Thailand holds an important position in the rim of free countries ringing Red China, and Eisenhower wants to keep it that way. The CIA has set up a dummy firm to train Thai police in guerrilla warfare and sabotage operations. Ex–U.S. ambassador Peurifoy is himself an ex-CIA man with an intimate network of relationships with top-tier Thai politicians. By the time Max arrives, there are upward of two hundred CIA agents in Thailand, the cumulative effect of which is to launch an even more virulent strain of anti-Americanism.

Max watches all this with a guarded eye. "I am thoroughly convinced ██████ is a spook," he writes in his diary. "Took me about a month to figure out. He's pretty clever about it—or was at first. Thinks I have the mentality of a juvenile and has gotten a bit sloppy. Someone should reprimand him about this. I'm sure there's a full file on me now in Bangkok."

Soon his own diary entries began to read like intelligence briefings. "The US supports General Pibul with guns and training, but the middle class, students, and intellectuals are very discouraged. They say the US is directly and indirectly suppressing them. Needless to say, the middle class, students, and intellectuals are ripe for communism." To his mother, Max cautions, "Please don't ask me anything about this in your letters and DO NOT repeat it. Please don't have any of my letters published, or any information that I may send. It's okay to tell people, but don't let it get into print. I have a good reason for this."

Meanwhile, Max continues to write for the *News Record* with an eye toward the shifting Asiatic sands. He covers topics like the growing threat of Communism in Singapore. The burgeoning nationalist movement in the Philippines. Thailand's culture and economy. For a twenty-two-year-old from Grove, Max shows a surprising facility for geopolitics.

And for making contacts: "I'm getting to know quite a few interesting people," he writes. The daughter of the prime minister. The director of the National Defense College. The American vice consul. A Thai intelligence agent who takes Max to the section of the city where they sell imported goods from Red China.

When the winter term concludes, the AUA director calls him into the office and gives him a new assignment: university troubleshooter. The AUA program is run under the auspices of the U.S. Information Agency—a propaganda arm of the State Department. Fueled by a budget of two billion dollars, the USIA is the largest full-scale public relations agency in the world, working to promote American interests and counteract the insidious creep of Communism.

"Troubleshooter? Does this mean I'll be out shooting Communists and tigers?" Max jokes.

In fact, Max will be traveling to university outposts with administrative difficulties. Up north, enrollment in the AUA program is falling—fast. Udorn is considered the wild frontier of Thailand, overrun with gangs, gamblers, smugglers, and drug addicts. Because the people here are known to be passive, it is considered particularly susceptible to the Communist threat.

But Max's presence in Udorn has no effect on falling enrollment. He writes letters browbeating the AUA for more money, promotes the school every chance he gets, rejiggers the curriculum—to no avail. He is beginning to suspect that they dispatched him up here to get rid of him, and he is almost certainly right. Like all other bureaucracies, the AUA has a way of doing things. And Max is a bit *too* rigorous.

By the time the Udorn program is shut down, Max has been abroad for fifteen months and is ready to return home. Percy has written about a couple of good job prospects in Washington for Max, and Max has asked his parents to orchestrate the details with Percy, cautioning them not to refer to either job by name from now on, because the letter might fall into the wrong hands. "Mrs. Ruby Portugal is with job number 1. And job number 2 is you-know-who." Just to be safe, he requested they forward his mail to the American embassy.

In his year abroad, Max has contracted malaria and the flu, skin rashes and blistering boils, fevers and chills—but has long since ceased to be the susceptible boy from Grove. Something in him has deeply changed. By the time he flies home on August 17, 1957, Max has traversed over fifty thousand miles, picked up a language, and dispensed with his Oklahoman drawl and innocence.

"If I don't get the job in Washington, I might try school again," he writes Dolly. "With a Masters, I'd be just a skip away from being a doctor. Doctor Copeland! I've always wanted a title like that."

CYRUS

On my third night in Grove, Owen popped a DVD into the computer, and flickering images of my father sprung to life. There was the Asia group palling around on the deck of the SS *Cleveland*, flirting with the camera, all coy smiles and lit cigarettes. And there were Percy and Alberta. I was shocked at how short Percy was, yet clearly the master of ceremonies. And handsome. Percy had the kind of face that belonged on money. Suddenly my father's face fills the screen in a close-up so close you can almost see his pores.

"That's Max. That's Old Soupy," Owen said.

With horn-rim glasses and a wide smile, Max looked less like a spy and more like a lanky goofball. A succession of tinted images followed: Alcatraz. The Golden Gate Bridge. Percy and Max ringed with pink Hawaiian leis. Footage of Max standing on a water buffalo as it blithely lumbered through the fields. "Your father and I and Percy would pull pranks and do things no one else would do," Owen said. "Max in particular would tell you something and leave you hanging and wondering about it."

Or not tell you something and leave you wondering about it.

After three days of traveling the length and breadth of my father's hometown, searching for clues about the boy he was and the man he became, my hunger to know about Max's life now bordered on obsession. I'd retraced his steps to school. Just yesterday, on the kind of brisk sunny day when I imagine my father had herded cattle across hill and dale with his dog Pup, I visited the Copeland ranch. Sadly, the ranch house had burned to the ground only months before, and in its place was a small pile of con-crete slabs and brick. It was a hole in the center of a glorious landscape that stretched out in all directions.

"I used to visit Max there," his friend Juanita Lee recalled. "We used to ride horses to Woodward Hollow and herd cattle to another pasture, through the woods. I loved that old house. Downstairs was a ping-pong table where we played for hours. Max could step back from the table and whip around and knock you off.

"You know, your father was fairly quiet, but he could joke and cut up. Didn't go in for sports or the band. Really nice and polite. Very intelligent. Mannerly. Treated you with respect, and smart as they come. He loved the outdoors and hunting and fishing. Is there any truth to the rumors?"

"Sorry?"

"I heard he was a CIA agent," she said with considerable forthrightness. "Someone said he was held for ransom at an airport. I heard he was killed by the Vietcong."

Max—killed by the Vietcong? I laughed. Then realized: Juanita had gotten the details wrong, but the CIA rumors had traveled all the way back to Grove. And they didn't match up with the *Tehran Times* story. Which made me wonder if perhaps the secret to my father's CIA past was buried here in his hometown.

So I started asking around.

"I can't say for certain, but I always thought Percy was the CIA's rep on campus—and that he'd recruited Max," Andy Coats told me. Coats was dean of the University of Oklahoma Law School. "They used to call us the Boulevard boys. We'd gather in the afternoon for a quick coffee on Univer-sity Boulevard with all the other fraternity brothers. Have you talked to Bill Comfort?"

Bill Comfort was a high-powered financier who'd been on the same trip as Max. "There wasn't any doubt in my mind that your father was CIA," he said. "Or that Percy used our trip to recruit him. It was just an accepted fact. He paid an unusual amount of attention to your father. Percy had an effect on people—he was quite charismatic and good-looking. Spitting image of Rudolph Valentino. We all fell under his spell. And my God, what an ego!

"Your father was one of the smartest men I knew. He shot out of Grove like a cannonball—imagine what a boy like that was doing in Grove? He couldn't stay there. But then you gotta ask: What was a young man of twenty-two doing in Thailand, taking a year out of his life to learn an obscure language that had zero application elsewhere? It was Percy. He was grooming him for other things. Didn't you ever ask Max directly if he was CIA?"

"No."

"Why not?" Bill said, utterly astonished.

Stupidity. The disinterest of an adolescent. The desire to forget all about the worst chapter of our lives.

"And Max never talked about Percy being CIA?"

"Never."

"Makes sense. You don't accuse the guy who brought you to the party."

Martha Watson, Katie Elliott, Lonnie Chestnutt—one by one, I reached out to the students who'd been on Percy's trip and heard the same thing: Percy was CIA and had probably recruited Max. The only one who didn't suggest it was Owen, who perhaps found it hard to imagine his professor and best friend had held out.

I reread Max's yearbook, letters, and journals for signs he'd been cultivating a career in intelligence. Several things struck me:

1. Max had been president of OU's foreign student program under Percy's tutelage. There were 225 international students in the program, but Max and Percy hatched a plan to double the number. "Only a year old, under the direction of Max Copeland, the program has flowered into a full-time job for Copeland," a *Daily* editorial read. OU's international program would have been prime fishing grounds for the CIA.

2. The year Max went abroad, the CIA began a covert practice of using American journalists overseas. The journalists provided a range of covert services to the Agency—from simple intelligence gathering to serving as go-betweens with undercover agents. The journalists ranged from Pulitzer Prize winners from the *New York Times*, Time-Life, Hearst, Reuters, and *Newsweek* to everyday correspondents who found their association with the Agency helped their work. Carl Bernstein had documented the practice in an explosive *Rolling Stone* piece. The operation had a name: Mockingbird.

3. Whether Max was a part of Mockingbird is unknown, but from the moment he stepped onto the SS *President Cleveland*, Max began filing stories—on families returning to Communist China, on Asiatic views of U.S. foreign policy, on Filipino politics and culture, on the declining Communist influence in Malaya, on the creep of Communism in Thailand.

4. In his year abroad, he had cultivated an impressive set of contacts—presidents, prime ministers, businessmen, mayors, professors, missionaries, and of course General Sudasna, who'd invited Max to teach at the Army Defense College where he'd "met every general in Thailand."

5. Max had a good eye for international forecasting. "I predicted trouble in Singapore and they're having the devil. I predicted a new U.S. policy toward neutralist nations, this has also come true. A better U.S.-Filipino relationship after Richard Nixon's speech, bad relations between American tourists and Thais—all of which have come to pass."

6. Then—the red herrings, the maddeningly opaque allusions to secret jobs in Washington and repeated admonishments to his parents

about staying mum. "I've got a little surprise for you pretty soon. As soon as I get a little information I'll tell you. Must swear you to the strictest secrecy, tho." "Some friends of Percy's are here. Seems they saw him not too long ago. They've been trying to find me for about three weeks . . ." "I'm applying for a job with the US Information Agency this coming week . . . but job No. 2 is still my desire."

And then there was Percy. By now I'd become a bit infatuated with the missionary-turned-professor who looked like Rudolph Valentino. He was long dead. I found a clipping from the *Oklahoma Daily*, Wednesday, June 13, 1956: My dad is pictured on the front page in a grainy black-and-white photograph, alongside Owen, Percy, and Alberta. They are loading luggage onto a bus. *Students Start Tour of Asia*, the headline reads. Looking closely at the photograph, I saw a young man with a duffel bag, lighting out for the future.

"Our trip will be the proving grounds in more ways than one," my father had written in his journal that night. "It will point out our strengths and weaknesses. And it will show Percy what we are capable of doing, individually speaking."

None of this was proof, of course. I was cherry-picking through my father's past, and he could as well have been aiming for a career in international journalism, or diplomacy. There was no smoking gun. But just when I was getting ready to admit that this had been a lovely if indeterminate trip filled with hearsay and circumstantial details, I saw a sentence in his journal that I'd missed.

In Yokohama we met up with Don Buchanan at the home of Mr. and Mrs. Vick Briggs.

Unbeknownst to anyone in Grove, Percy Buchanan had a son. Don Buchanan was now living in Massachusetts—and according to his Facebook page, he was enjoying retirement from a thirty-year career at the Central Intelligence Agency.

And with that revelation, my father's past began to unravel.

"THAT'S MY UNCLE! Norman Briggs. Ruth and Norman Briggs. I remember that house . . ."

The voice on the line sounded friendly, a bit gravelly and avuncular. I had reached Don Buchanan over his morning coffee, and coincidentally he had been reading Percy's letters and memoirs—the effect of which had put him in a nostalgic mood. For a good hour we raised our fathers from the dead. He told me that Percy was an accomplished composer and judo master. A practical jokester. A friend of Albert Einstein. They used to perform at Princeton parties, Percy singing while Einstein accompanied him on the violin ("not very well," according to Dad), after which Percy often sent his daughter Ruth over for help with her math homework. Don also told me stories about his own career in counterintelligence in Japan, India, and Vietnam—"looking for the Commies who were looking for us." CIA agents by nature aren't talkative, but retirement had evidently cured Don of any laconic tendencies.

"So . . . was Percy CIA?" I finally asked.

"In Japan when I was growing up, everyone thought we were spies. We weren't. We were missionaries. Dad didn't believe in mixing God and politics. It was only later that he did intelligence work for the Agency. They tapped Dad for a couple of assignments. First Korea to study the psychology of Reds in combat. Later at OU, Dad was what we called an OO contact. As an operations officer, basically he would keep his eyes open and report back to us. Percy would recruit and handle sources with access to vital intelligence."

"Did Percy recruit my dad?"

"He would never say—and I would never ask—but that was his job,"

Don said matter-of-factly. "My father had excellent people skills; he was good at identifying sources and putting them to work. If your father was in a position to get information to the U.S. government, my father was willing to get him to do it."

It was as close to a CIA confession as I was likely to get. I thanked Don and hung up, promising to stay in touch.

A FINAL READ-THROUGH of Max's diary provided one last clue. The morning of June 16, 1956—the day he'd set sail—Percy had arranged for Max to interview with the Asia Foundation in San Francisco. The foundation had been founded two years earlier to support development and citizen diplomacy in Asia. On the surface, the foundation was a bright-eyed outreach program that arranged student exchange programs, academic symposiums, and research scholarships designed to promote interest in the East. But the foundation wasn't what it appeared to be. It wouldn't become known for another decade, but the Asia Foundation was one of several covert dummy organizations the CIA used as a front for recruiting foreign agents and new officers.

"Come see us when you return stateside," they told Max.

If there was a more obvious link to my father's association with the Agency, I didn't know what it was.

AND SO MY FATHER'S Experiment in Understanding was the beginning of my own. It had taken a trip to Grove, but I finally cracked open my father's past—and the light of recognition that shone through the cracks illuminated subsequent events. After Max returned to Washington in 1957 and married my mother, he became a Fulbright officer, sending hundreds of scholars to countries like Egypt, Afghanistan, Cyprus, Turkey, Greece, and Iran. During that time he lived in Arlington, a mere forty miles from

Langley. Later, as director of the Pahlavi-Penn program, he recruited over 350 professors to return to Iran and made a name for himself in Iranian-American circles—then moved to Iran.

Like Thailand in the fifties, Iran in the seventies was a fast-changing country where the West had a significant stake. Both countries were buffers against Communism with ex-CIA ambassadors, CIA-trained police forces, a small army of CIA agents on the ground, and a growing strain of anti-Americanism. Both had monarchs who purchased millions in American military equipment. As he'd done fifteen years before, Max hunkered down in close proximity to military resources—teaching ESL at an army command center while working for Hughes Aircraft, and later Westinghouse.

I remembered other things—business trips. Thumbing through his passport, I saw that it was scarred by a steady stream of stamps from London, Munich, Helsinki, Amsterdam, Philadelphia, all within a year of the revolution. Max had returned from these trips with stories about West End shows, gourmet meals, and winning a hundred pounds at blackjack in London—all of which hung like a promissory note. *Let's get through this revolution, kids, and head back to the good life.* That was October 1979 and he'd returned a newly energized man.

Within a month he was languishing in prison.

OVER THE NEXT WEEKS, I continued chatting with Don, feeling like I'd wandered into an emotional support group for CIA sons. At eighty-five, Don was still piecing his father's life together, and he sent me chapters from Percy's unpublished memoir. They contained nothing revelatory—other than Percy's impression of Max as an "adventurous jokester." Alberta was "quiet and helpful." There was no mention of a heart attack, shared bank account, secret jobs in Washington. It wasn't for lack of space. He devoted a full page to talking about coconuts.

A slew of information flew back and forth—e-mails, files, photos—all driven by the insatiable need to know our fathers. I eventually told Don about Percy's heart attack, how he'd requested Max to scatter his ashes at sea, and Don got quiet.

"That's just what I did," he said after a few seconds, his voice cracking with emotion. "Flew up a plane and flung his ashes into the ocean." Our fathers had been linked in life and death, and now as we retold their stories, we were too.

The professor and his protégé. I wondered if Max and Percy had somehow orchestrated this friendship between Don and me in a bid to have their secret lives finally known and celebrated. Percy had labored for twenty-three years at OU without much recognition. The administration had routinely passed him over for promotions and salary bumps. In 1971, the university had given him a plaque and a party and sent him off to retirement. Having befriended world leaders, launched covert operations, signed up agents, and battled Communism, Percy retreated to a senior community in Oxnard at age seventy, where he spent the balance of his mornings gazing out across the Pacific.

"It was one thing after another with Percy," his colleague Russ Buhite recalled. "He made contacts easily and was well known in Asia. And he had an astounding capacity to make contact with people and energize relationships—and some students. But he wasn't a scholar. I think he published one book. Frankly, I'm shocked to hear that he was CIA."

"Yeah, I'm kinda shocked that my father was CIA, too."

"Oh?"

"I mean, you hear about all those 'enhanced interrogations,' the assassinations and extraordinary renditions and black sites . . ."

Professor Buhite set me straight. "Back then there was no stigma to the CIA. Remember, the cold war was serious business in the fifties. We had a real enemy in the Soviets and Chinese. Most people in policy positions and even academe saw the Soviet Union as having taken the place of Nazi Germany, and confronting that was a badge of honor.

"The CIA was more of a classical spy agency in those days, not a paramilitary operation. Oh, I have little doubt that they were involved in many black-bag operations and assassinations. In the fifties, the CIA blew up a plane carrying high-ranking officials of the People's Republic of China. They did lots of nefarious things back then that we don't associate with democracy, but not the same ways that we've seen since September 11. I had a student who joined the CIA in 1979. I didn't consider it a mark of dishonor that he took this job, but I think if I had a student now with the Agency, I wouldn't be happy with it. Your father probably did it for patriotic reasons," Professor Buhite said.

And to leave Grove, I thought.

To a rancher's son fueled by "a virtual fear of being a failure," it must've sounded like a lifeline. Secrecy and fear collided with knowledge and adventure, and out of this cold war cocktail my father emerged bright and lucid, looking for his place in the world.

ONE MORE THING. I can't tell you how many times—over drinks, at dinner parties and barbecues—I heard the same refrain spoken by Max's friends who saw Max in the way I moved, spoke, and looked. "You are your father's son." All my life I'd worked hard at emulating my mom, her exuberance and talent at life, so it was a shock to discover that my father had filtered through anyway. I began to count the ways this was true. His checked emotion. His hunger for the horizon. His astonishing capacity to lose himself in a country and adapt, chameleon-like. His faithful trust in his own intellect, his almost devotional love of nature, his insatiable love of travel . . . the list went on.

Even more surprising, as I read his diary, I calculated that I'd followed in his footsteps—literally. Seven years ago, in Thailand, I'd found myself standing before the AUA school where he had taught English exactly fifty years ago. In Bali, I'd somehow managed to book myself a villa a stone's throw from the palace where Prince Agung had put up the Okies. Had I been following in my father's footsteps all my life? Sometimes at night, I am gripped by the fear that life has stalled. The fear sinks from my head down to the pit of my stomach—and at times like this, I realize I am fundamentally alone. This is my father's fear. I know that. He must have felt very alone in those final months in Iran, his friends and compatriots and colleagues long gone, his embassy occupied, "Death to America" ringing out in a daily chorus across rooftops. The echo of those months in Tehran weighed heavily on him, but he rarely spoke of it. Who dies of a heart attack at age fifty-seven? The doctors said it was a congenital heart defect, but secretly, I wondered if it wasn't the cumulative weight of all those years of unvoiced secrets.

CIA fathers and their sons. Art and Kevin Callahan. Percy and Don Buchanan. It's classical, how we become our parents. I did not follow in these footsteps, of course. But when I called Katayoun to recount my findings, she had a surprise of her own. Apparently Max had tried to plant the seeds of a CIA career with *her*.

"I just always got the sense that he was nudging me in that direction—he thought I'd be good at it," she said.

Katayoun is now a federal prosecutor, a career she wryly ascribes not to our father, but to me. I shouldn't have tormented her so much as a child, she says. All those days during the revolution when I came up with countless nicknames for her? This is the consequence.

There was one more call I needed to make before flying back to Manhattan.

I told her everything. His childhood. The pranks. Number 31 on the football team. The Experiment in Understanding. Everything. She'd heard some of it before, but she listened silently as I drew the brush one last time over the canvas of Max's life. My mother had never been to Grove. Shortly after she got married, Max's parents moved to Texas, and so Max's childhood lay there, contentedly, on the ranch where cattle and sheep once roamed, under the boughs of sycamore, near the lake where he'd once fished, and overlooking the stream in which watercress still grew.

"So you finally agree your father was CIA, then?" she said when I finished the tale.

"I think it's extremely probable that he was an operative, yes."

"It all goes back to that professor; he signed Max up."

"Percy. Yes. Did you ever meet him?"

"I didn't need to. Max spoke about him. I just knew."

Again she grew angry, and again we talked about Dad's association with the CIA. But this time I found myself in a slightly different position, not of defending Max, but insisting that it didn't really matter anymore. Maybe all this was never really about the CIA. Maybe in true-to-movie form, "Max's Radar Affair" was just a device that launched the journey—which was far more consequential than the truth. It was classic Hitchcock. A Max-Guffin. What mattered was I had a dad who'd done some cool things with his life, ventured out into the world, married a remarkable woman, and made a life at the fault lines of East and West. And now I knew him a bit better.

A couple seconds of silence elapsed on the line. "You're just like your father," she finally said.

Then: "I'm glad you went to Grove."

BACK IN MANHATTAN, a letter from the CIA was waiting.

The CIA can neither confirm nor deny the existence or non-existence of records pertaining to your request . . .

The Glomar response was used in matters of national security when any denials by the Agency would confirm that such files exist. It didn't matter. I had already found out everything I wanted to know about my dad.

Someone once told me that on the walls of the CIA headquarters in Langley is an inscription from the apostle John. *Ye shall know the truth and the truth shall make you free.*

But I already knew that.

PARADAIZA LOST

EPILOGUE

Recently, I saw a video on YouTube about a fascinating outer space phenomenon. Seeing our little orb hanging in the darkness, a swirl of blue and white with a paper-thin atmosphere, some five hundred astronauts have reported an epiphany about the profound interconnectedness of everything. From that vantage point, you don't see religious or racial distinctions or national boundaries—rather the beauty and fragility of our planet. You see the dancing curtains of Aurora, passing electrical storms, and the ever-moving line that distinguishes day from night. You see the earth as one living, breathing system. The Overview Effect is a cognitive shift in consciousness, and as I watched the video, I found myself wondering how it was for Max. Was he still proudly American in the afterlife, or had death opened a larger perspective to him?

Thirty-five years after the revolution that tore our family asunder and created a schism between Iran and America, I am at turns disheartened, amused, and exhausted by the energy it takes to demonize another country. Watching Iran and America duke it out on the international stage is like being a child of divorce—Mom says Dad is the Great Satan; Dad calls her the Axis of Evil. All of which guarantees a lengthy therapeutic process for me—three-plus decades on the geopolitical couch. I am Iranian-American. I am the hyphen caught between two homelands that hate each other.

Iranians have another word for people of two cultures: *do-rageh*. Two-veined. But the thing about veins is this: They all lead back to the heart from which they come. What do you do when your homelands hate each other? I can't really launch myself into outer space in search of perspective, but I can do something as simple as visit Iran—six thousand miles that is about as far from America as I can travel. In doing so, maybe I might see my own childhood, and the country that blasted me out of it, anew.

For the record, the State Department strongly counsels against this. But then they have been leading me on for a year and a half now, so I am not likely to take their word on anything.

"Don't go, it's a bad time," my mother cautions. "Sanctions have hit hard. Tensions are high. People are miserable."

Plus: I am the son of a CIA operative.

I buy a ticket anyway. The countdown begins. I shut down my Facebook page—I don't want either government tracking me—and spend the weeks leading up to my departure in a gift-buying frenzy familiar to all returning Iranians. Starbucks mugs. Abercrombie hoodie. Tylenol. Calvin Klein underwear. Cole Haan wallets. I say my good-byes. "Be sure and bring me back some *lavashak*," Katayoun instructs. She loves the pressed sour cherries that burn and color her tongue.

"How about myself safely?" I counter.

Happily in the two weeks that I am in Iran, no one threatens to take me hostage, hurls invectives, or shouts "YANKEE, GO HOME!" On the contrary, perfect strangers invite me to dine. They buy me saffron ice cream and give me agate rings. And despite my vociferous protests they try to set me up—incessantly, which, come to think of it, might well be a form of terrorism after all. In my time in Iran, I come to fear nothing quite so much as the approach of a well-intentioned matchmaker with a gleam in his eye.

Every morning, my cousin wakes me to freshly brewed tea, quince preserves, and unleavened *barbari* bread still warm from the baker. Today the Maleki money is all gone, but you would never know it from the profusion of parties the family hosts in my honor—their tables groaning under the weight of mouthwatering vegetarian stews, grilled fish fresh from the Caspian, sweet-and-sour rice, and sticky rosewater ice cream pressed between wafers. They come bearing gifts. They forgive my mistakes in Farsi. (My favorite: "So, you fucked and fucked until you conceived? Congratulations!")

My ideal place to spend an afternoon is Tehran's Grand Bazaar. An interconnected hive of two thousand shops that harks back to Ali Baba, the bazaar is a four-hundred-year-old living museum of commerce, with pockets of light that fall in from the carved ceiling—creating luminous pools on the ground through which rug merchants, shoeshiners, spice sellers, and thousands of shoppers step lively. Women in chadors float through these corridors like grounded ghosts. Canaries sing. Merchants haggle as only a bazaar merchant can. At six-foot-four with Western looks, I am considerably out of place here.

"Hello, meester, ver ahr you ferom?" the shopkeepers call out.

"Ten thousand *tomans* if you guess," I reply in Farsi, and a lively game ensues. Germany? France? Australia? No one ever guesses right, so I give them a hint:

"Death to . . ."

"Israel?"

"No, the other one."

"America!" they cry in unison, and there is joy at this revelation—all of the revolutionary rancor gone, drained, dead. An American in their midst! What brings me here? Where did I learn Farsi? Have I ever met Jennifer Lopez?

But except for the bazaar, I cannot locate the touchstones of my childhood. Kentucky Fried Chicken? Pizzeria? The Ice Palace? Gone. Instead there are huge congested freeways. Gated houses in northern Tehran that evoke Beverly Hills—a counterpoint to the slums down south. Internet cafés have sprouted. No one has their fist in the air, certainly not the youth who seek out illegal satellite TV, underground parties, or the anonymous freedom of cyberspace. Where is all the passion? The angst? The collective beauty of outraged citizenry? I look around to discover that all the anger, the rancor, the sweet fire of revolution has died—replaced by humdrum lives where people buy pastries, take taxis, and read books as if they hadn't launched Islamic fundamentalism onto an unsuspecting world thirty-five years ago. My first day in Tehran is Valentine's Day and I am pleasantly shocked to find the capital full of young couples clutching roses en route to posh restaurants. *What, did you think that a day of love was only for the West?* my cousin says.

The best proof that the past is the past? Home. Standing outside our old house, I see it has shape-shifted into the oddest thing: the Sudanese embassy. *Our home belongs to Africa.* Inside I find a sleepy custodian and a ghost land. Our kitchen is stacked with brochures inviting you to discover Sudan, covered with a thin veneer of dust. (Has Iran discontinued relations with Sudan as well? The vague mustiness, the lack of bureaucrats behind desks, all suggest another international relationship . . . lost.) The living room is curtained off. Looking up, I see the air-conditioning ducts into which my six-foot-three father crawled to escape on a hunting expedition. My own bedroom is a classroom with desks facing a chalkboard where my John Travolta poster once hung.

I am having a tough time recognizing Iran—like Alice afoot in a wonderland where nothing is as it seems. Come see what is behind the curtain, I am advised when expressing amazement at the nonstop rotation of American movies and TV dramas piped in from Dubai; Iran isn't what you think. Here doublespeak is an art. Public and private lives split. The Great Satan is derided and loved. Here the party line prohibits alcohol, Western music and movies, but behind the curtain? Another party where Beyoncé rules and whiskey flows. Come dance!

Iran is neither the mirthless country of mullahs nor the gleeful country behind the curtain, but a third country that holds the contradiction. On TV, stern-faced women read the news. In the streets, stunning women— some sporting the telltale bandage of rhinoplasty, for in the decades since I left, Iran has become nose-job capital of the world—stop to adjust their headscarves, which fall back in defiant measures to reveal gloriously dyed locks. I see men bowing to Mecca. I see muscular peacocks at the gym. Mullahs in the streets wrapped in billowing robes. Garbage collectors doing calisthenics at two A.M. Yogis lit from meditation. I see a feeble woman in the bazaar wrapped in a chador, clutching a purse emblazoned with Leonardo DiCaprio's face.

A week into my stay, I am beginning to suspect I am on a fool's errand, looking for my past in a country that has rewritten history.

"Iranians have two different storylines today—the story and the truth," Morteza says. We are in a coffee shop hunched over his 110-year-old family album. It is the loveliest fossil, its pages frayed and spotted and alive with history—mostly focusing on his uncle, who clearly had a great sense of humor. Here he is posing as a painter. A hunter. A Cossack. Morteza keeps the album under his bed alongside other relics from the past. "People ask me why I do this, collect and catalog the past. Because the truth is important to me, I answer. It offends me when people lie about history. After the revolution, the government effectively turned Iran's clock back to year zero and rewrote her history. Everything. Street names. University books. In school, I would argue with other kids about this and they'd say: Who knows the truth better, a history book or you? The answer is me."

In a bid to know my own Maleki history, I visit the Malek Museum—founded by the patriarch Haj Hossein Agha Malek, and located in a gated enclave in the National Garden in central Tehran. As I stroll through the collection of paintings, books, ancient Qurans, and tiny coins that go back to the foundation of the Persian empire, I remember a story my mother told about how the queen of England wanted to purchase his coin collection. "It's not for sale," Haj Hossein Agha replied, then with Maleki panache informed the queen that he should be happy to buy *hers*. Iran was for Iranians, he believed. At the time he died at age 101, his endowments to the public were estimated at well over $100 million.

Upon leaving the museum, I find myself directly facing a majestic Greco-Roman edifice, but with classical Persian accents.

"That's the Foreign Ministry," a passerby informs me.

The Foreign Ministry? The very place where my mother repeatedly sparred with Sadegh Ghotbzadeh? I stand there for the longest time, astonished that these two buildings are directly parallel to each other. My bloodlines and the bedrock of international relations. Several times during the course of my stay, I will arrive at a place or a particular moment and feel that it is some kind of marker—a sign that I am on a sort of path, and all I have to do is pay attention. I will come to discover Iran is a particularly responsive country in this regard. Many times I think of a food, a person, a book—and moments later there it is. This is different. In a city of two thousand square kilometers, it seems highly improbable that these two buildings should face each other like graceful adversaries, as Shahin and Sadegh once had.

A WORD ABOUT THE MAN who once ruled the ministry. They say the revolution eats its children, and Sadegh was no exception. Three months, that's how long it took for him to fall from dizzying political heights to *persona non grata*. The month after Sadegh saw Shahin for the last time, he told the Soviet Union if they did not withdraw from Afghanistan, Iran would arm the Afghan *mujaheddin*. The KGB retaliated by circulating forged letters about Sadegh's complicity in freeing the Argo diplomats, leaking rumors that Sadegh had taken a six-million-dollar bribe for helping smuggle them out of Iran, and producing a cache of false documents showing that Sadegh was a CIA agent. A forged check also surfaced. The check bore an interesting notation in the memo line: "For release of American hostages."

Whether it was the actions of the KGB, or the militant students at the embassy, or Khomeini himself that was the source of Sadegh's undoing is unclear. Whatever the cause, in the summer of 1980, he resigned.

Sadegh went into publishing. He founded a newspaper titled *Valiasr*, named for the Quranic verse imploring Moslems to turn to faith. The mullahs shut it down.

Sadegh went on TV and exhorted the people to revolt. He was imprisoned.

Released from prison, Sadegh began planning a countercoup—but his plan was the biggest open secret in Iran. When Khomeini got wind of it, he declared those who fought against the revolution were "corrupt criminals of the earth" and would be put to death.

A cowboy, that's how Hamilton Jordan remembered Sadegh. But unlike a movie cowboy, Sadegh did not ride off into the sunset. That spring, he rented a house 150 yards from Khomeini's residence and instructed a rebel group to aim rockets at the venerated ayatollah's home. Sadegh intended to blow his onetime mentor to smithereens. But he was caught and imprisoned again. Hauled before the cameras, Sadegh spoke in a soft monotone.

"I was seeking to overthrow the government, not the Islamic Republic. From the beginning, I expected the plan to kill Imam Khomeini, but then I reconsidered. I wanted him saved, but I didn't know how to go about it. The final decision was to have been made in the days following my arrest."

He didn't apologize. Sadegh's final words echoed that of an American revolutionary: "Free me or execute me."

And so they executed him. In the Oedipal tradition, the son kills the father, but the revolution proved Iran would no longer follow in Western footsteps. After a kangaroo trial, Sadegh was executed at daybreak—shot from the legs up. It took him five hours to die.

In his forty-five years, Sadegh had traveled the world, met with renegades like Yasser Arafat and Muammar Qadaffi, and planned to build an Islamic coalition that would change the world. Instead he found himself undone by forces beyond his control or comprehension. Just before his execution, he asked a prison guard to smuggle a note out. "I want the record to be clear that I saw the light and tried as best I could to undo the damage I had done by supporting the satanic regime of mullahs."

Sadegh's body was tossed in an anonymous grave outside Tehran. But by then Sadegh had died and been reborn dozens of times. Death was nothing. It was a chrysalis—a cocoon from which he would reemerge to fight another fight. Even in death Sadegh lived. When pictures of his corpse appeared in newspapers the following day, people whispered it wasn't him. In his final months, he'd grown a bushy black beard, but in the photo his beard was entirely white. There were reported sightings of him in Paris. Beirut. Syria. All his old haunts. As though Sadegh's ghost were still earthbound, hoping to jump-start yet another revolution, another fight, another call against the marauders who'd butchered and betrayed the cause.

AFTER A WEEK IN TEHRAN, I hop a plane to Shiraz—the idyllic, sun-soaked city where I'd spent five years of my childhood. Dubbed the City of Wine and Roses by Hafez, Shiraz had a reputation for bacchanalia that wasn't without merit. The city had given birth to the Shiraz wine grape, a purple muse that fed the imagination of poets and plebes and put down roots in the earth's farthest corners—only to be excommunicated from her now-dry home. But I was a boy here once and am back in search of other treasures: The cherry soft-serve at Chencheneh. The outlying gardens heavy with fruit. The cinema where I glimpsed my first flash of nudity when *Sunday Bloody Sunday* premiered and I, age ten, fought to see nakedness through the fingers of my mother's covering hand.

I book a room at the Hotel Homa. We had stayed here when we first moved here in 1974. Back then it was the Kourosh Hotel, the finest, with five glittering stars, meandering gardens of tangerine and orange, and waiters who asked if you wanted a second café glacé. The Shah had built the hotel for the twenty-five-hundred-year festivities at Persepolis. Today, there are more impressive hotels in Shiraz, but I booked the Homa for nostalgic reasons. Almost immediately, the past yields a familiar face.

"Mr. Cyrus, is that you? *Ya Allah!*"

Kazem Khan was our first driver—and now stands outside the hotel where we met so many years ago. The years have carved wrinkles into his face and colored his hair white, but he still has the same insouciance. "Life's been hell," Kazem Khan says, laughing. "And forty years later you have the decency to return? How considerate."

For a good hour we linger outside the hotel, trying to compress four decades. A bon vivant, Kazem Khan tells me how one night he got drunk and cussed out the mothers, fathers, and sisters of all the revolutionaries he knew. The next morning a couple of soldiers tossed a gunny sack over his head and took him to jail.

"Where are you from?" he asked his first interrogator.

"Abadan."

"Hey, me too. I am a child of Abadan!"

When the second soldier came to question him, Kazem Khan was from Tabriz, then Meshad, and so on. None of the soldiers would admit that they wanted to release him because he was from their own city. Once freed, he went home and popped open another bottle of whiskey.

"They're just a bunch of know-nothings," he says of the soldiers. "Young and harmless. Stupid, orphaned, uneducated . . ." and the cussing continued. He despises them. "But you know who I love? Bill Clinton. Promise me if you ever meet him, you'll tell him he has an admirer in Shiraz?"

Our conversation meanders until lunch, when he takes me to his car, pops the trunk, and extracts a bottle of Clorox. We go to a nearby restaurant for lunch, during which he stashes the Clorox under the table and, when the waiter turns his back, mixes it with Pepsi in extravagant ratios.

"It's really Johnnie Walker," he whispers, undeterred by recent memories.

In Shiraz, the holiest sight is Shah Cheragh—a shrine that draws millions of pilgrims every year. Need a miracle? Shah Cheragh is your man. Here, wounds are healed. The lame walk. Mute girls chant the *salawaats.* The barren are seeded. Cancers and cataracts vanish. Even Sunnis are

---

*Prayers and blessings for the Prophet.

healed. Whenever a miracle occurs, the Miracles Registration Office is notified and Shah Cheragh's beloved servants, the *khudams*, beat the kettle drums in celebration.

"People tie themselves to his tomb and don't leave until their wishes are granted," my mother once told me. "They talk to him directly, like you'd talk to a family member. *Shah Cheragh, help me, cure me.* I visited his brother Imam Reza before leaving Iran; I asked him that I might have a decent life and that I wouldn't miss my parents too much."

After Ahmad ibn Moussa was martyred in 835 A.D., an old man saw a light flickering from inside his grave. When the Shah came to see what the hullaballoo was all about, the old man addressed him ("Shah!"), then pointed out the light ("Cheragh!"), and from then on, Ahmad ibn Moussa was known as King of Light. Nowadays his tomb is the second-holiest site in all Iran, packed with an escalating number of pilgrims—come to worship, come to pray, come to beg a miracle.

When I arrive, it is late morning and the courtyard adjacent to his shrine is humming. Picture an Emerald City—but turquoise—with glittering domes and spires rising dramatically. Vaulted mirrored ceilings that reflect a storm of light. Tiled courtyards with cooling fountains. A library. A seminary. Plush Persian carpets upon which pilgrims pray. Everything you'd need to spend a day here—or a life.

Just as I enter the courtyard, I feel someone touch the back of my neck, but when I turn around no one is there. A few seconds later it happens again. Once more, I have the distinct impression that this is a sign—but of what?

Through the courtyard and past the fountains I go, drawn toward the golden spire beneath which Shah Cheragh's bones lie. A boy approaches, wondering if I need help. He takes my hand and leads me toward the shrine. Off to the side a mullah is marrying a couple. It is a humble marriage—he just reads a few words from his threadbare Quran and joins their lives. Beside them an elderly *haji* is praying. We pass through silver

---

*Honorific title given to a Moslem who has been to Mecca.

doors, under thousand-watt chandeliers and walls studded with mirrors and tiles—the ceiling in particular is like a kaleidoscope of light, cut with a hundred thousand pieces of mirror, each angling light in a different direction so that the effect is at once dazzling and exceedingly humbling. In the center of it all is the tomb itself, a silver rectangle that rises ten feet, surrounded by worshipful men. It glows green.

Is this how devout Catholics feel upon entering St. Peter's Basilica?

The boy spins me around and dusts off my bottom. "You must be clean for Shah Cheragh," he says, then scampers off.

Face-to-face with the tomb, I grab hold and wait for revelation.

Inside this mausoleum are the bones of the second-holiest man in Iran. People grasp the silver grate surrounding the tomb, insert their fingers into the latticework, and kiss the lock. Men touch the grate and wipe their faces as if their hands are dripping with holy water. Children climb on their shoulders and form devotional pyramids. All around me, people are in a state of tearful prayer and meditation. Men are wailing, praying, lost in an emotional catharsis that is somewhat unsettling to a New Yorker with a healthy sense of boundaries. But I am determined to be one of these lost and found men. People often tie themselves to the tomb, and while I have no intention of doing that, I have not traveled sixty-five hundred miles simply to gawk at the faithful and walk away. So I close my eyes and redouble my efforts. *I will not go until you bless me.*

A couple years back, I visited the tomb of St. Francis of Assisi and felt overwhelmed with a sense of brotherhood. But at Shah Cheragh I feel nothing other than a quickening of the heart and blood rushing to my head—and a slight sense of resentment. All these people pressing toward the tomb with naked love, desire, adulation, adoration of the eighth saint's brother, they're making it impossible for me to connect with him.

Eventually I let go of the lattice and watch the tomb recede as I am drawn backward, unblessed.

Outside, I sit near the cooling fountains and gather my thoughts. The very part of Islam that I admire, its communal spirit, is also the part I fear.

I don't blame the revolutionaries for this. I have carried this sense of trepidation since I was ten and received my first Quran, and realized I didn't quite fit into the prayerful masses, but it flared and stayed with me after 1979. My fear is this: that my voice will be subsumed by the collective and God will not hear me. It's been decades since I prayed with anyone. Somewhere deep inside, I associate group prayer with fundamentalism. Men who speak in a single voice are anathema to me.

In successive years, I flirted with Sufism and read Rumi and Hafez—Islamic mystics who boasted of a personal relationship with God. But now I had a thought: Standing apart means *being* apart.

And isn't that the whole goal of mystical thought—union with everything?

At just that moment, boys begin unrolling crimson-and-white carpets in the courtyard for prayer. Rug after rug, and soon the eastern quarter is blanketed. When the muezzin's call to prayer echoes through the complex minutes later, I think: *Why not?* Walking back into the shrine, I pluck a *mohr*˙ from the collection, take my place with another group, and wait for the prayer to begin.

A few feet away, a pool of orange, pink, and red light filters through a stained-glass window. It is so iridescent and beautiful that I can't help but pick myself up and sit right inside the pool. Soon men take their place on either side of me, and the prayer starts.

Hands to temple. Bow low. Sink to my knees. Salaam. Up again. This is how Moslems have greeted God for fourteen hundred years. As the sole prostrate American in a crowd of hundreds, I feel a bit conspicuous. And I am praying in Arabic instead of the abridged English version I usually recite. I cannot match the words with the individual meanings but there is a bigger meaning blossoming inside me—a oneness of spirit that blindsides me. It's gone as soon as I notice it, but for that moment I feel like a drop that has rejoined the ocean. For several fleeting seconds on these commu-

---

˙A small clay tablet on which Moslems touch their foreheads during prayer.

nal carpets, I lay down my differences—and discover that no one else is paying attention to them either. How has such fear lived and bloomed inside me for four long decades? All because a few revolutionaries marched under God's name? I am the one who excommunicated myself from Islam.

Halfway through the prayer comes the part where you greet your neighbors. To my left, I shake hands with a mullah. To my right, a boy who appears to be about ten.

A mullah.

A ten-year-old boy.

And me in the middle. It dawns on me that my placement here is no accident, that I have stepped into a luminous space bookended by a man of Islam and a boy who is the same age I was when my fears blossomed. In an instant, I understand that no matter how much I might hold myself apart, I will still be part of the collective, a Moslem among Moslems. But the sweetest epiphany, the thing that goes to my very core and produces a monsoon of tears the mullah and boy kindly pretend not to notice is this: The thing I fear most about group prayer—that God isn't paying attention to my life—is the thing that is disproved only when I take my place here among the collective.

For this is assuredly a God-constructed moment, too rich in irony to be anything else.

After the prayer ends, I retire to a small vestibule in the shrine, where I encounter a boy who is crying such deep and voluble sobs that my first inclination is to flee.

"My mother, my mother," he cries. "Would that I were in her place. Shah Cheragh, only you can deliver her from this . . ."

It's not clear what "this" is, but I lay a tentative hand on his shoulder and soon find myself crying alongside him—again. Years before, I had placed my hands on my mother's shoulders in much the same way. She had been in an auto accident and was about to be wheeled into surgery. In that moment, my hands locked onto her body and I felt a rush of energy, pulled through me into her. I never felt it again, but now with my hand resting gently on the boy's shoulder it seems to be working in reverse, and I can feel the great dark depths of his sadness. So I sit with him and we pray for his mother.

Afterward as I exit the shrine, I come face-to-face with the mullah.

"Excuse me—are you the man who was praying next to me?"

I tell him I am.

"You dropped your card. Come."

He walks me to a small office adjacent the shrine. And when the attendant there returns my business card to me—this small rectangle of personal identity—I have to laugh at Allah's sense of humor. I am standing at the Lost and Found.

"I'm Cyrus," I tell the mullah. "I've come from America to say a prayer here."

"My name is Abdullah," the mullah says. "May your prayers be accepted. May you be ever successful."

That day, the kettle drums remain silent. No one comes rushing out of the Miracles Registration Office to take my story. But I know that a small miracle *has* happened—that Shah Cheragh has visited. Not as a vision, but as the collective in whose embrace I feel transformed. People pray for very specific things, but for me prayer itself is the answer.

"INTRODUCE YOURSELF. Say, 'Hello, I'm Cyrus and I've got an eating disorder,'" Ali instructs.

Doesn't matter that Ali is soda-straw thin (and I am middle-aged thin); we are attending a group for Fat People with Lost Names. Or as they're known stateside, Overeaters Anonymous.

"Ali, I don't have an eating disorder!"

"Doesn't matter, just say it. Tell them you've had a disorder for just twenty-four hours."

"You say it."

"I did—years ago when I joined."

"Aren't you, like, forty kilos? You're barely a teenager."

"Thirty-five kilos. Down two! Admitting you're powerless is the first step."

So the twelve steps have come to Iran. I survey the crowd in rickety chairs, rising one by one to speak unsentimentally about their grades, their ambitions and loves and common humanity. No one is fat. Overeating is a small lie they tell each other that allows them to connect on a deeper level. "Hi, I'm Reza and I've been an overeater for three years." By which Reza means: *I'm hungry for the milk of human kindness, for connection to my citizens, for a sign that I'm not alone in this life.*

In America people lie about their addictions to avoid facing their feelings. Here people declare false addictions to broadcast them. Proof? At Overeaters Anonymous, no one talks about food. Trust me, you *wanna* talk about Iranian food. Maybe in the face of unemployment, repression, censorship, sanctions, and a hardened regime that sees past them, impersonating an addict is a solution to life's powerlessness? Like *Fight Club*—but Islamic. Which means sexes are divided and chairs face forward.

There are real addicts too, of course. Later I meet Navid, a lithe man of thirty-five who got lost in drugs and looks a good decade older than his age. Heroin had lured him with its elysian promise until he found himself lying, stumbling, and stealing his way back to that first feeling—only to discover it was no longer there. Rock bottom was homelessness. Now he works three jobs, including construction and teaching yoga, to keep afloat. Navid attends Narcotics Anonymous religiously, meditates, and keeps a meatless diet. Yoga *and* Twelve Steps? Facing a plethora of difficulties, Iran's youth have swung the gates of healing open—to the East and West—and found a way to contend. Quietly.

Ali has accompanied me to OA on the instruction of his parents, Marjan and Ghassem. After the meeting we head home for dinner. A sprightly man of thirty-five, Ghassem has a boundless amount of energy and bright eyes. "Before I found OA, I would lie and cheat and insist women cover themselves. Now if Marjan found a lover, I would pray for her happiness. Do you know when the last time I got upset was? Five years ago!"

That night, Marjan prepares a vegetarian feast for her OA friends: *oliv-ieh* salad with egg, potato, and pickles; *addas polo* with rice, raisins, lentils, and cinnamon; and *kuki sabzi*, a Persian frittata with fresh herbs and wal-nuts. The conversation turns both East and West—first to India. Had I heard about people who live on sunlight? About the masters who retreated for six months, no nutrients, into a state of meditation and emerged alive? Matters of spirit are of great interest here. "If we live cleanly and without harming other life, the world will change," Shahab says. A divorced ac-countant, he is a strong proponent of vegetarianism. "It is an affirmation of life, and a repudiation of war, because all life has value." Whereupon he reaches over and gives me a hug. A word about OA hugs: They last a long time—uncomfortably long for an American.

"You really hug people with your whole self," I say, typically butchering Farsi, but it gets a laugh.

"The way you speak is cute," Shahab replies.

How is the economy in America? Does Obama have an agenda for black people? When do people get married? America is an object of ceaseless fas-cination. In fact, the whole world is a source of curiosity for Iranians—all the more for how the sanctions have basically cut them off and made their lives miserable, forcing them to work two and three jobs just to stay afloat. Gas. Meat. Bread. Electricity. The prices of staples have skyrocketed. In recognition of this, the government gives each person forty-five thousand *tomans* a month—the equivalent of about $15, but that is hardly enough. The rich just get richer while Davoud, one of the OA brood, works at an elevator company during the day and moonlights as a cabdriver after work.

There is hardly any part of the economy that the sanctions have not laid waste to—from cancer drugs to spare parts for airlines. Even wildlife. Soraya has plans to start an ecotourism company for the dwindling popula-tion of Persian leopards and cheetahs, but the sanctions have cut off funding. "There are only about forty to seventy Persian cheetahs still left. We are trying to protect these species in danger of extinction, but the international measures have made that impossible."

"They think we want to make nuclear bombs," Davoud interjects. "Have you seen anything in your travels that would lead you to believe that? Looking back on the past two hundred years, Iran has never attacked a country without being attacked first. Never. Can America say that? It's true that the regime has done itself no great favor with its cries of 'Death to America', 'Death to Israel.' It is just posturing. And perhaps anger at the policies of America and Israel to insert themselves into the affairs of Islamic countries and ruin our Palestinian brothers. Even Khomeini says that nuclear weapons are *haram* according to Islam. Perhaps they're scared of Iran because we support the Moslems that Israel suppresses? Perhaps they think this is the country of *Argo*?"

Ah, *Argo*. *That* movie. I remember David Smallman mentioned that the film was made with the cooperation of the CIA, and how it was designed to embarrass the Iranians. Indeed, everyone has an opinion about it here— generally not a good one. "It was a very low-quality way of telling the truth," Davoud says. "No one is disputing that taking hostages is bad. But looking at this film, you think Iran is a country of lunatics."

I recently had a revelation about the sanctions. For almost two weeks, I've been coasting on a strong dollar. Four-course meals for $10. Five-star hotels for $50. Spending money in Iran, I feel absolutely immense—from which one might infer how Iranians with their devalued currency and alienation from the world feel. Cut off. Unappreciated. And barely scraping by.

Yet here they are inviting *me* to dinner.

Oddly, they do not resent America for driving them to the brink of economic despair. During dinner, Marjan gets a phone call. "We have an American guest," she tells the caller.

"Does he know how much we love America?" the caller asks.

"He does," she whispers. And I do. I've made a point of telling people I am American—thinking myself a goodwill ambassador. Do Iranians assume America is a combative country unwilling to bend to the culture and customs of others, or learn the intricacies of their language? I negate that. I reject that. I am a smaller, more personalized variant on American foreign policy come to life. To my great surprise, I discover that Iranians are nothing but welcoming—inviting me to dinner and expressing great enthusiasm and curiosity about the country whose sanctions have dealt them a crippling blow. I do not understand this.

Later we watch a video of Ghassem preparing vegetarian entrées. He tells me about traveling the country and holding seminars on vegetarianism, dieting, spirituality, twelve steps, and a new world order. Their movement is thirty thousand people strong and growing, he says.

A while ago, I read an account of how caterpillars become butterflies. Embedded in the caterpillar's body is a set of imaginal cells operating on a different frequency. The cells are so threatening that the caterpillar's immune system begins to attack and eat them, but the cells continue to regenerate. The imaginal cells begin to cluster, exchanging information and feeding off the nutrients of a dying society. Clusters become clumps and when they reach a critical mass, an evolutionary leap happens. From death and decay, a butterfly appears.

Tonight, I have come upon an imaginal cluster—rare and aberrant cells bonding in the closed-off chrysalis of Iran.

AFTER A FEW DAYS IN SHIRAZ, I am exhausted.

"How about a sauna," the hotel concierge suggests when I virtually limp into the hotel on my third afternoon. I had visited my old school, the bazaar, my neighborhood, the Shah's palace, and the park where Katayoun and I used to play—all in one day, all on foot, for I wanted to approach the markers of my childhood slowly.

"Just be careful of the pipes," the concierge adds. "They're old and you don't want to burn yourself."

Sure enough, on my way out of the sauna, I knock loose a pipe, and the resulting jet of scalding steam on my ankle produces an instant blister the size of a small plum.

As luck would have it, there is a burn hospital nearby where a nurse bandages my foot with practiced efficiency. His name is Mr. Jafari and he is a revolutionary. I know this because of his beard, his demeanor, and his considerable portrait of Khomeini that hangs above him.

I am being treated by a revolutionary, I think to myself. *Cool.*

The following morning, Mr. Jafari drops by the hotel to check on my wound. He will not take money. During this visit I learn he had been a nurse in the Iran/Iraq war. "The chemical warfare was horrible," he says. "Mustard gas. Men with severed limbs and burned faces . . . and we treated them in the most primitive conditions. Tents of injured soldiers from here to the horizon. It went on for years, and all the time everyone was wondering: Why isn't the world saying anything? It was only after a team of German doctors reported back that these tactics were acknowledged—and then hundreds of doctors from Germany, France, and Italy volunteered for the front."

He looks humbly to the ground.

"The chemical weapons were furnished by the U.S. Sold through a clandestine network to Argentina, then Germany, then finally to Iraq."

"And here you are dressing my wounds."

"I have no quarrel with Americans. Your foreign policy, yes—but your people are decent."

Mr. Jafari is standing by the window. He stands like all revolutionaries—humbly, hands clasped in front. When I offer him money, he refuses it once again. It seems he is grappling with something. Having heard of the atrocities of America, he is now faced with one of its wounded. It helps that I am wounded. It helps that I speak Farsi. We take a picture together and he tells me I am like his brother. Not in features, but in feeling, he says, thumping his heart.

These days, I am feeling both bigger and smaller—more like Alice than ever. The dollar makes me feel bigger. Dinner for four dollars. Suede pants for fifteen. I am amazed at how rich I am and think nothing of spending money. I feel immense.

And then tiny and grateful—humbled by Iran and her healers, drivers, pseudo-addicts, and saints.

ON MY LAST DAY IN SHIRAZ, I visit Pasargadae.

I'd been here once before in 1974. When we first arrived in Iran, my father thought it would be a good idea to pay homage to the country's father, Cyrus the Great, and so one spring afternoon he drove us to his tomb a hundred kilometers outside Shiraz. That afternoon, as was Max's frequent habit, he gave us a history lesson. Under Cyrus's rule in the sixth century BC, the Persian empire stretched from Libya to India. Cyrus's brilliance was to unite disparate cultures under a single rule, but he left them their gods and languages.

"But the really cool thing about Cyrus was that he gardened the way he governed. Look around," Max said, gesturing across the barren landscape. Except for the freestanding sepulcher said to contain Cyrus's remains, and six broad steps that framed it, there was nothing here but the parched plains that stretched toward the Zagros mountains. "This tract was once the world's finest garden. Cyrus imported trees from the farthest reaches of his empire and planted them—oh, right about where you're standing. Cypress trees from Egypt. Cherry from Caucasus. Orange trees from Southeast Asia. Cyrus wanted his gardens to reflect his internationalist beliefs, and his conviction that true prosperity lay in peaceful coexistence."

My father went on to describe how from the king's throne, a broad, tree-lined avenue ran for about a mile, bisected by four limestone waterways that gave way to reflecting pools and quadrants populated with lush and fragrant gardens.

"And do you know what he named his garden?" my father asked, striding up and down the barren landscape as though the gardens and pools were suddenly extant and flourishing. *"Paradaiza."*

"Paradise?" Katayoun whispered.

My mother smiled knowingly. She loved the fact that Max knew Iran's history so well, and now brought it alive for us.

"Bingo," Max answered. "It was the very first Persian garden!"

Fascinated that there was once a paradise on earth, I read up on my namesake. As Cyrus's empire grew, his version of paradise soon spread to other cultures and languages. The word was translated into Greek (*paradeisoi*), then Latin (*paradisus*) and from there reincarnated into the European languages. The French called it *paradis*, the Germans *paradies*, and the English, of course, paradise. *Paradaiza* meant "walled space," and it became a blueprint not only for the classical Persian Garden but a succession of equally astonishing gardens in other lands. The Greek gardens of the Seleucids and Alexandria took their design from *Paradaiza*. The biblical Eden too, with its four sections that mirrored the four quadrants of *Paradaiza*, and four waterways that represented the four rivers of paradise—water, wine, milk, and honey. The Taj Mahal and the Alhambra gardens were direct descendants of Cyrus's garden. The seeds from *Paradaiza* blew into the pages of history, germinated into so many other cultures and languages—until finally they landed in our backyard.

That week in March 1974, Max began work on his own walled paradise, tilling and softening the earth behind our new house and planting the Burpee seeds he'd brought from the States. Morning glories. Chrysanthemums. Tulips. And because he was equally a practical man, he planted cucumbers, tomatoes, and squash. He filled our tiny, turquoise-tiled pool and populated it with goldfish. Every morning he fed them. Then he knelt down to inspect and water the seedlings.

By the first blush of summer, the sprouts shot up a couple of inches—then stalled. Max fertilized the garden with donkey droppings and added special nutrients to the water. By sheer willpower, he coaxed a few more inches from his flowers, until it looked as though they might make it through the summer. A few morning glories climbed halfway up the wall.

Then one morning a construction crew began work on the lot next door, and the rising structure darkened our fledgling garden. Now only the noontime sun delivered a shifting square of light to the plantings. Construction was a blur of broken glass, noise, bricks, and metal beams. One day, Max came home to find his garden blanketed in chalk. The chalk had crushed the morning glories, stained the freshly hung laundry, and bleached his little oasis a ghostly white. It had also settled in the pool and poisoned the goldfish. They floated belly-up.

Max flew into a rage. I never heard my father cuss so passionately or so long. His anger was a magnificent, volcanic thing. He plucked the chalky laundry from the clothesline and deposited it on our neighbor's doorstep, demanding it be laundered. The neighbor was a general whose four stars neither daunted Max nor cooled his anger. The following day a basket of our neatly folded clothes showed up at our doorstep.

But the Persian garden was gone—and with it a piece of Max's spirit.

From then on, Max went up into the mountains and down into the valleys, luxuriating in God's natural creations. Who wanted a walled garden anyway? Wasn't a shared vista a more impressive thing? And so it was that, having seen the demise of his own private paradise, he came to discover in those mountainous treks the closest version of paradise on earth I had ever seen. It was the autumn of 1976 when my father packed Katayoun and me into the car and drove us to the valley he'd discovered.

AND NOW AS I STAND before Cyrus's tomb at Pasargadae, I cannot stop thinking about it. It dawns on me that this is the through-line I've been looking for—a link that connects me to my childhood, my mother's homeland, my father, my namesake king, and twenty-five hundred years of history. A valley.

Alas, I have long since lost the map my father drew.

"Is there a lush valley outside Shiraz, with trees and a river?" I ask Kazem Khan. "Maybe a couple hours outside the city, leaving from the Quran Gate? The trees have circular leaves that turn gold in the fall. That's all I recall about it."

"You mean *Beheshteh Gom Shodeh*?"

"*Beheshteh Gom Shodeh*," I repeat, stunned.

It means: the Lost Paradise.

With that name, it is too much of a coincidence to be anything but my valley. I can't help but laugh. Two and a half centuries after Cyrus had designed the original version of paradise, had Max somehow discovered its ancestor? Kneeling at his tomb, I wing a prayer for King Cyrus skyward. Minutes later, we are back in Kazem Khan's car, speeding toward the Lost Paradise.

En route to the valley, Kazem Khan has cracked open another bottle of Clorox and is on the verge of throwing his arm around me.

"Do you consider yourself American or Iranian?" he asks. "Are you Moslem? Your father grew up on a ranch—but your mother is a Maleki." He is being unusually personal, but we have long since left *Driving Miss Daisy* protocol behind us. "Who is Cyrus? How do you contain all these parts? I'm just a child of Tabriz."

In my experience there are two kinds of inebriates. The obnoxious kind, and the kind that somehow locks into an ineffable grid of spiritual empathy. He has drunkenly tapped into a question that has long plagued me.

The truth is that I occupy two walled spaces, Iran and America, and the walls are not coming down anytime soon. I have spent a lifetime proudly claiming my differences. American in Iran. Iranian in America. And these days, being Moslem anywhere. I relish how I don't fit into the mainstream. As time passes and the animosity between Iran and America has deepened, so too has my sense of being an outsider. "Hey, it's your favorite Iranian," is how I often answer the phone back home—or occasionally, "Hey, it's your favorite Islamic terrorist." "Get bombed with your favorite Iranian" is how I'd invite you to a party. And if you were my paramour and wanted to leave? I'd threaten to take you hostage. Were you to laugh at me, as most do, I'd advise you: Never laugh when an Iranian says he'll take you hostage! Do you want another international incident? In America, I groom and exaggerate my sense of otherness—a self-appointed goodwill ambassador from a maligned country. Here in Iran, I proudly flash my blue American passport. The anti-hero! A cool identity, perhaps, but not a cohesive one—dependent on prejudice, opposition, misinformation, and location. In neither country do I feel fully at home.

Cyrus had created paradise out of trees from the farthest reaches of his empire, and knit the world a little closer with his gardens, but I can't even fuse the worn threads of my own heritage. Maybe because I enjoy this role of ambassador of a misunderstood culture too much? Carl Jung defined the shadow as that part of our personality we reject out of fear, ignorance, or shame. Essentially, the shadow is the person you'd rather not be. I have inverted my shadow—taken that aspect of myself that incurs judgment from the world and flipped it. My shadow is my skin. I advertise it as much as possible. And maybe that is equally unhealthy? Jung said that there is only one way to integrate our shadow and heal our fractured psyches: "[We must] struggle with evil, confront the shadow, to integrate the devil."

Well, it doesn't get more devilish than the Great Satan and the Axis of Evil.

Truthfully, I have no idea how to do that. When Kazem Khan asks if I am Iranian or American, I have no answer for him. I do not know how to integrate both aspects of my bloodlines into a healthy, whole psyche, for they are contradictory in every way that two countries can contradict each other. They are perpetually at odds. But then I remember something from my new twelve-step friends.

The first step is introducing yourself and telling your story.

THE ROAD DRONES ON—an endless ribbon through the plains corsetted by the Zagros mountains rising just beyond. I am beginning to feel a bit sleepy but every few minutes, Kazem Khan takes a swig of Clorox, so I need to stay awake. A bit farther on we pass a lone store outside of which stands the strangest thing—a freestanding mannequin in a bridal dress. On either side of the mannequin, miles of shrubbed earth stretch into the distance. It occurs to me that Iran is like this mannequin—sidelined, waiting patiently for her beauty to be seen.

An hour or so later, Kazem Khan's sedan is chugging across a dirt road toward a hill that looms larger as we approach. It is still February, but patches of green sprout along the way. In the distance two hills intersect, and where they cross, a triangle of gold and orange glints in the sun. We round the first hill and all at once find ourselves in a tunnel of trees. When we clear the foliage, Kazem Khan pulls aside.

"Welcome to *Beheshteh Gom Shodeh*," he says.

It looks nothing like my valley. The trees are all knotty and overgrown, more than fifty feet tall. The streams have united into a river dammed with pools of fallen leaves. Everything is massive, aged, and unrecognizable to me. But just when I begin to think he has it wrong, I get a whiff of something fecund and woodsy, with a hint of decay.

That's it. The scent of the best day of my childhood.

Kazem Khan pulls a blanket and several cans of food from the trunk, and we walk upriver under boughs of mostly naked trees. A canopy of leaves clings to the upper levels. There are successive pools at each elevation—like Cyrus's reflecting pools. Occasionally Kazem Khan stoops to point out wild mint, sweet onion, or mushrooms. He picks up and cracks open a walnut with his bare hands and gives me half the meat. When we come to a clearing by a waterfall, he ceremoniously spreads the blanket and lights a small fire over which he heats a can of tuna fish. When the oil is bubbling, he squeezes a fresh lemon over it, spoons it into naan, and hands me a sandwich.

After our makeshift lunch, I excuse myself and wander upriver. I had thought that the trip to Grove was my farewell to Max, but now it seems like this is where the long road of discovery should rightfully end. In Persian poetry, the garden is always the spirit's final destination. Sitting on a rock, I skip a few pebbles into the river, then thank Max for being my father. I thank him for teaching me how to be an adventurer in search of hidden beauty, and for showing us this unbounded valley with its rich soil and raging river, fecund scent, and pools that reflect back a fundamental truth. Let the Great Satan and the Axis of Evil play their games. Out beyond their political grasp is an untended valley that contains multitudes, and we fallen angels are just trying to make our way back.

On the ride back to Shiraz, Kazem Khan and I are silent.

"When you return to America, you'll tell everyone you had a bad time," he says after a while. It's a classically Persian thing, a way of fishing for compliments.

I assure him that this has been my loveliest day.

Then once again we settle into silence, because I myself was drunk on the beauty of paradise, age-old kings, and had found a way to say good-bye to my father—and in the covergence of these things, discovered a kind of peace that I wanted to savor a moment more.

AUTHOR'S NOTE

Countless books have been written about the hostage crisis. I read many, trying to understand the context against which our story unfolded, before realizing ours is not a traditional work of history. It is, rather, a very personal event told from three perspectives—four if you count the adult me. Our tale is a footnote in the history of U.S.–Iran relations, and by definition, an elaboration of the details of a bigger story. I've done my best to get the historical facts straight, but this book is not meant to be a detailed and expert account of U.S.–Iran relations. It is a personal story told in an idiosyncratic way.

Frankly, I'm not sure I know of any books structured like this. It is tricky writing a memoir, trickier still if you are writing the story of your parents and your fifteen-year-old hormonal self. My chapters were relatively easy to write and I found myself lapsing into my boyhood in Iran almost effortlessly. But recounting the events of one's parents' life is complicated—partly because I wasn't there for much of it, and because I wanted to get it right for them. For my father's chapters, I relied on our conversations, letters, notes and chapters of his unpublished story, diaries, newspaper articles I dug up from 1956, and conversations with other sources. My mother is an exquisite storyteller and has recounted the events of her life to me many times.

From time to time, I used Farsi words to give the reader a taste of life in Iran. Dialogue and details have been reconstructed. Time periods compressed. Names and identifying details changed for protection.

The careful reader will note that the events of 1979–80 are told in the present tense, lending a sense of immediacy to those scenes. Thirty-five years have elapsed since that fateful time—and while I've done my best to get it right, there are undoubtedly errors of both omission and commission here. But the story of what happened to us Copelands is true, and committed to the page to the best of my abilities. As I was researching, I found I was also telling the story to myself, and in the process drawing a line from childhood to adulthood. Maybe that's what happens when you teeter on fifty. Only instead of having a torrid affair or buying an age-inappropriate car, I wrote a book linking past to present—which in no way lessened the emotional pratfalls along the path.

SOURCES

Mirrors of the Unseen: Journeys into Iran by Jason Elliot (St. Martin's Press, 2006)

The Destined Hour by Barry and Barbara Rosen and George Feifer (Doubleday, 1982)

Legacy of Ashes: A History of the CIA by Tim Weiner (Anchor, 2008)

The Houseguests: A Memoir of Candian Courage and CIA Sorcery by Mark Lijek (CreateSpace, 2012)

The Man in the Mirror by Carole Jerome (Key Porter Books, 1987)

Guests of the Ayatollah by Mark Bowden (Grove Press, 2007)

Our Man in Tehran: The True Story Behind the Secret Mission to Save Six Americans During the Iran Hostage Crisis and the Foreign Ambassador Who Worked with the CIA to Bring Them Home by Robert Wright (Other Press, 2011)

Iran–U.S. Claims Tribunal Report, Vol. 33 (Cambridge University Press, 1997)

Persian Mirrors: The Elusive Face of Iran by Elaine Sciolino (Free Press, 2005)

Argo by Tony Mendez (Penguin, 2013)

The Game Player by Miles Copeland (Aurum Press, 1989)

Persian Oil: A Study in Power Politics by Laurence Paul Elwell-Sutton (Greenwood Press, 1976)

Time magazine archives

The *New York Times* archives

The *Economist* archives

Wikipedia

Encyclopaedia Iranica

Ken Hannigan's letters on Westinghouse's Iran program

"The CIA and the Media" by Carl Bernstein (*Rolling Stone*, October 20, 1977)

"Escape from Iran" by Jessie Hyde (*Men's Journal*, August 2011)

"Persia in the History of Civilization," speech by Will Durant

"The Influence of Translation on Shakespeare's Reception in Iran: Three Farsi Hamlets and Suggestions for a Fourth," dissertation at Middlesex University by Abbas Horri

"The BBC Persian Service, 1940–1953, and the Nationalization of Iranian Oil" by Hossein Shahidi, *Journal of Iranian Research and Analysis*, Vol. 17, No. 1, April 2001

"A Not So Silent Partner: Thailand's Role in Covert Operations, Counter-Insurgency, and the War in Indochina" by Arne Kislenko, *Journal of Conflict Studies*, Vol. 24, No. 1, Summer 2004

The letters, diaries, notes, and newspaper articles of Max Copeland

ACKNOWLEDGMENTS

My extraordinary parents, Shahin and Max, who taught me how to have a remarkable life by example.

My elegant sister Katayoun, fellow guardian of Copeland history, who always carries strength and beauty into the fray.

Gene Taggart for his talent with words, unflagging enthusiasm, and friendly intelligence, and for helping lift this book (and my spirits) with great humor.

My editor at Blue Rider Press, David Rosenthal, for his encouragement, keen suggestions, and gentle curiosity, and for seeing the book's potential from the first word. "He is the perfect editor for you," a Balinese fortune-teller told me, and this has proven to be true.

The Blue Rider team for their sharp professionalism and infectious enthusiasm: Phoebe Pickering, Linda Rosenberg, Linda Cowen, Jason Booher, Claire Vaccaro, Aileen Boyle, Brian Ulicky, and Wesley Salazar.

David Smallman for sharing the journey and expertly steering me through the choppy waters of Washington.

Barney Karpfinger for finding this book its perfect home at Blue Rider.

Erica Barnes for finding the game-changing memo.

Jess Taylor for his canny advice on just about everything.

Albert Naglieri for always being there.

Pierre Moreau Peron for being my number one cheerleader. You kept insisting I write this book—so I did.

Joe Scholtz for his hospitality and friendship.

Bob Weil for his astute questions, on-point suggestions, and insistence that I go to Grove.

ACKNOWLEDGMENTS

The Sooner gang: Owen and Claudia Butler, gracious hosts and keepers of my father's history; Ron Young for his connective kindness; Mark Lee (good luck on the Copeland ranch!); Mary and Norma for sharing their memories over Claudia's crab cakes; and Juanita Lee, whose innocuous question lit a path toward the truth.

Bill Comfort, Martha Watson, Anne Rutledge, Lonnie Chestnutt, and the Experiment in Understanding posse for sharing their recollections of my father and that fateful trip.

Professor Russ Buhite, David Levy, and LeaAnn Quirk at Oklahoma University for their generous assistance.

Donal Buchanan for his long-distance friendship and recollections of his fascinating father.

Westinghouse veterans George Beck, Jack Geikler, Jack Tyman, and Ed Yoder, and Emily Demougeot and Ruth Bright for patiently answering my questions.

Professor Hugh Wilford at California State University for sharing his knowledge of the early CIA years, and Jennifer Hoar at IGI for her sleuthing help.

Readers who hunkered down with my manuscript and offered thoughtful suggestions: Lois Atkinson, Erica Barnes, Alejandra Cisneros, and Jess Taylor.

Mark Lijek and Roger Lucy for lending their Argo expertise, and Professor Robert Wright for generously sharing his own research from *Our Man in Tehran*.

My cousins in Iran for their extraordinary kindness.

My friends, who have heard this story in its many iterations. You know who you are.

About the Author

Cyrus M. Copeland, a former advertising executive, is the editor of two collections of eulogies: *Farewell, Godspeed* and *A Wonderful Life,* and the author of *Passwords: The Essential Guide to a Heartfelt Eulogy.* When not scouring the globe in search of adventure, he lives in New York City—and in the digital domain: cyruscopeland.com. (Drop by for a visit.)